RECLAIMING THE BODY: MARÍA DE ZAYAS'S EARLY MODERN FEMINISM

BY
LISA VOLLENDORF

CHAPEL HILL

NORTH CAROLINA STUDIES IN THE ROMANCE
LANGUAGES AND LITERATURES
U.N.C. DEPARTMENT OF ROMANCE LANGUAGES

2001

Library of Congress Cataloging-in-Publication Data

Vollendorf, Lisa.
    Reclaiming the body: María de Zayas's early modern feminism / by Lisa Vollendorf.
    p. cm. – (North Carolina studies in the Romance languages and literatures; no. 270).
    Includes bibliographical references.
    ISBN 0-8078-9274-2
    1. Zayas y Sotomayor, María de, 1590-1650–Criticism and interpretation. 2. Women in literature.   3. Violence in literature.   4. Sex role in literature.   5. Feminism and literature.   I. Title.   II. Series.

PQ6498.Z5 Z967 2001
863'.3–dc21   2001030246

Cover design: Heidi Perov

© 2001. Department of Romance Languages. The University of North Carolina at Chapel Hill.

ISBN 0-8078-9274-2

DEPÓSITO LEGAL: V. 2.376 - 2001

ARTES GRÁFICAS SOLER, S. L. - LA OLIVERETA, 28 - 46018 VALENCIA

THIS BOOK WAS DIGITALLY MANUFACTURED.

UNIVERSITY OF NORTH CAROLINA AT CHAPEL HILL
DEPARTMENT OF ROMANCE LANGUAGES

NORTH CAROLINA STUDIES
IN THE ROMANCE LANGUAGES AND LITERATURES

Founder: URBAN TIGNER HOLMES

Editor: CAROL L. SHERMAN

Distributed by:

UNIVERSITY OF NORTH CAROLINA PRESS

CHAPEL HILL
North Carolina 27515-2288
U.S.A.

NORTH CAROLINA STUDIES IN THE
ROMANCE LANGUAGES AND LITERATURES
Number 270

RECLAIMING THE BODY:
MARÍA DE ZAYAS'S EARLY MODERN FEMINISM

For my parents, Carol and Henry Vollendorf,
and my grandmother, Charlotte Hillas Vollendorf

TABLE OF CONTENTS

	Page
Acknowledgements	11
Titles of María de Zayas's Prose Fiction	13
Introduction: *Reclaiming the Body*	15

PART ONE: FLESH AND BLOOD

I. *Social and Literary Contexts of Corporeality*	35
II. *Violence Denaturalized: Feminist Readings of the Body Imperiled*	83

PART TWO: THE BOUNDARIES OF GENDER

III. *Women's Place in the Social Order: Public, Private, and Convent Life*	125
IV. *Crossdressers, Avengers, and the Performance of Gender*	158
Conclusion: *Feminism Embodied*	197
Works Cited	216
Index	229

ACKNOWLEDGEMENTS

I was still an undergraduate when H. Patsy Boyer gave me a copy of her translation of María de Zayas's fiction and set me on a path that would lead to this book. Throughout my educational career and into my professional life, Patsy inspired me to be a better teacher and scholar. I am only sorry that she did not live to see the book in print.

Patsy was one of many people–teachers, colleagues, students, and friends–who contributed to this project. I am especially thankful to Marina S. Brownlee, who advised me from start to finish. While my book was in press, both Marina's and Margaret Greer's books on Zayas were published. As these publications suggest, a community of Zayas scholars has emerged over the past decade. The many exchanges I have had with other *zayistas* in this time have sustained and nurtured my research.

I am grateful to my institution, Wayne State University, and to the Program for Cultural Cooperation between Spain's Ministry of Education and Culture and United States Universities for grant support that made this publication possible. My colleagues–particularly Beatriz Cortez, Michael Giordano, and Charles Stivale–supported my research agenda with genuine enthusiasm. Anne J. Cruz, Mitchell Greenberg, Larry Malley, Denise McCoskey, Kathleen McNerney, Mary Elizabeth Perry, José Regueiro, Teresa Soufas, Joyce Tolliver, Valerie Traub, Nancy Vosburg, and Alison Weber gave me encouragement and offered much-appreciated advice about the perils and pleasures of publication. David Gies and Constance Sullivan graciously rescued me from a bibliographical quandary in the eleventh hour.

Amy Williamsen has been supportive in more ways than I can count. Both she and the other, anonymous, reader for UNC Press gave incredibly generous criticism. In conjunction with the kind guidance of series editor Carol Sherman and proofreader Sandy Judd, the readers helped me turn a manuscript into a book.

The Newberry Library has provided me with an intellectual home away from home. Without the help and good humor of John Aubrey, John Brady, Susan Fagan, John Powell, and the rest of the library staff, this book might not have seen the light of day.

I want to thank the editors of *Hispania*, *Revista Canadiense de Estudios Hispánicos* (RCEH), and *Cincinnati Review* for granting me permission to reprint revised versions of the following articles: "Reading the Body Imperiled: Violence against Women in María de Zayas," *Hispania* 78.2 (May 1995); "Our Bodies, Our Selves: Vengeance in the Novellas of María de Zayas," *Cincinnati Romance Review* (May 1997); and "Fleshing out Feminism: María de Zayas's Corporeal Politics," *RCEH* 22.1 (Winter 1997). I would like to extend a special thanks to Richard Young, editor of *RCEH*, for his assistance in editing and revising my work.

The deepest debts I owe are personal. Nicola Ash, Denise K. Buell, and Mark Schuhl have been my closest friends and kindest cheerleaders for many years. The phone company is probably as thankful as I am for these far-flung friendships. A source of great happiness in my life, Jade Yee-Gorn has given me faith that the future is in the hands of intelligent, kind young people. For such a little boy, my nephew, Fisher Rae Vollendorf, has brought me an inordinate amount of joy. Fisher's mother, Kim, has inspired me with her tireless optimism. My wonderful brothers, Sean, Patrick, and Daniel Vollendorf, have laughed at me and with me for many years, and I am grateful for their friendship.

For years, Elliott J. Gorn has kept me abreast of the wins and, more commonly, the losses of the perennially mediocre Chicago Cubs. He has also given me his intellectual support and his love. There is little more I could ask for.

My parents, Carol and Henry Vollendorf, and my grandmother, Charlotte Hillas Vollendorf, have been my greatest teachers. I dedicate this book to them as a token of my love and appreciation.

TITLES OF MARÍA DE ZAYAS'S PROSE FICTION

Novelas amorosas y ejemplares

1. Aventurarse perdiendo
2. La burlada Aminta y venganza del honor
3. El castigo de la miseria
4. El prevenido, engañado
5. La fuerza del amor
6. El desengaño amando y premio de la virtud
7. Al fin se paga todo
8. El imposible vencido
9. El juez de su causa
10. El jardín engañoso

The Enchantments of Love

Everything Ventured
Aminta Deceived and Honor's Revenge
The Miser's Reward
Forewarned but not Forearmed
The Power of Love
Disillusionment in Love and Virtue Rewarded
Just Desserts
Triumph over the Impossible
Judge Thyself
The Magic Garden

Desengaños amorosos

1. La esclava de su amante
2. La más infame venganza
3. El verdugo de su esposa
4. Tarde llega el desengaño
5. La inocencia castigada
6. Amar sólo por vencer
7. Mal presagio casar lejos
8. El traidor contra su sangre
9. La perseguida triunfante
10. Estragos que causa el vicio

The Disenchantments of Love

Slave to Her Own Lover
Most Infamous Revenge
His Wife's Executioner
Too Late Undeceived
Innocence Punished
Love for the Sake of Conquest
Marriage Abroad: Portent of Doom
Traitor to His Own Blood
Triumph over Persecution
The Ravages of Vice

Introduction

RECLAIMING THE BODY

As the author of bestselling tales of violence and desire, María de Zayas has captivated readers for over three hundred and fifty years. Zayas's *Novelas amorosas* (*Enchantments of Love*, 1637) and its companion volume, the *Desengaños amorosos* (*Disenchantments of Love*, 1647), immediately enjoyed great success in Spain and abroad. These twenty framed novellas so decidedly captured attention that they were rivalled only by Cervantes's own *Novelas ejemplares* (*Exemplary Novels*) in Europe. Although Zayas's texts were nearly squeezed out of the canon when they were deemed vulgar by nineteenth-century critics, the twentieth century rescued them from oblivion. In the past two decades, Zayas has emerged as the most heavily studied woman writer from Spain's early modern period. The popularity of her writing among readers and critics alike is easy to explain: the texts have all the amorous intrigue of a supermarket novel and all the literary mastery of fine baroque prose.[1]

---

[1] In her introduction to Zayas's *Desengaños amorosos*, Yllera mentions that in spite of many claims to Zayas's nearly unsurpassed popularity, many of the editions that were thought to exist probably never did. Undoubtedly, Zayas was a bestselling author of fiction in Spain, and as Yllera summarizes, "Se ha indicado que, después de las *Novelas ejemplares* de Cervantes, fueron las suyas las novelas breves españolas más difundidas en el Occidente de Europa o bien que fue el autor de libros de pasatiempo más leído después de Cervantes, Alemán o Quevedo" (64) [It has been indicated that, after Cervantes's *Novelas ejemplares*, Zayas's novellas were the Spanish novellas that enjoyed the widest diffusion in western Europe; she might well have been the most widely read author of 'recreational' books after Cervantes, Alemán, or Quevedo]. Yllera's list of known editions of Zayas's prose constructs a publishing history that, at the very least, confirms the intense European interest in Zayas until the mid-nineteenth century. It should be noted, however, that partial editions of her texts were published regularly throughout the period from

While some of the ten stories in the *Novelas amorosas* deal with violence and deception, most tell of love lost and love found. This theme takes a decidedly violent turn in the *Desengaños amorosos*, in which all ten novellas contain horrifying representations of violence against women. Replete with graphic descriptions of abuse, rape, torture, and murder, this second volume of women's disillusionment in love aims to convince readers of the need for social change. As the bodies pile up, the message becomes clear: cultural and individual reform must take place for women's safety to be guaranteed.

Cast as a response to the violence of the texts, a heavy dose of didacticism runs through the collection. Before, during, and after the stories, female frame tale characters urge women to defend themselves against men. They also call on men to change their deceptive, violent ways. During the course of the two soirees that serve as the setting for both volumes, the protagonist Lisis issues one of many protests of the treatment of women:

> ¡Ah, señores caballeros!, no digo yo que todos seáis malos, mas que no sé cómo se ha de conocer el bueno; demás que yo no os culpo de otros vicios, que eso fuera disparate; sólo para con las mujeres no hallo con qué disculparos. (*Desengaños* 331)

> [Oh, gentlemen! I don't mean that you're all evil, but I don't know how to recognize a good man. I'm not blaming you for other vices, that would be foolish; but for your treatment of women I find no way to excuse you. (238)]²

By the end of the *Desengaños amorosos*, Lisis becomes so convinced that good men are hard to find that she refuses to marry her fiance. To substantiate her claims about the dangers facing women, Lisis catalogues the violence experienced by the female protagonists of

---

1847 to 1948, when no complete editions were published. See Whitenack ("Introduction") for information on scholarly interest in Zayas.

² Throughout this study, citations for Zayas's *Novelas amorosas* are taken from Amezúa's edition. I cite Yllera's excellent critical edition of the *Desengaños amorosos*, following the restored order of the novellas. With some modifications (indicated by "mod." after the page number), all translations of Zayas are based on Boyer's English editions of *The Enchantments of Love* and *The Disenchantments of Love*. For clarity, I indicate after each Spanish citation which volume I am citing, but for brevity's sake I do not do so for the English counterpart. Unless otherwise noted, translations from all other Spanish texts are my own.

the novellas. Her list details the circumstances of those who have been beaten, raped, tortured, poisoned, decapitated, and stabbed.

Having heard these tales of women's victimization, Lisis sets her own self-preservation as a priority. In the final pages, she rejects the current state of gender relations and declares that she will enter a convent. Lisis also suggests that other women choose a similar course of action in order to ensure their own survival. Lisis's example makes explicit the pro-woman didacticism present in the *Novelas amorosas* and, more obviously, in the *Desengaños amorosos*. With directly stated protests, this collection of exemplary novellas seeks to bridge the gender gap by speaking on behalf of victimized women and by advocating women's basic rights.

Working against cultural prejudice that figured woman as corruptible and corrupting, Zayas's texts flesh out many characterizations of women and validate women's capacity for intellectual and physical freedom. Her characters take adamant stands on women's issues by criticizing men's behavior and men's refusal to grant women access to education, arms, and justice. Zayas denounces violence against women, calls for legal and educational reform, and represents the convent as a safe haven. In political terms, Zayas's fiction marks one step forward in the centuries-long development of feminist consciousness in western Europe. Her ideology marks a huge leap forward for Spanish letters; because of her outspoken protests and calls to action, she has been hailed as a founding feminist figure in Spain.[3]

To speak of feminism in the early modern period is not to invoke modern social movements aimed at dismantling the very foundations of patriarchy. The many feminisms that exist in modern societies have taken centuries to develop, and discussions of feminism in a historical context require a recognition of this evolutionary

---

[3] Critics who have dealt specifically with Zayas's position as a key feminist figure include, but certainly are not limited to: Barbeito Carneiro, Boyer ("Introduction" and "The War"), Cocozzella, Foa (*Feminismo y forma narrativa*), Heiple, Lockert, and Williamsen ("Engendering Interpretation" and "Questions of Entitlement"). Zayas's defense of women is emphasized in Mancuso's *Donna María de Zayas y Sotomayor: una donna in difesa delle donne nella Spagna del Seicento*. Citing Teresa de Cartagena as an example, Yllera correctly points out that Zayas was not the first woman to defend women's intellectual capacity (48 n. 21). As I will argue throughout this study, Zayas is revolutionary in that she does much more than merely defend women's intellect: she aims to correct the practices and structures that subordinated women to men.

process. Elucidating this development, Gerda Lerner has laid out the basic components of what we now understand to be a full-fledged feminist consciousness:

> the awareness of women that they belong to a subordinate group; that they have suffered wrongs as a group; that their condition of subordination is not natural, but is societally determined; that they must join with other women to remedy these wrongs; and finally, that they must and can provide an alternate vision of societal organization in which women as well as men will enjoy autonomy and self-determination. (*Creation* 14)

Like María de Zayas, other early modern feminist writers were aware of their mistreatment as a group, protested their subordination in the natural order, and often called for women to join together. Zayas's representations of men as violent matches up with other women writers' concern with the "perversions" of patriarchy.[4] Yet, historically speaking, the seventeenth century was too early for a full articulation of an emancipatory agenda similar to those we have seen in recent Western feminisms, too early for claims on "autonomy and self-determination" for all people, regardless of race, ethnicity, and class.[5] It is with an awareness of historical processes and of the role that early modern women played in the formation of a feminist consciousness that Zayas's texts are herein referred to as feminist.

---

[4] A general consideration of pro-women writings in the early modern period presents infinite contradictions. Many humanists–including Erasmus and Juan Luis Vives–favored a limited expansion of women's education that would make them better wives and mothers (cf. McKendrick, *Woman and Society* 1-44; Foa, *Feminismo* 1-54; Jordan, *Renaissance Feminism* 11-64). As Jordan reminds us, some feminist writers rejected "the literature of patriarchal authority . . . (and) characterized patriarchal attitudes as *perversions* of a legitimate vision of sex and gender relations as egalitarian rather than hierarchical" (272). Zayas certainly could be included in this group of writers.

[5] The idea of a feminism based on emancipation for all people, regardless of sex, race, ethnicity, religion, class, or nationality, belongs, of course, to the late twentieth century (cf. Fraser, *Justice Interruptus*, ch. 7). For more on feminist thinking in Spain, see Camps's *El siglo de las mujeres*, and Perona and Castillo Santos's "Pensamiento español y representaciones de género." Studies that adopt an historicized approach to feminism in Spanish literature include the following edited volumes: Zavala's *Breve historia feminista de la literatura española*, Pérez's *Feminist Encyclopedia of Iberian Literature*, and my *Recovering Spain's Feminist Tradition*.

While some aspects of Zayas's feminism are expressed in direct language, others are expressed indirectly. Perhaps due to its many contradictions and varied assertions, Zayas's feminism has been discussed in countless ways over the years. In the seventeenth century, for example, one censor praised the didactic element of Zayas's fiction while simultaneously insulting women. Pointing to the exemplarity of the collection, Dr. Juan Francisco Genovés characterizes women as indiscriminate and careless:

> le veo lleno de ejemplos, para reformar costumbres, y digno de que se dé a la estampa, que en él (ya que el ocio de las mugeres ha crecido el número a los libros inútiles) la que se ocupare en leerle, tendrá ejemplos con que huir riesgos, a que algunas desatentas se precipitan.
>
> [I see that it is full of examples of ways to reform people's habits. It is worthy of print, since–given that the sloth of women has increased the number of useless books–she who reads it will find examples of how to avoid the risky situations into which some inattentive women throw themselves.][6]

While praising the moral value of Zayas's texts, this censor blames women's reading tastes for the abundance of "useless" books. He also glosses over Zayas's insistence on men's responsibility for social ills. Instead, he places the burden on women to avoid unnecessary risks, presumably in matters of love and desire.

It is tempting to imagine Zayas herself reading such remarks. Did the author of these pro-woman texts agree with Genovés's opinions of women as indulgent readers? Did she interpret the

---

[6] These comments by Genovés appear in the 1659 combined edition of the *Novelas amorosas* and the *Desengaños amorosos* (fol. 4). In contrast to Genovés, the censor of the 1648 edition of the *Desengaños* notes that lessons for both sexes are contained in the texts, which, he says, offer "un asilo donde puede acogerse la femenil flaqueza más acosada de importunidades lisonjeras, y un espejo de lo que más necesita el hombre para la buena dirección de sus acciones" (*Novelas* 5) [an asylum for that feminine weakness most given to flirtation and trouble, and a mirror of what man most needs for good guidance of his actions]. To varying degrees, both censors' remarks reflect dominant views on women's reading in the period. As Cornilliat indicates in "Exemplarities," "Humanist cultural propaganda does not see the romance reader as a nobleman in search of a model but as a 'damoiselle' indulging her private fantasy and seeking only her own pleasure" (615).

comments as we might today, as further evidence of the sexism that permeates Western cultures?

As a woman author of unusually outspoken, violent texts, María de Zayas has inspired many to imagine who she was, to speculate about the most intimate and mundane aspects of her life. For decades, critics have lamented the fact that little to nothing is known about this anomalous personage in Spanish literary history. Working with little concrete evidence, people have made educated guesses and wild claims about Zayas's life. She was probably born in Madrid in 1590, but there is no record of her death.[7] We can infer from poems left by Lope de Vega, Pérez de Montalbán, and other writers that she was accorded great respect in important literary circles. On the other hand, well-known assertions about her supposed loneliness, bitterness, and ugliness, as well as about her entry into a convent, amount to nothing more than conjecture.[8]

The Spanish writer Azorín devoted an essay to speculation about Zayas. In *Los clásicos redivivos* (*The Classics Revived*), Azorín imagines an old woman living alone with a half dozen cats. In this re-creation, Zayas has sacrificed artistic excellence to popular taste. Declaring that nothing she wrote after the *Novelas amorosas* had any literary merit, Azorín imagines that Zayas produced thirty or forty volumes of popular fiction and then finally died in utter solitude and poverty, apparently as punishment for her literary sins.

---

[7] A baptismal certificate from September 12, 1590, bears the name of María de Zayas and probably belongs to our author. There are at least two death certificates with this name: one from 1661 and the other from 1668, yet neither seems to correspond to her. See Yllera's introduction for an extensive discussion of these biographical issues (11-21).

[8] For tangible evidence of Zayas's literary merit, we can turn to Amezúa's edition of the *Novelas amorosas*, which includes the prefatory poems written for Zayas by other authors (including Ana Caro, Alonso de Castillo Solórzano, and Juan Pérez de Montalbán). The conflation of fiction with autobiography is a common tactic in reading women's literature, of course. The association between Zayas and her frame tale protagonist Lisis is perhaps the most salient example of this dubious critical strategy. According to Yllera, Amezúa first suggested in his prologue to the *Desengaños amorosos* that Zayas entered a convent. Rincón, Hesse, and Montesa repeated the speculation. Hesse and Martínez del Portal both suggest that Zayas suffered her own disenchantment in love. Since Zayas foregrounds the female body and women's experiences, it is somewhat understandable that many subsequent critics have tried to create a biography for her that coincides with her fiction. For a summary of previous assertions that confuse fiction with biography, see Yllera's introduction (esp. 18-21).

The anomaly of Zayas's identity as an educated, productive, successful woman writer continually provokes critics and readers to venture comments on her personal history and, in the absence of real information, to draw this history out of her fiction. As Azorín's scenario confirms, this fascination belies a collective voyeurism: we want to know more about the woman who dared to write such shocking, bloody, outspoken fiction. The intense urge to explain Zayas's existence closely relates to the voyeurism that often accompanies interest in women intellectuals. In Zayas's case, we want to understand how it is that a woman in seventeenth-century Spain came to write prose as packed with action, sex, social criticism, and violence as a novel we might pick up at a local bookstore today.

I have heard and read many reactions to María de Zayas: she was indiscreet, a sellout to the book market, disillusioned with love, disgusted with the literary scene, not feminist enough, not the "right" kind of feminist. Such judgments and speculations recall the burdens traditionally placed on female writers, especially those who write with remarkable style and political consciousness. In addition to the obviously troubling conflation of woman with text, it is a testament to Zayas's unique, and perhaps threatening, status as a popular woman writer that she and her texts have been the subject of so much curiosity. Fundamentally, the vigorous polemic over the formal, thematic, and political elements in Zayas attests to the complexity of her literature.

The fervent interest in Zayas relates most directly to the powerful politics and dramatic aesthetic of her texts. Given the renewed commitment to recuperating women's literature and history, it is no surprise that she has come to the fore as one of the most important subjects in Spain's early modern period. There is an ever growing bibliography on her fiction and her one authenticated play (*Traición en la amistad* [*Friendship Betrayed*]), and graduate programs have begun to add her to their reading lists.[9]

---

[9] The past twenty years have seen numerous publications on Zayas, including dozens of articles, Williamsen and Whitenack's edited volume (*María de Zayas: The Dynamics of Discourse*), and Foa's *Feminismo y forma narrativa*. In 2000, Brownlee's *The Cultural Labyrinth of María de Zayas* and Greer's *María de Zayas Tells Baroque Tales of Love and the Cruelty of Men* were published; I do not deal with them here because my book was in press when they came out. These publications, in conjunction with a total of over twenty-five dissertations on Zayas in the past few

This rising interest notwithstanding, Zayas has yet to be inserted into the historiography on women and feminism in Europe.[10] To begin to rectify this oversight, we first need to situate Zayas's woman-centered politics within the ideologies and strategies of other women writers in western Europe. To do so, we can turn to the most complete book on the topic to date, Constance Jordan's *Renaissance Feminism*, which provides a framework for thinking about early modern feminist thought:

> Renaissance feminists spoke of powerlessness and objectification, but they tended to see the wretched condition of women as the consequence of the moral perversion of men, who failed to live up to the challenge of being fully human. They sought recognition for women as females and exponents of the feminine but also as a reason to reform the distorted humanity of men, to bring the other half of the human race into line. (9)[11]

Inasmuch as her female characters lack access to safety and justice, Zayas depicts women as disempowered. She also urges men to reform their moral decline and seeks recognition of women's basic rights.

Zayas's critique of women's powerlessness matches up with those of other feminists examined by Jordan. Like other early modern feminists, Zayas does not call for a complete dismantling

---

decades, speak to critics' renewed interest in this author. Times have changed since 1972, when Vasileski wrote in *María de Zayas y Sotomayor: Su época y su obra* that Zayas was understudied (9). Whitenack alludes to Zayas's absence from graduate reading lists and courses in the United States even as late as the 1980s, but also notes her rising popularity ("Introduction" 1-2).

[10] Some of the most influential work in this field–including Jordan's *Renaissance Feminism*, King's *Women of the Renaissance*, and Lerner's *Creation of a Feminist Consciousness*–does not mention Zayas at all. She does figure, however, in Anderson and Zinsser's *A History of Their Own*. Interestingly, a juvenile reader of brief biographies includes a sketch of Zayas's life (cf. Benedict and Covington's *The Literary Crowd*).

[11] Jordan's analyses and categorizations have been praised for their ambition and criticized for their imprecision. In particular, the discussion of androgyny, the lack of analysis of readership and reception, and the assessment of women's lack of property ownership as a primary hindrance to their autonomy have been criticized for their lack of historical contextualization and nuance (cf. Maclean). Nonetheless, Jordan's is the most comprehensive study on Renaissance feminism to date, and it certainly represents a solid point of departure for further consideration of the many manifestations of and departures from feminist discourse in the period.

of patriarchy. Rather, she envisions women's inclusion in the institutional workings of society. Put simply, she wants a guarantee of safety, education, and justice for women. Zayas's novellas seek a reconfiguration of social relations and, like other texts analyzed by Jordan, they are "devoted to securing for women a status equal to that of men" (11).

While unique in Spain, a large part of Zayas's feminism is consonant with western European feminism of the period. In fact, Zayas's fiction shares many similarities with various ideological and literary discourses of the early modern period. Like Christine de Pizan and other pro-feminist writers engaged in the debate on the "woman question" (*querelle des femmes*), Zayas presents lists of famous women and endorses women's solidarity. The theme of domestic violence, which is prevalent in Zayas, also appears in Hélisenne de Crenne's *The Torments of Love* (*Les Angoysses douloureuses qui procedent d'amours*, 1538), Margaret Cavendish's *Convent of Pleasure* (1668), and Madame de La Fayette's *The Princess of Clèves* (*La Princesse de Clèves*, 1678). In terms of the novella genre, Zayas's prose follows in the tradition of Giovanni Boccaccio, Marguerite de Navarre, Miguel de Cervantes, and Lope de Vega. Like her Italian contemporary Moderata Fonte and late seventeenth-century English writers Mary Astell and Aphra Behn, she has pointedly feminist moments in her texts. And, like many of her Spanish contemporaries, she laments the sociopolitical consequences of the decline of the Spanish empire. As even these brief comparisons suggest, it is possible to connect Zayas to many authors with regard to ideology, literary style, and genre.

Based on a rigorously politicized treatment of sex and the body, Zayas's highly original aesthetic differentiates her from other writers of the period. Framed by statements about the need to reform gender relations, most of the novellas contain descriptions of the physical and emotional perils of love. The number of characters who are injured or killed speaks to the high stakes of desire in Zayas's texts: over three dozen women and men fall victim to violence in the novellas. Most of these victims are women who suffer at the hands of jealous and protective husbands, lovers, brothers, and fathers. Others–including servants and slaves–get caught in the whirlwind of violence that befalls many of the households in the tales. A few male victims die in flurries of violence that include women's own acts of vengeance. This brief catalogue of victims testifies to the major role played by sexuality and violence in Zayas's texts. This reliance on sex and violence has led many to call the novellas vulgar, improper, and, in the *Diccionario de literatura española* of 1953, "frankly obscene."[12]

Having little to do with procreation (for there are few children here) and everything to do with gender relations, sexuality and corporeality are used to criticize social dysfunction. Such criticism is connected intimately with the honor code and with men's claim on women's bodies. As female characters fall victim to men, the texts protest the hypocrisy and proprietariness that inform dominant values about women's place in society. These representations of victimization, hypocrisy, and injustice focus our attention on the body. From this schema of representation and didactic intervention, the body emerges as the cornerstone of Zayas's feminism.

Since Zayas's texts insistently defend women's right to education and social justice, many critics have commented on the nature of her feminist beliefs.[13] Some scholars claim that reading Zayas as a feminist is to read anachronistically (Perry, *Gender and Disorder*), to be duped by her rhetoric (Griswold), or to underestimate the sophistication with which she uses language (Brownlee, "Postmodernism"). Others (such as Boyer, Greer, and Maroto Camino) point to the privileging of the feminine in her fiction as testimony to her feminist ideologies. Some critics in this camp call her feminism conservative (Foa and Yllera) or claim that Zayas contradicts her own commitment to feminism (Redondo Goicoechea, "Introducción"). This debate persists because Zayas's texts are, as Brownlee has highlighted, quintessentially baroque, and also because the particularities of Zayas's politics have yet to be addressed within a theoreti-

---

[12] The full quote from the *Diccionario de literatura española* speaks to the concern for the eroticism in the texts: "María de Zayas no siente reparo alguno ni temor para tratar las cuestiones eróticas, hasta llegar, en ocasiones, a una franca obscenidad" (760) [María de Zayas does not have any qualms or fears about dealing with erotic issues and, on occasion, she even reaches all out obscenity]. To the editors' credit, they do cite Sylvania's 1922 assessment of the feminist elements in Zayas's texts.

[13] In addition to the critics previously mentioned (cf. note 3), Díez Borque ("El feminismo") and Spieker have discussed the structural importance of Zayas's feminism, and Stackhouse ("Narrative Roles"), Greer ("Who's Telling this Story Anyhow?"), and Alcalde have addressed the various narrative techniques and styles in her work. Moreover, Cocozzella, Heiple, and Salstad have signalled the important fact that Zayas's feminism is circumscribed by her engagement with literary tradition.

cal model that accounts for the interplay between her aesthetic and her feminism.[14]

As the most compelling and unique aspects of these novellas, sexuality and corporeality form the basis for Zayas's politicized aesthetic. Based on this initial assessment, *Reclaiming the Body* articulates the feminist agenda put forth in Zayas's novella collection and contextualizes the aesthetic through which this feminism is communicated. This book uses feminist theory as a tool for teasing out and interpreting the various feminist tenets of the *Novelas amorosas* and the *Desengaños amorosos*, two volumes which are read here as a unified collection.[15]

Specifically, my theoretical framework relies on "sexual difference" feminists, thinkers who have historicized and contextualized the role of the female body vis-à-vis individuals and their cultures. As Elizabeth Grosz summarizes in *Volatile Bodies*, this loosely configured group of contemporary feminists is

> concerned with the *lived body*, the body insofar as it is represented and used in specific ways in specific cultures. For them, the body is neither brute nor passive, but it is interwoven with and constitutive of systems of meaning, signification, and representa-

---

[14] Perry says that Zayas "cannot really be considered a 'feminist' in the modern sense" (*Gender and Disorder* 74). Griswold rejects Zayas's "feminist posturing" as "purely rhetorical" (100). In "Postmodernism and the Baroque," Brownlee points to the complex exploration of subjectivity in Zayas: "Instead of an exclusive focus on the gender of the speaker or character, she undertakes an analysis of the many discourses (sexuality and gender as well as socioeconomic status and racial identity) whose conflicting imperatives collectively define the unstable boundaries of the individual subject of baroque culture" (119-20). While I agree with Brownlee's analysis, I am arguing that Zayas's feminist ideology is the driving force behind her aesthetic and her politics. For more on female subjectivity, see Otero-Torres's "The Construction of the Female Subject in the Spanish Golden Age."

[15] Methodologically, this reading of both volumes together depends on the argument that, like the two parts of *Don Quijote*, Zayas's texts must be read as part of one unified collection. Ten years separate the publication of the *Novelas amorosas* from that of the *Parte segunda del sarao y entretenimiento honesto* (*Second Part of the Soiree and Honest Entertainment*, popularly known as *Desengaños amorosos*). The volumes are joined by a single frame story that is resolved at the end of the *Desengaños*. Both volumes have similar structures (i.e., frame narrators tell ten tales in each) and deal with similar subject matter (i.e., gender relations). These structural and thematic reasons suggest that, to understand Zayas's aesthetic, we must treat the two publications as one long volume of framed novellas. In most complete editions from 1659 forward, the *Novelas* and the *Desengaños* have been published together in one volume.

tion. On one hand it is a signifying and signified body; on the other, it is an object of systems of social coercion, legal inscription, and sexual and economic exchange. (18)[16]

This is a useful framework through which to approach Zayas's texts precisely because the *Novelas amorosas* and the *Desengaños amorosos* invest meaning in the body. The texts show the body to be the primary point of contact and dissension in gender relations as well as in the cultural construction of the category of woman. Moreover, the texts manifest an awareness of the constraints and freedoms that inform men's and women's behavior, as well as an interest in challenging many of the values and practices that inform relations between the sexes.

Since *Reclaiming the Body* deals with depictions of sexuality and the construction of gender, it is important to consider the categories of sex and gender as they operated in Europe during Zayas's lifetime. Given the import and influence of Thomas Laqueur's arguments in *Making Sex* that gender was subsumed under the larger category of sex in the early modern period, the introduction of postmodern feminist philosophy in analyses of pre-eighteenth century texts raises questions of legitimacy and historicity. For over a decade, the notion of a one-sex model of the human body has been used to claim that only the concept of 'sexual' difference–that of sex and not of gender–existed in the early modern period. These and other assertions about the influence of the one-sex medical model have marked an important turning point in thinking about the changeability of conceptualizations of the body.

Without diminishing the importance of this work, I do, however, agree wholeheartedly with the editors of *Feminist Readings of Early Modern Culture* in their assessment of current scholarship. Valerie Traub, Lindsay Kaplan, and Dympna Callaghan have argued that, although the analyses of the "one-sex, no gender" model offer a legitimate reading of scientific beliefs, these discussions have resulted in a critical tendency to ignore the importance of gender as a

---

[16] Grosz describes the "sexual difference feminists" as distinct from two other main groups: "In contrast with both egalitarianism and social constructionism, a third group can be discerned. Its participants include Luce Irigaray, Hélène Cixous, Gayatri Spivak, Jane Gallop, Moira Gatens, Vicki Kirby, Judith Butler, Naomi Schor, Monique Wittig, and many others" (17-18). Unless otherwise noted, all citations from Grosz are from *Volatile Bodies*.

category of analysis. In their introduction, the editors state that they "reject the now prevalent argument, based on the theory of physiological homology between the sexes, that there existed only one gender in early modern culture" (4). As they assert, and as feminists have suggested in many contexts over the years,

> gender exists as a term of definition even when it is not specifically articulated; it operates according to the exigencies of various discursive domains, and relates to and interacts with other axes of social formation. (4)[17]

This analysis is particularly applicable to Zayas's texts, in which issues of compliance with and resistance to gendered codes of behavior influence much of the plot movement and character development. By focusing on gender relations, sexuality, and violence, *Reclaiming the Body* examines Zayas's self-conscious and explicit engagement with issues of gender–including the mutability of both masculinity and femininity.

As the analyses of social context, violence, space, discourse, and transgression in the following chapters suggest, Zayas depicts the female body as a site of simultaneous overinvestment and devaluation. Men are shown to treat women as bodily vessels, as objects to be guarded and contained. In discussing the protest of such practices, I argue that Zayas's political and literary strategies urge readers to recognize embodiment as common ground between the sexes. Ultimately, Zayas focuses on this common ground as a way to convince readers that something is amiss in a culture that does not guarantee women's integrity and survival.

Aimed at expressing Zayas's feminism through a theoretical model that focuses on her deployment of the body, *Reclaiming the Body* is divided into two sections. Part one, "Flesh and Blood," examines the uses and meanings of violence and the body in early modern Spanish culture and in Zayas's texts. The first chapter, "So-

---

[17] In *Cross Dressing, Sex, and Gender*, Bullough and Bullough also reject the one-sex model. Challenging Greenblatt's claim in "Fiction and Friction" that women were seen as imperfect men and that "modern notions of sexual difference developed only later" (cf. *Shakespearean Negotiations*, 66-93), Bullough and Bullough state, "This theory, however, ignores the gender experimentation that was taking place during the same period" (76). For a related argument, also see Park's "The Rediscovery of the Clitoris."

cial and Literary Contexts of Corporeality," begins with an analysis of the discourses of corporeality that were available to Zayas in seventeenth-century Spain. The chapter relates Zayas's representations of violence and gender to other bodily discourses and practices. The analysis also establishes a theoretical connection between Zayas's own deployment of the body for feminist purposes and what Elizabeth Grosz terms "corporeal feminism." This kinship–in which Zayas is shown to anticipate later feminist developments in precise and startling ways–is used as the basis for a discussion of the import of bodily discourse in Zayas's preface to the *Novelas amorosas* and in the first tale of the *Desengaños amorosos*.

Chapter two, "Violence Denaturalized: Feminist Readings of the Body Imperiled," complements the initial discussion of the body's many meanings with a comprehensive analysis of violence in Zayas's novellas. This discussion considers the implications of theoretical frameworks that take women's corporeality as central to female existence and of Zayas's own close association between corporeality and women. This chapter lays out the ways in which Zayas denaturalizes violence and deconstructs the metaphors of the homogeneous category of woman in Western cultures. As in the other chapters, the display of the body is read here as an integral aspect of Zayas's feminist agenda: by denaturalizing violence against women, Zayas's texts encourage the reader to come to terms with the particularities of women's humanity and the realities of women's disempowerment.

Part two, "The Boundaries of Gender," interprets Zayas's intense engagement with gender issues through an historicized analysis of early modern gender relations. Chapters three and four seek to delineate the boundaries of gendered behavior in Zayas's fiction. These chapters argue that Zayas's exploitations of dominant constructions of gender are based on the politicization of baroque writers' expression of individual disillusionment. By focusing on confinement and transgression in Zayas's texts, these analyses link Zayas's fictional women to discursive constructions of women in the period. Chapter three, "Women's Place in the Social Order," argues that the interstices between space and violence in Zayas's texts demystify the notion that the home is a safe place for women. The violation of women's bodies in public and private spaces throughout the novellas suggests that women are left to fend for themselves in a society that fails to include them fully in the workings of the social order.

Chapter four, "Crossdressers, Avengers, and the Performance of Gender," examines the challenge put to gender codes and social control by characters who defy culturally proscribed boundaries of behavior. Based on Zayas's tales of crossdressed characters and women avengers, the chapter posits that these plots expose the constitutive elements and processes of gender construction. Highlighting models of acceptable behavior, Zayas's novellas mirror the components of desirable (and undesirable) femininities and masculinities.

The conclusion lays out the components of Zayas's claim on the body as feminist territory. Integral to this assessment is a consideration of the parameters and implications of Zayas's feminism. Emphasizing the multiplicity of female characterizations, this chapter discusses the range of political stances made available in the texts. The feminist advocacy present in the frame tale provides the focus for this final assessment of the feminist agenda of the collection.

When examining Zayas's politics, we should keep in mind that the texts are remarkably nuanced in their representations of gender. Not all men are portrayed as dangerous or violent and not all women as virtuous and good. Such varied depictions force the reader to recognize the individual and cultural forces at work in the subordination of women. In Zayas's schema, men, women, and social norms all contribute to women's disempowerment and endangerment. As Lisis's rhetoric attests, the novellas criticize men *and* society for sanctioning the mistreatment of women:

> ¿Pues qué ley humana ni divina halláis, nobles caballeros, para precipitaros tanto contra las mujeres, que apenas se halla uno que las defienda, cuando veis tantos que las persiguen? (*Desengaños* 504)

> [What human or divine law enables you, noble gentlemen, to so hurl yourselves against women that you can hardly find a single man to defend them and when you see so many men persecute them? (400, modified translation)]

This statement encapsulates some of the issues at stake in Zayas's texts. The system demands that women depend on men, yet, as the many victims in the novellas show, men fail to comply with their obligations to the women around them. Rather than categorically dismiss men or the social system, Zayas constructs her criticism so that blame falls on individuals–anyone who treats women with disrespect–and on society–which fails to protect members of either sex.

With the *Novelas amorosas* hinting at the tension and occasional violence between the sexes, the *Desengaños* depicts these problems almost exclusively in terms of victimization. The patterns of victimization highlight the structural and individual problems that Zayas wants to correct. Rather than grant reprieves for what might otherwise be seen as isolated acts of violence and deception, Zayas depicts men as having control over women's bodies in every way and in almost every imaginable space. The texts argue that, since there is limited accountability for this mistreatment, women must take measures to protect themselves from abuse, and everyone must begin to take responsibility for a flawed system that allows for such abuse.

The chapters that follow seek to contextualize–historically, textually, and theoretically–the feminism of María de Zayas's novellas. Integral to this analysis is the larger question of what exactly is accomplished (and sacrificed) when gender emerges as the privileged category of identity. In addition to Zayas's treatment of class and ethnic difference, for example, her representation of violence against women, emphasis on woman as body, and depiction of women as agents of violence are all relevant to our own era. Like questions of social justice and basic human rights, these issues continue to spark debate among contemporary feminists.[18]

* * *

It is a poignant fact of literary history that a woman who wrote powerful prose aimed at improving society's estimation and treatment of women would herself nearly disappear from the historical record. A masterful storyteller who structured her entire collection

---

[18] Although I refer to many feminist thinkers throughout the book, the following list should serve as a shorthand bibliography for the basic issues engaged by Zayas that contemporary feminism continues to debate. For questions of representational violence, see de Lauretis's *Technologies of Gender*; for a summary of the dilemma of reading woman as body see Grosz's *Volatile Bodies*; for a discussion of questions of sexual difference, see Irigaray's *An Ethics of Sexual Difference*. On international social justice and the problems of coalitional politics, see Butler's *Bodies that Matter*, Fraser's *Justice Interruptus*, Gatens's *Imaginary Bodies*, Nussbaum's *Sex and Social Justice*, and Rupp and Taylor's "Forging Feminist Identity."

on the telling of purportedly biographical stories, Zayas's own biography is but a sketch. Again and again, critics have scoured her texts for clues about her life. This strategy is legitimated in a few isolated instances in which the authorial voice is heard, when Zayas breaks away from the other narrative voices to refer to the act of writing and to her readership. At the end of the *Desengaños amorosos*, for example, she refers to, and perhaps even anticipates, her own disembodied relationship with the public and with posterity. Threatening to take up the sword just as she has taken up the pen in defense of women's good name, this voice insists that we know the speaker by her writing, but not by sight ("me conocéis por lo escrito, mas no por la vista" [*Desengaños* 507]).

In spite of her efforts to insert women into the realm of social justice, the fact remains that, while we have records of Cervantes, Quevedo, Lope, and other great baroque authors, recent archival searches have yielded little about Zayas. Although she represents a body lost to the historical record, Zayas continues to grip our attention and pique our curiosity. While the details of this remarkable author's life seem to have disappeared, her fictions lay claim to a corporeal feminism that calls for the reevaluation and validation of the collective female body. Her incisive critique can be seen as a building block for more inclusive visions of social justice. In arguing for the protection of men and women, Zayas touches on a central issue of liberal philosophy: societies need to invest in all of their constitutive identities, to value every body that makes up the whole.

Reclaiming the Body theorizes the union of corporeality with feminism in a comprehensive study of the *Novelas amorosas* and the *Desengaños amorosos*. This approach endorses the re-embodiment of feminist theory and practice. I hope that this book will encourage a more expansive evaluation of the development of feminism and of the points of contact between early modern and postmodern feminisms. Along with H. Patsy Boyer's translations and recent books by Marina S. Brownlee and Margaret Greer, I hope that my discussion will encourage scholars of early modern Europe to look again at Spain, and that it will inspire Hispanists to look more closely at women writers, most of whom remain outside the canon. Above all, I hope that this book will help to secure María de Zayas a well-deserved place in feminist history.

Part One

FLESH AND BLOOD

CHAPTER ONE

SOCIAL AND LITERARY CONTEXTS OF CORPOREALITY

> *Every body is marked by the history and specificity of its existence. It is possible to construct a biography, a history of the body, for each individual and social body.*
>
> Elizabeth Grosz

LIKE many early modern authors, María de Zayas holds the body up for scrutiny, demanding that we read its multiple cultural and historical meanings. The *Novelas amorosas* claims to have the explicit purpose of entertaining Lisis, the frame tale protagonist who is recovering from an illness. Dubbed *maravillas* ("marvels" or "enchantments"), these stories describe the perils and joys of love.[1] In spite of the carefree connotations of the term *maravilla*, some characters are beaten, raped, and killed in these tales. The description of the battered woman Hipólita, the female avenger of "Al fin se paga todo," exemplifies the attention given to bodies and violence in this first volume.

---

[1] In the *Novelas*, the narrator explains that Lisis's mother calls the tales *maravillas*, "que con este nombre quiso desampalagar al vulgo del de novelas, título tan enfadoso que ya en todas partes le aborrecen" (31) [In using this term she wanted to avoid the common term "novella," a title so trite it was now entirely out of fashion (8, mod.)]. This generic refashioning, attributed to Lisis's mother in the *Novelas amorosas* and to Lisis in the *Desengaños*, represents a strategic move by Zayas to distance her fiction from the many other novellas of the period. In this respect, Zayas follows the lead of Cervantes, who promises originality and innovation in his use of the term "novela ejemplar" or exemplary novel. As to the titles of the novellas proper, it should be noted that Zayas gave titles to all of the *Novelas amorosas*, but only entitled "La esclava de su amante" in the *Desengaños*. As Yllera points out, the titles, including that of *Desengaños amorosos*, were added to the 1734 Barcelona edition (127 n. 1). For the sake of convenience and clarity, the titles have been used subsequently by editors and critics. See Williamsen's "Questions of Entitlement" for a discussion of the implications of imposed titles in Zayas and Sor Juana.

Recounting the beating that her ex-lover gave her,

> la hermosa dama mostró a don García lo más honesta y recatadamente que pudo los cardenales de su cuerpo, que todos o los más estaban para verter sangre [...]. (*Novelas amorosas* 323)
>
> [As modestly and as chastely as she could, the beautiful lady showed don García horrible bruises all over her body, almost all of which looked like they were ready to spill blood. (237, mod.)]

Hipólita reveals the unmistakable signs of violence in these bruises. On the verge of bursting open, her skin barely holds the blood below the surface. With its tension between revelation and containment, this description suggests that women must bear the weight, as well as the pain, of men's abuse.

In terms of both detail and number, the second volume of the collection contains more explicit representations of violence. The principal narrator describes that, at Lisis's mandate, the female frame characters will tell tales about women in the *Desengaños amorosos*:

> [Se dispuso que] ... los que refiriesen fuesen casos verdaderos, y que tuviesen nombre de desengaños .... Fue la pretensión de Lisis en esto volver por la fama de las mujeres (tan postrada y abatida por su mal juicio, que apenas hay quien hable bien de ellas). (*Desengaños* 118)
>
> [(She said that) ... the stories they told should be true cases, and they should be called "disenchantments." ... Lisis's intention in this was to defend women's good name (so denigrated and defamed by men's bad opinion that there is scarcely anyone who speaks well of them). (37)]

Following guidelines that mark a clear break with the tone of the previous volume, Lisis and her cohort narrate morbidly violent *desengaños*. The perpetrators of this violence are almost exclusively men.

In "Mal presagio casar lejos," for example, the Spanish woman Blanca asks her Flemish husband and his father why they have treated her with such cruelty. Weary of her complaints, the husband

> se descompuso con doña Blanca, no sólo de palabras, mas de obras, maltratándola tanto, que fue milagro salir de sus manos con la vida [...]. (*Desengaños* 356)

[became violent with doña Blanca not only with words, but also in action, beating her so much that it was a miracle that she escaped from his hands with her life. (260, mod.)]

As this passage suggests, the most striking (and frequent) manifestation of bodily discourse in this volume is that of the violated female body. In the *Desengaños amorosos*, women's bodies are described as incorruptible in death, as bleeding from beatings, and as seething with worms from decay. While some men are victimized as well, their bodies do not receive similar narrative treatment. Instead, the volume emphasizes men's role as aggressors.

Male characters in the *Desengaños* carry out every type of violence imaginable as they imprison, rape, poison, torture, strangle, stab, and behead the women closest to them. It seems likely that Zayas and her readers were familiar with such dramatic confrontations with the corporeal. In addition to the public violence of executions and *autos de fe*, readers of many baroque texts took in similarly vivid representations of violated bodies. By approaching Zayas's fiction from a combined literary and cultural perspective, we can see that she mobilizes various discourses of corporeality in her fiction, ascribing meaning to bodies in ways that connect her texts with the presentation and utilization of the body in art, politics, and religion. By examining various discourses of corporeality with which Zayas and her readers would have been familiar, we can begin to understand the points of contact between the author's aesthetic and the deployment of the body in seventeenth-century Spain.

Signalled by the disruption of physical and/or psychical integrity, violation occurs in seemingly infinite variations in the period. In addition to the Catholic hagiographic tradition, in which saints (and their pious followers) graciously withstand tremendous physical pain and martyrs' relics constitute a commodity unto themselves, representations of bodies can be found in any number of literary texts in the period. Perhaps the most public, performative literary examples of bodies on display can be found in the wife-murder plays. This subgenre of *comedia* posits the female body as the principal site of contestation for issues surrounding sexual and political anxiety.[2] Among abundant examples on the stage, we find

---

[2] In *Fatal Union*, Stroud focuses on thirty-one wife-murder *comedias* dating from 1575-1675, pointing out that "it is very likely that there are others still not

Lope's Casandra killed by her lover in *El castigo sin venganza* (*Punishment without Revenge*) and Calderón's Mencía sacrificially bled to death in *El médico de su honra* (*The Physician of His Honor*).

Bodies also emerge as the site for subversion and challenge in the literature of the period. The popularity of crossdressing provides one example of this questioning of gender roles. Some of the best known Golden Age female characters, including Rosaura in *La vida es sueño* (*Life Is a Dream*) and Laurencia in *Fuenteovejuna*, break down gender roles by dressing and/or acting like men, taking honor into their own hands, and usurping the traditionally masculine role of avenger.[3] Among Cervantes's fascinating female characters, Marcela (in *Don Quijote*) and Preciosa (in the *Novelas ejemplares*) stand out because they cross traditional gender boundaries by asserting their will and speaking their minds.

In spite of the differences among these transgressive fictional characters, the one thing they have in common is that they were penned by men. And, as Sheila Fisher and Janet Halley summarily state in *The Lady Vanishes*, "for a male author to write women in these periods was to refer not to women, but to men" (4).[4] The use of the body by these and other early modern authors tells us many things, but one conclusion we can make about *comedia*, poetry, and other literary genres and cultural phenomena is that bodies acted as signifiers for a variety of dominant (i.e., patriarchal) ideologies in the seventeenth century. Put simply, bodies had meaning. And, in the cultural and social realms, men controlled the production and presentation of that meaning.

In early modern Spain, an age in which male authors, the Inquisition, and the state used bodies for varying aesthetic, didactic, po-

---

considered" (19). In *Woman and Society*, McKendrick has cautioned against extrapolating from these plays to real social conditions of women (3-44). By invoking this group of *comedias*, I merely want to recall the fact that theatergoers often were faced with the spectacle of violence on the stage.

[3] The woman warrior Catalina de Erauso's anomalous life also presents an intriguing story in terms of the body. Given the recent translation of her memoir, *Historia de la monja alférez* (*Lieutenant Nun*), the escapades of this cross-dressed woman seem to have captured the imagination of modern Americans as well. For more on the body in early modern drama, see Greenberg's *Canonical States, Canonical Stages* and Yarbro-Bejarano's *Feminism and the Honor Plays of Lope de Vega*.

[4] Similarly, Harvey uses the concept of ventriloquism to discuss the literary transvestism that occurs when male authors create women characters (cf. *Ventriloquized Voices*).

litical, yet ultimately patriarchal, purposes, María de Zayas issued her own response to male dominance over discourses of sexuality, gender relations, and justice. Using violence and bodily discourse to convey a feminist message, Zayas's novella collection incorporates the spectacle of violence seen in public life, literature, and theater, and the aestheticization of violence seen in hagiography. In the *Novelas amorosas* and the more daring *Desengaños amorosos*, Zayas turns to the stories of the body referred to by Elizabeth Grosz in the epigraph. Through fictional women characters, Zayas offers up women's stories with the effect of constructing what Grosz calls "a biography, a history of the body, for each individual and social body" (142). Forging a connection between women's voices and bodies, Zayas tells the story of women in her society. Through this connection, she lays out the tenets of an early modern corporeal feminism that engages and politicizes the female body. Through the portrayal of women as victims of violence and of male-oriented values, Zayas inserts herself into the gender debate that had raged since the late Middle Ages in western Europe. Mary Elizabeth Perry has observed that Zayas entered this debate by focusing on interpersonal relations, "where violence becomes entrenched" ("Crisis" 24).

Zayas's characters articulate a variety of ideological positions, and from these we can cull a list of core feminist components of the texts. These include: advocacy for women's access to education, an emphasis on women's autonomy, an endorsement of the convent as a safe haven for women, a cohesive subtext of female solidarity, and a condemnation of masculine violence. These fundamental tenets are complemented and sometimes contradicted throughout the collection. In spite of occasional ideological tension, which I discuss in detail in the final chapter, these positions represent the skeleton of Zayas's feminist agenda.

Zayas expresses much of her complex ideology through representations of violence. This politicized aesthetic begs an analysis of the relationship between Zayas's violent, corporeal aesthetic and the availability of similarly violent images in the author's culture. The scathing critique of patriarchy communicated through representations of violence against women–depictions claimed to be based on truth–raises the issue of which source materials and influences might have served as the basis for Zayas's aesthetic. Previous critics who have raised this point have turned to the Italianate novella, tracing many of Zayas's tales to their Spanish, Italian, and French origins. While an exhaustive source study has yet to be done on Zayas's novellas, Edwin Place and others have discussed many of the tales in a comparative context, primarily in relation to male-authored texts of the period. If Zayas incorporates *comedia* tropes as well as medieval miracle tales into her fiction, she also follows in the tradition of great novella writers such as Boccaccio, Marguerite de Navarre, Timoneda, Cervantes, Lope, and Castillo Solórzano. Reworking stock plots and exploiting generic conventions, Zayas forges a unique form of feminist exemplarity that relies heavily on an aestheticized presentation of the female body.[5]

The use of the framed novella genre for this combination of stock plots, violence, and feminized discourse differentiates Zayas from other writers. Indeed, her texts stand out as the most overtly feminist novella collection of this period in western Europe (cf. Donovan). While we cannot pretend to know what exactly made Zayas turn to the body as a framework for her feminist didacticism, it is possible to outline the different models of corporeality in the period. This approach to corporeality addresses the relationship between Zayas's aestheticized representations of the body and the cultural context of the first half of the seventeenth century. By considering these models of bodily discourse, we can historicize the perception and understanding of the body in early modern Spain.

In many instances, Zayas's texts provide the historical context– of an empire in decline, a nation in decay–for the reader. In an analysis of Zayas's attitudes toward her society, Foa has noted in *Feminismo y forma narrativa* that Zayas's references to the declining state of affairs are typical of seventeenth-century authors, and yet generally are not as forceful as those that appear in other writings of the

---

[5] Those who have considered Zayas's sources and/or analyzed her work in conjunction with other writers of the period include: Bourland, Brownlee (*The Cultural Labyrinth*) Chevalier, Felten (*María de Zayas*), Foa (*Feminismo* and "Humor and Suicide"), Grieve, Kohn, Montesa, Otero-Torres, Pérez-Erdely, Place, Senabre Sempere, and Serrano Poncela. Comparisons of Zayas's work with canonical texts are useful in determining her own points of contact with both Spanish and foreign literature, as well as with other dominant discourses (cf. Salstad). Recently, studies that compare Zayas to other women authors have become more common. See, for example, dissertations by Cushing, Jiménez, Kothe, Langle de Paz, and Walliser; and comparative articles by Ordóñez and Donovan.

period (76).[6] Although the pointed criticism in Zayas's oeuvre is baroque in its expression of disenchantment and its awareness of social decline–as William Clamurro has laid out convincingly in "Ideological Contradiction"–, her critique undeniably focuses on problems associated with gender relations in the period.

The historical grounding provided by various references anchors the texts in their time and culture. This historical information communicates the baroque sentiment of disenchantment while also suggesting that the calls for social reform relate to cultural realities of the period. In addition to statements that decry the decay of the times, several facts and figures refer the reader to seventeenth-century Spain. As Boyer has noted, "The multifarious effects of Spain's militarism on society in general hold a prominent place in Zayas's works" ("Introduction" xxxiii). The expulsion of the Moors in 1609, the Catalan revolt of 1640, and the Duke of Alba's scourge of Flanders specifically are mentioned in the texts, for example. These events signal the ethnic and political unrest that afflicted Spain during much of the century. Reflecting a common idealization of the past, Zayas's characters yearn for the age of Charles V and Philip II, and make reference to the nation's moments of glory under the Catholic monarchs.[7]

Presented as a stark contrast with the golden days of old, the dynamics of violence and victimization in the novellas proper reflect the practices of criminal justice, particularly as they were im-

---

[6] In *Feminismo y forma narrativa*, Foa reaches this conclusion after looking at various texts of the period for their statements on disillusionment and general social decay (55-77). She also indicates that Alemán, Gracián, and Quevedo all focus on the war between the sexes, with the fundamental difference being that Zayas focuses on woman as victim whereas "para ellos la mujer es la responsable de todos los males, y el hombre es la víctima" (78) [for them, the woman is responsible for all problems, and the man is the victim]. For more on the baroque sentiment of *desengaño* and gender relations, see Maravall (*La literatura picaresca* 639-97) and Montesa (139-80). Also see Cruz's "Feminism, Psychoanalysis, and the Search for the M/Other" for a provocative analysis of the differences between men's and women's writing in the period.

[7] References to Spain's glory days and to the social and political decline of the mid-seventeenth century appear several times throughout the collection, particularly in the *Desengaños* (e.g. 124, 229, 505, etc.). For a list of historical figures mentioned in the texts, see Yllera (37 n. 96). Scholars who have explored the connection between Zayas's negativism and the political and cultural decline of seventeenth-century Spain include Boyer ("Introduction"), Clamurro ("Ideological Contradiction"), Foa (*Feminismo*), Montesa, and Yllera.

plemented by the Inquisition. Zayas's women characters often are presumed guilty upon accusation of sexual "impurity" and are punished severely for transgressions they may or may not have committed. Women who are punished or killed because men view them as tainted by extramarital sex or rape include: Camila ("La más infame venganza"), Roseleta ("El verdugo de su esposa"), Inés ("La inocencia castigada"), Elena ("Tarde llega el desengaño"), and Magdalena ("Estragos que causa el vicio"). This incomplete list of victims suggests that men's perceptions of women have little or nothing to do with women's behavior. Through these and other representations of violence, Zayas particularizes the prevailing baroque sentiment of cultural decadence by turning it into a protest of the treatment of women in society.

Given their cultural references and political agenda, these novellas beg a closer examination of the points of contact between the fictional representations and the historical realities of gender relations. Among others, Fisher and Halley have addressed the issue of historicity, saying that feminist scholars need to critique the "contemporary economic, legal, political, and religious systems and codes articulating the parameters of women's access to power and self-determination" (6).[8] In other words, the reconstruction of the "textuality of social context" facilitates a richer understanding of women's history as well as a closer, more accurate reading of texts written by and about women (6). In this case, an analysis of the discourses of corporeality incorporated into Zayas's fiction suggests several intersections between the texts and the cultural context in which the author developed her body-based, politicized aesthetic.

Part I of this chapter theorizes that, in writing the collection comprised by the *Novelas amorosas* and the *Desengaños amorosos*, Zayas re-shapes the discourse of the body as it was espoused by seventeenth-century cultural authorities. That is, Zayas exploits the available discourses of corporeality by adapting them to her own

---

[8] Fisher and Halley's discussion of historically contextualized research on women and literature provides an overview of the trajectory of the emphasis on historicism in the late 1980s. Fisher and Halley's collection is emblematic of the historicist impulse of feminist scholarship on early modern Europe (cf. Dolan's *Dangerous Familiars*, Cruz's "Studying Gender," and Traub, Kaplan, and Callaghan's *Feminist Readings*). In the Spanish context, Cruz has called for the examination of extraliterary texts in order to understand the forces shaping women's access to power in the Golden Age ("Studying Gender" 206).

political and artistic agendas. Part II analyzes the preface, the frame tale, and the first novella in the *Desengaños* in order to elucidate the techniques by which Zayas adapts dominant cultural practices and ideologies about women and the body to her own feminist ends. With these complementary analyses of the body in baroque culture, we can begin to uncover the ways in which Zayas, like feminists of our own period, constructs an interpretive history of the collective female experience.

I. THE BODY AS TRUTH

In the past two centuries, critics have been hard pressed to explain the corporeal aesthetic of the *Novelas amorosas* and the *Desengaños amorosos*. What does it mean exactly that a woman wrote popular fiction containing numerous descriptions of women's victimized bodies? Much skepticism has been thrown Zayas's way in response to the excesses of violence in her novellas, and many critics of the nineteenth and twentieth centuries read her representations of sex and violence as obscene, shameless, and tediously detailed.[9] Strong criticism about the inappropriate content of her writings might be explained, as Patricia Grieve has argued, by the mere fact of Zayas's gender. Specifically, Grieve has suggested that the focus on bodies and women in Zayas's work led her to be "labeled offensive and the tone of her message strident" (104). Aside from positivist rejection of the shameful content of the texts, Zayas's critics have rarely been in agreement. Until recently, much of the scholarship read her texts as realist or *costumbrista*.[10] As Juan

---

[9] The negative judgments of Zayas's novellas give testimony to critics' anxiety about this woman writer. While Place found her work overly detailed, Ticknor and Pfandl were offended by its immodesty and shamelessness. For a discussion of such criticism, see Blanqué (esp. 921-42), Grieve (92 n. 13), and Kaminsky (378-79 n. 6). Williamsen traces the influence of negative readings of Zayas in "Challenging the Code" (esp. 147-48). By not reiterating these negative comments, I follow Williamsen's convincing suggestion that sympathetic critics have done a disservice to Zayas by repeating harsh and speculative criticism over the years (cf. "Challenging the Code" and "Engendering Interpretation").

[10] Popularized–or, as Goytisolo suggests, canonized–during the nineteenth century, readings of Zayas as realist or *costumbrista* persisted until the late-1970s (cf. Amezúa [Prólogo to the *Novelas amorosas*, 1948], Pauley, Sharp, and Vasileski). See Yllera for a discussion of previous interpretations of Zayas as realist (40-43).

Goytisolo points out in "El mundo erótico de María de Zayas" ("The Erotic World of María de Zayas"), the tendency to read Zayas's novellas as realist fiction for many years obfuscated more nuanced interpretations of her work (63-70).

The debate now has shifted to a focus on the feminist elements of Zayas's texts and to a general skepticism about her depictions of violence against women. More precisely, the focus on bodily violation in her texts has been interpreted by contemporary critics as "unmask(ing) the victimization of women" (Kaminsky 377), "the inscription of obsessive desire" (Gartner 100), "crueldades y violencias gratuitas que Zayas parece acumular por el simple gusto de horrorizar al auditorio" [cruelty and gratuitous violence that Zayas seems to accumulate for the mere pleasure of horrifying her audience] (Levisi 451), "militant feminism" (Chevalier 31), and "an exaggerated commentary on the situation of women" (Clamurro, "Ideological" 44). Understandably, critics tend to express reluctance and discomfort when reading texts that narrate violence against women and display women's violated bodies. After all, the violence in the texts could be a marketing ploy meant to widen the audience and could be aimed, like the "Prólogo de un desapasionado" ("Prologue by an Objective Reader") to the *Novelas amorosas*, at selling more books. Yet this reading of the excesses of violence and sexuality overlooks the didacticism and obscures the role of violence in the articulation of Zayas's feminism. A more fruitful approach lies in an integrative analysis that takes into account the predominant role of the body in these tales about love, sex, marriage, and family.

I would like to explore the possibility that Zayas's fiction engages the ideologies of corporealism of which she (and probably her readers) had some knowledge. Here we can consider various practices of disciplining the body used by the church and the state. This list includes bodily mortification of Catholic saints and religious followers, and public performances of penal and Inquisitional "justice." Of course, artistic representations of the body–which include everything from hagiography to poetry to a general baroque aesthetic of degradation–must be considered as well.

If we examine the prominent role of the body in the traditions and practices that occupied a fairly visible position in early modern culture, we can see that Zayas's use of the body as the cultural script upon which the dangers of the patriarchy are written is a legitimate and highly sophisticated choice. By writing through the body, Zayas builds on one of the most accessible and prominent sites of meaning, one that was exploited by the Inquisition, the church, and the state, and had increasing cachet in the baroque period. In this regard, it is important to understand that Zayas's focus on the body echoes and perhaps even grows out of various cultural discourses of corporealism. Responding to stock literary plots, religious discourse, and various mechanisms of social control, Zayas feminizes her social critique and focuses on violence as a means to make the reader rally around calls for social reform. This appropriation of such discourses and their strategic adaptation to a feminist agenda serves the dual, and conceivably competing, purposes of making her fiction appeal to readers and of communicating an unapologetic feminist message.

Like Sor Juana in *La respuesta* (*The Answer*), Zayas responds to the devaluation of women in society through her writing. The foregrounding of women's experience in the texts constitutes a response to dominant, masculinist literary and cultural traditions. Zayas's fiction poses a challenge to the Renaissance claim on the discovery of "man" by showing the cost (paid by women through their bodies) of the unquestioned privileging of the male self. With texts that validate women's experiences as distinct from men's, in other words, Zayas exposes the fallacy of the universal, homogeneous man celebrated by intellectuals, artists, and theologians throughout the early modern period.

Zayas's texts contain a network of narrative commentary and plot elements that question the patriarchal power structure through direct criticism, representations of violence, and depictions of empowered women. Women's lack of recourse to justice comes under attack in both volumes, especially since much of the betrayal and violence that could be criminally prosecuted goes unpunished. And even when the justice system punishes wrongdoers and assists victims, many individual characters take it upon themselves to impose their own personal forms of punishment. This emphasis on injustice and suffering encourages the reader to sympathize with the victims.

Zayas's portrayal of transgression is more complex than one might initially assume. Many men and a few women get away with murder (Pedro in "El verdugo de su esposa" and Aminta in "La burlada Aminta"), adultery (Florentina in "Estragos que causa el vicio"), and other criminal or amoral actions (such as rape and murder in "La más infame venganza"). In spite of the variety of contexts for violence and betrayal, the tales–with their sustained call for women's rights–consistently link women's victimization to deep-rooted social problems. Zayas's foregrounding of the body marks a strategy meant to encourage male and female readers to invest in the feminine and to question the cultural practices that endanger women.

One potent example of the subversive aspect of Zayas's poetics can be found in a comparison of her representations of violence with the recommendations about wife beating made by the sixteenth-century humanist Francisco de Osuna. Osuna's and Zayas's descriptions of violence against women narrate similar actions and contexts, but the authors' messages differ dramatically. In a treatise on Christian life, Osuna details the conditions under which he condones wife beating. If a wife of the middling classes ("de mediano estado") persists in disobeying her husband's wishes, is negligent in keeping house, and

> no le bastan [al marido] un par de puñadas para hacerla andar derecha, no habría yo por inconveniente metella en el palacio después de todos acostados, y cerrada la puerta dalle con su cordón, media o una docena, hasta que amansase.
>
> [it is not enough for the husband to punch his wife a couple of times to make her behave properly, I wouldn't have a problem if he put her in the parlor after everyone went to bed, and, with the door closed, hit her with his belt a half dozen or a dozen times, until she was tamed.][11]

---

[11] Osuna divides his dicta regarding wife beating into categories of class. According to this schema, nobles should hardly ever have occasion to beat their wives. A lower-class man, however, is licensed to beat his wife "cuando ella sale a bailar con alguno que le vedó su marido que ni aún mirase porque era su enemigo" (Vigil 103) [when she dances with a man whom her husband forbade her to even look at because they were enemies]. These injunctions against and endorsements of certain kinds of violence correspond to a similar phenomenon in England, where domestic abuse, particularly among the upper classes, was tolerated less and less throughout the seventeenth century. See Dolan's *Dangerous Familiars* (esp. ch. 3) for a discussion of how representations of domestic violence changed during the seventeenth century. Also see Dolan's "Household Chastisements"; Hunt's "Wife Beating, Domesticity, and Women's Independence in Eighteenth-Century London"; Pleck's *Domestic Tyranny*; Sharpe's "Domestic Homicide in Early Modern England"; and Vigil's *La vida de las mujeres* (92-105). In his *Tesoro de la lengua castellana*, Cova-

The fifth tale in Zayas's *Novelas amorosas*, "La fuerza del amor," exposes the brutality of the recommendations of humanists such as Osuna. This novella, related in its title and violent content to Cervantes's exemplary novel "La fuerza de la sangre" ("The Power of Blood"), could be read as a feminist response to the Cervantine novella in which a man is pressured to marry a woman he impregnated while raping her. Pictured in the final scene as a harmonious threesome, the family unit in "La fuerza de la sangre" owes its union to the cultural forces at work in sexual and familial dynamics.[12]

In Zayas's "La fuerza del amor," such pressures are articulated from the woman's perspective. Here, an adulterous husband beats his wife, Laura, who protests the injustice of a society that sanctions men's sexual freedom while controlling women. When Laura confronts Diego with his moral corruption, he perceives her as disobedient and acts with violence to make her retreat into submission. Unlike Osuna's callous recommendations about wife-beating, Zayas's narration evokes sympathy for the woman, who falls victim to her husband's ire:

> acercándose más a ella y encendido en una infernal cólera, (Diego) le empezó de maltratar de manos, tanto que las perlas de sus dientes presto tomaron forma de corales, bañados en sangre que empezó a sacar en las crueles manos. (*Novelas* 238)
>
> [moving closer to her and incensed in an infernal rage, he began to beat her with her hands, so much so that the white pearls of her teeth, bathed in the blood shed by his angry hand, quickly took on the form of red coral. (172, mod.)]

Zayas subverts Renaissance poetic tropes about women's bodies in this detailed narration of violence. As a result of the assault, Laura's pearl white teeth quickly take on the red hue usually reserved in literature for descriptions of women's flushed cheeks. The violent re-

---

rrubias defines "palacio" as "una sala que es común y pública" (845) [a living area that is shared and public], a usage found in the kingdom of Toledo and one that coincides with Osuna's meaning.

[12] For an analysis of Cervantes's representation of rape in this novella, see Welles's "Violence Disguised"; for a larger study on such representations in Spanish literature, see Welles's *Persephone's Girdle*. Wofford's discussion of "The Social Aesthetics of Rape" provides a fascinating perspective on the function of rape in male-authored texts.

working of the tropes echoes the chaos that male violence inflicts on the female body.

Laura has to endure physical and emotional anguish and abandonment by male family members before her tale finds a happy ending in the convent. The dynamics of violence against women in Zayas's novellas draw out the injustice by which the female body is sacrificed to the whims and desires of men. To use Osuna's terminology, Zayas's protagonist already is "andando derecha" when her husband cheats on her and then beats her. In fact, Laura's only offense lies in complaining about her husband's adultery. Rhetorically and ideologically, "La fuerza del amor" exemplifies the ways that Zayas's fiction enters into direct conversation with humanism and male-authored literature.

Zayas critiques the disempowerment of women with depictions of women as victims of physical and emotional trauma. In "La fuerza del amor," Laura voices this critique:

> ¿Por qué, vanos legisladores del mundo, atáis nuestras manos para las venganzas, imposibilitando nuestras fuerzas con vuestras falsas opiniones, pues nos negáis letras y armas? ¿El alma no es la misma que la de los hombres? (*Novelas* 241)

> [Why, vain legislators of the world, do you tie our hands so that we cannot take vengeance? Because of your mistaken ideas about us, you render us powerless and deny us access to pen and sword. Isn't our soul the same as a man's soul? (175)]

Laura's language again refers the reader to the issue of power. While she describes women's oppression in terms of lack of access to power, she adds nuance to the concept of *fuerza*: as a victim of masculine violence, Laura is forced into a humiliating and dangerous position by her adulterous husband. She later asserts her independence, though, when she makes a decision that thwarts male authority. Rather than reunite with her repentant husband, Laura moves to regain control over her body and her reputation by entering the convent. This mix of love, blood, and protest in Zayas exemplifies women's lack of power as well as women's capacity to act independently when given a chance to do so.

Laura's situation exposes women's dependence on men for their well-being. Directing herself to those at the very top of the social hierarchy, she points out that women's plight is perpetuated by the exclusion of women from the two major vehicles of self-empowerment, education and arms (*letras y armas*). These complaints reverberate throughout the novellas, in which women's inequality contributes to their suffering.

With its violent episode and feminist protests, "La fuerza del amor" delineates several key elements of Zayas's fiction. The comparison between the violence of the tale and Osuna's approbation of violence illuminates the connection between Zayas's fictional representation of men's treatment of women and a misogynist position articulated by some educated men of the period. As Mariló Vigil points out, many moralists condemned violence against women (92-105). Nonetheless, the issue was treated as a matter of household discipline, thereby reinforcing the Christian conception of marriage in which the submission of a wife to her husband was thought to be woman's obligation, her fulfillment of God's will.[13]

Humanists describe women's submission as one of body and soul. As Vicente Mexía succinctly states in his *Saludable instrucción* (*Healthy Instruction*) of 1566: when a woman marries, "she makes herself subject to her husband . . . and is no longer owner of her body."[14] The function of marriage as an institution that controlled women had been codified centuries before in Alfonso the Wise's *Siete partidas*, the legal code that remained in effect in Zayas's time. Alfonso asserts that marriage is necessary "to avoid quarrels, homicides, insolence, violence, and many other wrongful acts that would take place on account of women if marriage did not exist."[15]

We find a counterpart to this expression of containment of women's sexuality in the fourth *partida*, which explained that a man was allowed to kill his wife and her lover immediately if he caught them in the act of adultery. Renewed in the sixteenth-century (in the *Nueva Recopilación*), the uxoricide law granted the right to private justice to a husband or a father if he found his wife or daughter

---

[13] In addition to Osuna, Fray Vicente Mexía suggests that disobedient women run the risk of being beaten by their husbands if they get too far out of line (Vigil 102).

[14] The quote from Mexía appears in Perry (*Gender and Disorder* 63).

[15] I have used Perry's English translation of the *Siete partidas* (*Crime and Society* 182). The original states that marriage exists "por desviar contiendas y homecillos y soberbias: y fuerzas y otras cosas muy tortizeras que nascieren por razon de las mugeres si casamiento non fuese" (qtd. in Stone 40).

having adulterous sex. If he opted for such vengeance, the man was required to kill both parties (Vigil 139-55). Considered in relation to moralists' injunctions against women's disobedience, the persistence of the uxoricide law on the books confirms that the female body was a site of contestation for symbolic, as well as pragmatic, biology-bound, reasons. Indeed, as research on prostitution, sumptuary laws, convents, and crime has shown, the seventeenth century was a period of heightened social control, and women's bodies were subject to diverse regulations.[16]

The attempts to maintain tight control over individual behavior and cultural values signal a power struggle between the state and the people. This struggle centered, to a large extent, on the female body. The perception of woman as a threat to the social fabric lies at the center of many laws and religious doctrines of the period. From numerous decrees prohibiting women's veils to travellers' observations of women being locked up by their husbands to avoid scandal, the historical record leaves no doubt that the process of building the Spanish state involved a preoccupation with controlling women. Furthermore, many decrees and laws in the seventeenth century, such as those regarding the closing of brothels or the numerous prohibitions of *guardinfantes* (the farthingales of Velázquez's *Las meninas* fame), suggest that women repeatedly tried to free themselves from the cultural authority that attempted to enclose and contain them.[17]

Explaining the apparent rise in anxiety about women in the period, Anne Cruz and Mary Elizabeth Perry have called attention to

---

[16] As Nash describes in "Two Decades of Women's History," the field of Spanish women's history has grown tremendously in the last twenty years. I refer the reader to the following studies on the early modern period: Bilinkoff, *The Avila of Saint Teresa*; Haliczer, *Sexuality in the Confessional*; Kagan, *Lucrecia's Dreams*; Perry, *Crime and Society* and *Gender and Disorder*; *Religion, Body, and Gender in Early Modern Spain* and *La historia silenciada de la mujer* (ed. Saint-Saëns); and Sánchez Ortega, *La mujer y la sexualidad en el antiguo régimen*.

[17] In *Daily Life in Spain*, Defourneaux discusses various expressions of anxiety about women's clothing in the seventeenth century. He suggests that the *guardinfante* was outlawed in 1633 because it might have helped to conceal pregnancies (157). Under Philip II and Philip IV, the use of the veil was forbidden because it hid women's faces (159). Like other sumptuary laws aimed specifically at women, these communicate the state's attempts to regulate female sexuality through the control of the body. Defourneaux (145-62), Vigil (*La vida*), McKendrick (*Woman and Society*, ch. 1), and Perry ("Crisis and Disorder" and *Gender and Disorder*) discuss women and social control at length.

the perception of women as "the most dangerous threat to Christian morality" during the Counter-Reformation ("Introduction" xvii). Attempts at control of women partially had their roots in a rising concern for *limpieza de sangre* or purity of lineage, by which families would prove their "untainted," Christian bloodlines. Since this phenomenon depended on preventing contamination in one's family, it resulted in a heightened demand for women's sexual purity in order to ensure the survival of Christian male privilege. Cruz and Perry also point to a shift in Post-Tridentine culture, when "the Church and the State reinscribed misogyny by focusing on women's powers to lead men's souls to hell" (xviii). The preoccupation with securing one's place in this changing society manifested itself, in part, as anxiety about women's sexuality and power: prostitutes, widows, and rebellious single women could be placed forcibly in convents for reform of their behavior, for example, and all women except widows were prohibited from litigating on their own behalf.[18]

Women's bodies were the focus of extensive debate and were singled out as subjects of government and religious control.[19] Other paradigms of corporeal discourse can be related to the prominent role of the body in Zayas's texts as well. Arguably, the most dramatic public deployment of the body in early modern Spain was the *auto de fe*. This highly theatrical inquisitorial ceremony still existed well into the seventeenth century, although the number of executions diminished over the centuries. Most relevant to this discussion of violence is the emphasis placed on the accused's body during the *auto*: the prisoners often were forced to parade through town wearing penitential garments (*sanbenitos*), which bore a representation of their crime or the manner in which they would be executed. The

---

[18] As Kagan describes in *Lawsuits and Litigants in Castile*, the exclusion of women from the courts marked a significant barrier to their empowerment in an age of increasing reliance on litigation as a means of settling disputes (10-13). Chapter one of Sánchez Lora's *Mujeres, conventos y formas de la religiosidad barroca* analyzes the related phenomenon of the construction and oppression of the feminine in the Golden Age.

[19] In *Renaissance Feminism*, Jordan gives a detailed account of the standard theological justifications used to explain women's inferior position to men (21-34). With regard to marriage and violence, she indicates that most English marriage treaties "condone behavior that ratifies patriarchal discipline" (287). This stance appears in William Whateley's *A Bride Bush or A Direction for Married Persons* (1623), where the author allows for "a husband to beat his wife to the point of 'knocking her brains out'" (qtd. in Jordan 287).

unrepentant accused of more serious crimes fell victim to the stake. Particularly in the early stages of the Inquisition, *autos de fe* often, although not always, culminated with the burning of the condemned at the stake.[20]

The public nature of punishment in the period, reinforced by the choreographed ceremony of the *auto* itself, acted out the exercise of power onto the body that Michel Foucault has referred to in *Discipline and Punish*. In his discussion of pre-eighteenth-century criminal justice, Foucault points to the use of "the body and the spectacle for the reproduction of truth" (97). Indeed, the *auto* was meant to evoke penitence as well as the spectators' admiration of the Inquisition's power. The pictoral representation of one's crime on the clothing and the public nature of the punishment inscribed the power of the Inquisition directly onto the individual's body. In this justice system, as in the rest of Europe, the state appropriated, displayed, and violated the transgressor's body. As Foucault explains, "(T)he body of the condemned man became the king's property, on which the sovereign left his mark and brought down the effects of his power" (*Discipline* 109). Perry aptly summarizes the effects of such practices in Spain: bodies mutilated and punished by the Inquisition served as "gruesome reminders of the power of the city and royal governments to carry out violence against those who challenged their authority" (*Crime and Society* 143). In effect, the system exploited the exemplarity of corporeality to convey the message of its own power.[21]

---

[20] This description is taken from Flynn's "Mimesis of the Last Judgment: The Spanish *Auto de fe*" (esp. 282-83). Kamen also details the *auto* in *Inquisition and Society* (178-97), where he emphatically argues against the "legend of a bloodthirsty tribunal" (189) and says that reports of executions in the *autos* have been exaggerated over the centuries. By this account, the ceremony had lost most of its severity by the seventeenth century. In general, very few *autos* (under 2 percent in Valencia and Galicia, for example) culminated in the execution of the prisoners, with the penalty of execution being "heavily weighted against people of Jewish and Moorish origin" (189). The ceremony, albeit without the burnings at the stake, did take place during the period in which Zayas was writing. With this in mind, I mention the *auto* in order to highlight the performative aspect–or bodily display–that was integral to the spectacle, regardless of whether the prisoners were executed.

[21] The culture of violence in early modern Spain is analyzed extensively in Maravall's chapter on "Hostigamiento y lucha" (*La literatura picaresca*), Kamen's chapter on "The Urban Environment" (*Spain in the Later Seventeenth Century*, esp. 167-82), and Kamen's discussion of class and violence in *European Society* (171-78). Citing recent work on violence by Barker (*The Culture of Violence*), Amussen ("'Being stirred to much unquietness'" and "Punishment, Discipline, and Power"),

Given the display of the body for criminal justice, religious, and nationalistic purposes, it should come as little surprise that literature and plastic arts from this period also focus on corporeality. From religious iconography to noble portraiture, some of the most powerful images from early modern Spain rely on the power of the body to persuade and move. El Greco's strangely elongated bodies, Ribera's impulse toward naturalism, and Velázquez's stylized portraits all play with the meanings attached to their subjects' bodies.

As evidenced by many *comedias*, novellas, and poems, much of the baroque literary canon engages the body's potential for meaning. In a comment that calls attention to the power of the body to signify, King Pedro in *El médico de su honra*, uses four synonyms for Mencía's cadaver:

> Cubrid ese horror que asombra,
> ese prodigio que espanta,
> espectáculo que admira,
> símbolo de la desgracia.
>
> (l. 2876-79)

[Cover that startling horror, that frightening wonderment, shocking spectacle, symbol of misfortune.]

This reaction encapsulates a range of meanings associated with the violated body, which causes horror and wonder, but, ultimately, emerges as a symbol of disorder and disgrace. In many contexts on the stage, the body is indeed symbolic. When the king in *El médico* decides not to punish the murderous husband, the cadaver remains on stage as a reminder, a symbol, of the injustices suffered by women or, depending on the actors and the spectators, as a warning to women to keep their behavior in check. Revealed to the audience, Mencía's body demands an interpretation. What does her dead body symbolize? The male characters' reactions to the bloody scene

---

and others, Dolan's "Household Chastisements" provides an overview of violence in England that corresponds to the Spanish situation: "The evidence that early modern England was a 'culture of violence' comes, most obviously, in its reliance on public whippings, mutilations, burnings, hangings, and beheadings to punish crime and maintain order, and in the occasional violent rebellions against state power. In such a culture, violence is not inevitably transgressive; it can assert authority or impose discipline as well as betray a lack of control" (204).

lead us to think that there are several meanings to be found in this display of the body.

Judging from the amount of violence in Spanish *comedia*, playwrights had great faith in the potential of the altered body to produce *admiratio*: the Comendador's mutilated cadaver is paraded across the stage in *Fuenteovejuna* and Segismundo's uncivilized body is covered in animal skins in *La vida es sueño*, for example. Prose and poetry also explore the symbolism of physicality. A salient example of the crossover between the physical and the metaphysical arises in the disjuncture between reality and fantasy in *Don Quijote* as the hero's misadventures take their toll on his physical health. The preponderance of baroque poems dealing with aging and death bespeaks a fascination with the transient nature of bodily existence as well as a more generalized concern for degradation. Quevedo's moral sonnet on "Desengaño de la exterior apariencia" ("Deception of Outward Appearances") exemplifies the baroque aesthetic of degradation. The sonnet concludes with the familiar declamation of the physical and moral decay of the nobility: "pues asco, dentro son, tierra y gusanos" [they are but rot, dirt, and worms within].

These examples underscore what we already know about the period: the Renaissance idealization of the body devolves into baroque violence and decay. Think, for example, of the opening lines of Garcilaso's Sonnet XXIII ("En tanto que de rosa y azucena / se muestra la color en vuestro gesto . . .") ("While the colors of roses and lilies are still to be seen in your face"), and compare this to the employ of a similar conceit in Góngora's Sonnet CLXVI. While both poets draw on the trope of *carpe diem*, Góngora twists the conceits and corporealizes the threat as he warns that physical beauty will turn "no sólo en plata o viola troncada / . . . mas tú y ello juntamente / en tierra, en humo, en polvo, en sombra, en nada" [not only into silver or a crushed violet, but you and all of it together into earth, smoke, dust, shadow, nothingness].[22]

One unchanging bodily discourse readily available for consumption in Catholic Spain was that of piety, particularly as expressed in hagiography. With Christ's own bodily sacrifice as the model, inspiration for spirituality was found in the tales of those

---

[22] These poetry citations are taken from Elias Rivers's bilingual compilation, *Renaissance and Baroque Poetry of Spain*.

who had overcome great suffering in the name of Christianity. While Saint Agatha's clipped breasts and the *dolorosa* Virgin's ashen body commonly appear among the representations of women's suffering in the plastic arts, nuns' life stories (*vidas*) place heavy emphasis on practices of mortification.[23] On this note, both Margarita Levisi and Patricia Grieve have studied the similarities between the pictoral representations of women's suffering in Zayas and those in hagiography, and their analyses suggest numerous commonalities between the two. Levisi concludes that the specificity in Zayas's representations of violated bodies indicates that she "parece llevar al plano narrativo y secular las premisas que rigen en el nivel del arte plástico" (455) [seems to bring the premises that reign at the level of the plastic arts to the secular narrative of her novellas]. Grieve has analyzed the meanings of Zayas's incorporation of hagiography, suggesting that Zayas uses this religious discourse to subvert patriarchal norms, to encourage women to reject the "secular martyrdom" of marriage in favor of the protection of the convent (86-87).

Grieve's analysis of martyrdom in Zayas's novellas recalls the ways in which femininity was imbued with religious (and often corporeal) models of behavior in the period. A brief glance at one example of bodily mortification can help us contextualize the role of the body in early modern women's religiosity. Sor Jerónima de la Ascensión's *Exercicios espirituales* (*Spiritual Exercises*, 1661) tells us that she used to fast as a small child. Around the age of ten, however, she began to search for other ways to discipline her body in order to achieve proximity to Christ:

> La disciplina en esta niñez era de un manojo de hilo de alambre, que lo hallé en un cofre de casa, y me alegré, porque no tenía comodidad de tener disciplinas con el secreto que yo quería. Hacíame llagas muy penosas, de que yo andaba muy contenta de

---

[23] Depictions of both male and female saints as enduring great physical pain represent one prominent model of suffering in the period. The question of Catholic women's relationship to the body and religion has been dealt with by Bynum (*Holy Feast and Holy Fast* and *Fragmentation and Redemption*) and Warner (*Alone of All Her Sex*). For analyses of Spanish nuns' discussions of the body, see Arenal and Schlau's *Untold Sisters*, and Velasco's *Demons, Nausea, and Resistance*. Sor Jerónima de la Ascensión's text is available at many American universities as part of the microfiche catalogue, *Escritoras españolas* (Madrid: Chadwyck-Healey España, 1992-93).

tener siempre algo que me doliera. Destos mismos hilos de alambre y de hierro me ponía en los muslos muy apretados, al modo de quien engarrota. Esta era una penitencia harto penosa, porque se hundían, y metían en las carnes, y al quitarlos hacíame mucho mal. Mas si bien me acuerdo, tenía tanta gana de hacerme mal, que me los quitaba con harta violencia. (fol. 121-22)

[As a child, I used a bundle made of steel wire, which I found in a trunk in my house. I was happy when I found it, because until then I had not found a way to discipline myself with the secrecy I desired. I gave myself very painful wounds, and it made me happy to have something always causing me pain. I would put this wire very tightly around my thighs, in the style of someone who throttles another. This was an extremely painful penitence because the wires would dig into my flesh, and on taking them out, they caused severe pain. But if I remember correctly, I so wanted to cause myself pain that I would take out the wires with great violence.]

Emphasizing her suffering and, later, her own ability to withstand pain, Sor Jerónima presents us with a commonplace description of the spiritual quest to transcend the bodily condition.

In addition to the self-inflicted wounds described here, the issue of fasting also plays a role in women's displays of spirituality. As Caroline Walker Bynum has demonstrated in her extensive studies on spirituality, women's religiosity traditionally has manifested itself differently from men's. The abundant examples of self-starvation by nuns dealt with in *Holy Feast* and *Holy Fast* speak to one key difference: religious women's bodily experiences. Bynum also cites studies that point to the incorruptibility of the cadaver–the characteristic by which a dead body remains intact and supple–as a feminine virtue, "a virtual requirement for female sanctity by the early modern period" (*Fragmentation* 187).[24]

---

[24] Thurston's *The Physical Phenomena of Mysticism*, a study of saints from 1400 to 1900, discusses incorruptibility as a requirement for the six female saints canonized during this period. Along with Thurston and other religious scholars (e.g., Peter Brown, Jacques LeGoff, and Donald Weinstein), Bynum analyzes and contextualizes bodily practices that seem strange and even masochistic from the modern perspective: "Control, discipline, even torture of the flesh is, in medieval devotion, not so much the rejection of physicality as the elevation of it–a horrible yet delicious elevation–into a means of access to the divine" (*Fragmentation* 182).

Another possible source for Zayas's dependence on violence as a device to convey her feminist messages can be found in the rising incidence of violence in seventeenth-century society. In an echo of Zayas's fictional portrayal of epidemic violence, Henry Kamen's statistics bear out the rise of violence in Madrid. In particular, Kamen views the seventeenth century as a time of acutely violent crime in Spain. In support of this perception, he cites a 1639 testimony from Madrid:

> Not a day passes but people are found killed or wounded by brigands or soldiers; houses burgled; young girls and widows weeping because they have been assaulted and robbed. (*European Society* 176)

This speaker catalogues the everyday violence that, in his view, threatens men and women alike. The comment indicates that at least some people expressed concern over the increasing dangers of living in an economically and politically overextended society.

Zayas primarily deals with aristocrats, the traditional subjects of the novella genre, and Kamen points to the aristocracy as a whole as a perpetrator of violence. Discussing the high numbers of nobility in Spain, which reached 10 percent of the total population (compared with 1 percent in most other western European countries), Kamen concludes that this group's exclusive right to bear arms meant that they played a role in the violence of the times (*European Society* 95-96). In terms of violence and other criminal acts, it is important to recall that the monied classes had tremendous influence over the justice system. Easily corrupted by those with wealth and prestige, authorities were likely to drop cases in which noblemen were charged with wrongdoing.[25] In a related observation, José Antonio Maravall discusses the oppressive nature of baroque culture and postulates that only those "who were exempt or fiscally and judicially immune remained apart from those layers and free from the crushing weight of vigilance and punishment" ("From the Renais-

---

[25] Kagan's *Lawsuits and Litigants in Castile* explores the impact of widespread corruption in the courts (45-48). It is interesting to note that one crime that was punished in Spain regardless of social station was sodomy, as Herrera Puga describes in *Sociedad y delincuencia en el siglo de oro* (251). Also see Monter's discussion of "Sodomy: The Fateful Accident" in *Frontiers of Heresy* (276-99).

sance" 33). To the extent that they concern themselves with gender discrimination within the aristocracy, Zayas's texts criticize some of the injustices that have been shown to be historical realities. In addition to the institutionalized violence of the Inquisition, these indications of rising violence and power imbalance help explain and even legitimize Zayas's choice of the violated body as a sign of cultural decline.

Zayas capitalizes on religious traditions, cultural practices, and on the broader baroque aesthetic (or, according to Maravall, the cultural *phenomenon*) of degradation by incorporating violence into her texts. Piecing together the influences and elements of Zayas's corporeal aesthetic is crucial to understanding her two volumes of novellas as a cohesive textual unit dedicated to liberating the feminine voice and educating both sexes about the problems of patriarchy. The availability of violent images and the evidence of violent practices in seventeenth-century Spain suggest that the "textuality of social context" of Zayas's novellas–the relationship between the texts and their culture–can best be explained through the focus on the powerful signifying potential of the body. This connection serves as a baseline for analysis of dynamics of bodies and violence in Zayas's texts, for it provides a map of the most public and accessible discourses of the body–those that probably would have been familiar to Zayas and her reading public.[26]

As evidenced by the climate of intense social control and the performance of such control in the *auto de fe* and on the stage, the early modern Spanish public was familiar with the regulation of the body. In a more general sense, the public was familiar with the meanings given to the body through various practices and institutions. The victimized female body in Zayas's novellas signifies the power of men over women, just as bodies mutilated and punished by the Inquisition signified the power of the church over the individual. As a closer examination of violence and the body in the

---

[26] Except for the discussion of humors in the latter section of this chapter, I do not deal with scientific discourse and practice. Due to the limited audiences for anatomy texts and to the small numbers of people (men) actually practicing and observing dissections, I do not think these are likely sources for Zayas's representations of violence and bodies. Excellent scholarship has been done in the field of early modern anatomy and science, however, and I refer the reader to Sawday's *The Body Emblazoned*, and Hillman and Mazzio's edited volume, *The Body in Parts*.

texts will show, Zayas transposes some of her culture's beliefs and practices onto fictional women's bodies. This reliance on the body's power to evoke sympathy and to project a message relates to the role of the body as a *locus* of meaning in early modern religious, artistic, and cultural practices.

Drawing on a variety of contexts in which one might encounter a body invested with meaning in the seventeenth century, Zayas seems to anticipate her readers' ability to interpret and decipher the meanings assigned to bodies in her fiction. As the following discussions of the texts will make evident, there is a close proximity between Zayas's bodily representations and the bodily practices and depictions in early modern Spanish culture. Based on this proximity, we can see that Zayas borrows from the deployment of the body by the church and state, as well as from specific roles of the body in literary and artistic traditions. Zayas's focus on the feminine body and on feminist reform signifies the fashioning of her own authority out of dominant cultural codes. Borrowing from the larger cultural context, Zayas transforms dominant ideologies about the body's symbolic weight into the keystone of her feminist aesthetic. This schema of bodily representations provides a passageway through which we can step to further unfold the schematics of violence and feminism in these novellas.

II. Minding the Body

Zayas's texts draw attention to women's plight of physical danger and emotional hardship. The narrative structure of the Boccaccian-style framed novellas and the focus on women reinforce the didacticism of the collection. Like Laura in "La fuerza del amor," several characters express their frustration with their secondary status. Exercising their own power, especially as narrators in the seat of disenchantment (*asiento de desengaño*) in the second volume, the frame characters also comment on the need for social change.

One example of such advocacy occurs when the frame tale narrator Nise, in her introduction to "El verdugo de su esposa," advises men to stop seducing women:

> Caballero que solicitas la doncella, déjala, no la inquietes, y verás cómo ella, aunque no sea más de por vergüenza y recato, no te bus-

cará a ti. El que busca y desasosiega la casada, no lo haga, y verá cómo cuando no la obligue la honestidad, el respeto y temor de su marido, la hará que no te solicite ni busque. (*Desengaños* 200)

[You gentlemen who court a damsel, leave her alone, don't press her and you will see that she, from her sense of modesty and shame, will not seek you out. The man who chases and bothers a married woman, let him desist, and he will see that her respect for her husband and her fear, if not her modesty, will keep her from seeking him out or pursuing him. (114)]

Nise wants men to take personal responsibility for courtship and to stop exploiting their power over women. Her remarks underscore a key element of the ideology underlying the texts: for women's situation to improve, men must change. The powerlessness of women and the sovereignty of men over the female body are made explicit in Nise's tale, "El verdugo de su esposa," in which a husband kills his wife after his own friend unsuccessfully courts her. Such violence emphasizes the need for social reform, but the political and theoretical implications of the association of women with their bodies need to be explored in order to begin to reconcile Zayas's feminism with her corporeal aesthetic.

The emphasis on bodies in Zayas's texts forces the reader to come to terms with the symbolic baggage of the female body. This task has caused feminists great consternation over the years. The difficulties of reading bodies and interpreting sexuality in a woman author's work are compounded by the fact that women's relationship to their bodies and to the body social has long been problematic for feminist thinkers. As Grosz summarizes in *Volatile Bodies*, the absolute differentiation between mind and body, with its exaltation of the mind and denigration of the body, effected a "binarization of the sexes" at the very "threshold of Western reason" (5). In ancient sources viewed as foundational to Western thought, women are said to belong to the secondary sphere of matter, of the body, while men's territory is defined as that of reason and the mind. The persistence of such conceptions of women in popular and intellectual realms has quite justifiably made feminists wary of approaching the corporeal. Yet many feminists have taken on the project with grace and force.[27] In particular, contemporary feminist theory has

---

[27] Feminists have long focused on the body as a rallying point for politics and as

helped us refine our thinking about the relationships between mind and body and between body and culture.

In *Volatile Bodies*, one of the most broadly conceived books on corporeality and philosophy, Grosz addresses the complex history of women's relationship to the body. Grosz admits in the introduction, for example, that feminists are skeptical of putting too much stock in the body. This trepidation is borne out of the reality that, traditionally, women's bodies have been acted upon, culturally constructed and represented for us rather than by us (x). Issuing a feminist corrective to this corporeal colonization, Grosz examines mainstream philosophical discourse and explores the aspects of this tradition that might be used for the theorization of what she announces in her subtitle to be "corporeal feminism." Like Grosz's own philosophical explorations, Zayas's discourse is fundamentally corporeal, for she draws on the signifying powers of the body to convey a feminist message to the politically tense society of seventeenth-century Spain. And, just as Elizabeth Grosz responds to a masculinist philosophical tradition in an attempt to theorize a body-based feminism in *Volatile Bodies*, María de Zayas responds to the devaluation of the feminine in the intellectual and cultural spheres with a feminism based on women's corporeality.

Part of the difficulty of interpreting the body lies in the fact that the meanings of corporeality are culturally and historically bound. Philosophy and feminist theory of the past two decades are helpful in understanding the changing role of the body throughout history. We need only recall another of Foucault's influential explanations, in the first volume of *The History of Sexuality*, about physicality in pre-eighteenth-century Europe:

> At the beginning of the seventeenth century a certain frankness was still common, it would seem. Sexual practices had little need

---

a focus for theorization (cf. Conboy, Medina, and Stanburg, *Writing on the Body*). Some women who have made significant contributions in this area include Irigaray (e.g. *This Sex which Is not One*), Cixous ("Laugh of the Medusa"), Wittig ("The Straight Mind" and "One Is not Born Woman"), Butler (*Gender Trouble* and *Bodies that Matter*), Fuss (*Essentially Speaking*), Bordo (*Unbearable Weight*), Grosz (*Space, Time, Perversion* and *Volatile Bodies*), Gatens (*Imaginary Bodies*), and Bray and Colebrook ("The Haunted Flesh"). For an extensive study of the metaphors of the body that permeate Western philosophy, see Lakoff and Johnson's *Philosophy in the Flesh*.

of secrecy.... Codes regulating the coarse, the obscene, and the indecent were quite lax compared to those of the nineteenth century. (3)

Although much Foucauldian analysis has been challenged for its lack of consideration of gender and cultural specificity, this particular observation seems to hold true in the Spanish context, in which the "frankness" of Zayas's texts was not condemned decisively until the nineteenth century.

It is no coincidence that Zayas's prose, with its representations of sexuality and violence, went out of print in the middle of the nineteenth century after enjoying publishing success for two hundred years.[28] Emilia Pardo Bazán's cautionary explanation in the introduction to her 1892 partial edition of Zayas's novellas speaks to this shift in ideology:

> Nuestro recato exterior ha progresado tanto desde el siglo XVII acá, que temo, al presentar nuevamente á doña María de Zayas, que se la juzgue mal por culpa de algunas frases vivas y algunas escenas poco veladas. (15)
>
> [Our modesty has progressed so much since the seventeenth century that I fear, as I reintroduce María de Zayas, that she will be harshly judged because of a few lively sentences and some thinly veiled scenes.]

As Pardo Bazán's remarks imply, Zayas's focus on sexuality and on the tensions between the sexes has not gone unnoticed. Pardo Bazán's comments also draw attention to the gap between Zayas's conception of these issues and changing views toward the same issues over time.[29] In contemporary society, our impulse to regulate the body and its functions is so distinct from the attitudes toward

---

[28] For a detailed publishing history of Zayas's works, see Yllera's introduction to the *Desengaños amorosos* (64-93).

[29] In Azorín's speculations on Zayas, he suggests that Zayas gave herself over to market pressures, that her only "literary" work was the *Novelas amorosas* (72). And, like Pardo Bazán, he couches Zayas's projected loss of popularity with her reading public in terms of changing sensibilities: "Poco a poco el público distinguido, selecto, que tenía doña María se fué apartando de ella; era peligroso, sí, el leer sus novelas" (71) [Little by little the distinguished, the select public who followed doña María de Zayas began to part ways with her; indeed, it was dangerous to read her novellas].

the body in the pre-Victorian age that, even in the twenty-first century, we continue to overlook the important role of corporeality in early modern texts.

With this in mind, Zayas's self-conscious appropriation and deployment of the female body is examined here in an analysis of the preface, "Al que leyere" ("To the Reader"), to the *Novelas amorosas* and its ideological counterpoint, the first novella of the *Desengaños amorosos*. An initial analysis of the preface, "Al que leyere," provides the basis for an overview of the key narrative techniques that situate the feminine body at the center of the texts. Specifically, the first novella of the *Desengaños amorosos* is discussed as emblematic of the merging of body, voice, and text in Zayas's poetics. That is, Zayas's intertwining of women's bodies and stories creates a formidable political agenda that mobilizes the female body in a campaign to validate women's physical and psychical integrity.

Zayas's politicization of the feminine constructs a feminism that speaks of and through the woman's body. This feminism issues a challenge to the ideologies and cultural practices that dehumanize women, practices that position women on the body side of the mind/body split and that treat the female body as a male domain. Since Zayas's representations of women forge a close relationship among women's bodies, voices, and texts, they can be interpreted not only as a corrective to the prevailing devaluation of the feminine in the seventeenth century, but also as an anticipation of postmodern body-based feminisms.

From the beginning of the *Novelas amorosas* to the end of the *Desengaños amorosos*, Zayas politicizes her fiction both directly and indirectly and uses the body as the central point of reference for her feminist messages. Unlike the countless anonymous texts attributed to Virginia Woolf's much discussed female author "Anon," Zayas gives her readers no room to doubt her gender or her politics. At the beginning of "Al que leyere" in the *Novelas amorosas*, Zayas confronts the reader with her gender and then inserts herself firmly into the public sphere as a woman writer whose work has been legitimized by virtue of having gone to press:

> Quién duda, lector mío, que te causará admiración que una mujer tenga despejo, no sólo para escribir un libro, sino para darle a la estampa, que es el crisol donde se averigua la pureza de los in-

> genios; porque hasta que los escritos se rozan en las letras de plomo, no tienen valor cierto . . . . (21)

> [Oh my reader, no doubt it will amaze you that a woman has the nerve, not only to write a book but actually to publish it, for publication is the crucible in which the purity of genius is tested; until writing is set in letters of lead, it has no real value. (1)]

Aware of the potential criticism her work might receive because of her gender, Zayas does not stop with simply claiming the public space of publication.

In keeping with Renaissance discourse on the "woman question," Zayas also diminishes the supposed differences between the sexes as she asserts biological and spiritual equality between men and women. In this self-authorizing move, Zayas draws on prevailing philosophical and theological paradigms to validate her own intellectual exercise. Constance Jordan tells us in *Renaissance Feminism* that such merging of Scriptural and philosophical models was popular among early modern feminists, who questioned the discourses meant to perpetuate "existing social and political practices" (65).

By directly addressing the dominant ideologies (so-called natural laws) regarding sex and gender, Zayas indicts men for mistakenly viewing women as weak, inferior beings who should remain, as Fray Luis de León insists in *La perfecta casada* (*The Perfect Wife*), silent, chaste, and humble so as to please both their husbands and God. Zayas argues, for example:

> si esta materia de que nos componemos los hombres y las mujeres, ya sea una trabazón de fuego y barro, o ya una masa de espíritus y terrones, no tiene más nobleza en ellos que en nosotras, si es una misma la sangre, los sentidos, las potencias y los órganos por donde se obran sus efetos son unos mismos, la misma alma que ellos, porque las almas ni son hombres ni mujeres [. . .]. (*Novelas amorosas* 21)

> [whether this matter that we men and women are made of is a bonding of clay and fire, or a dough of earth and spirit, it has no more nobility in men than in women, if our blood is the same, if our senses, our powers, and the organs that perform their functions are all the same; our souls the same, for souls are neither male nor female. (1, mod.)]

Here, in an allusion to the Aristotelian and Galenic models that saw woman as a biologically defective man, Zayas highlights the sameness of male and female corporeality. In emphasizing corporeal equality, Zayas does not confirm a natural hierarchy as Aristotle does. Rather, she pinpoints a natural lack of sexual difference (a sexual *in*difference, as Irigaray would have it) that can then be interpreted as a sameness between the sexes.[30] The subsequent declaration of spiritual equality that desexes the soul expresses the late medieval and Renaissance essentialist belief, as discussed by Fisher and Halley, in an androgynous self (2).[31]

Throughout her preface, Zayas capitalizes on prevailing tropes of the day in order to validate her authority as a woman writer. Countering claims to men's superiority, she makes several arguments for equality. This includes the use of her own biological explanations to posit that women might be intellectually more capable than men:

> la verdadera causa de no ser las mujeres doctas no es defecto del caudal, sino falta de la aplicación, porque si en nuestra crianza como nos ponen el cambray, en las almohadillas y los dibuxos en el bastidor, nos dieran libros y preceptores, fuéramos tan aptas para los puestos y para las cátedras como los hombres, y quizá más agudas por ser de natural más frío, por consistir en humedad el entendimiento [. . .]. (*Novelas amorosas* 22)

> [The real reason why women are not learned is not a defect in intelligence but a lack of opportunity because if, in our upbringing, our parents gave us books and teachers instead of putting cambric on our sewing cushions and patterns in our embroidery frames, we would be as fit as men for any job or university professorship. Since intelligence consists of the damp humor, we might even be sharper because we're of a colder humor. (1-2, mod.)]

Here, Zayas invokes the discourse that described human nature in terms of humors, adapting this logic to her own purposes. Rather

---

[30] Taking sexual difference as the most challenging philosophical and relational conundrum facing us in the modern world, Irigaray's *An Ethics of Sexual Difference* argues for a reconceptualization of the categories of sex.

[31] Zayas repeats this trope of androgynous souls (e.g., *Novelas* 241 and *Desengaños* 317).

than merely inverting the antifeminist biological arguments, Zayas demonstrates the flexibility, and therefore the fallibility, of logic that claims to explain human nature. With such comments, she issues a challenge to readers of the preface, pressing them to see the flaws in dominant masculine discourse and simultaneously urging them to continue reading her texts.

Zayas does not limit herself to inverting popular assumptions about sexual difference; she also uses her femininity to ensnare her male readers. Here she appeals to their chivalrous obligation, for example:

> Te ofrezco este libro muy segura de tu bizarría y en confianza de que si te desagradare, podías disculparme con que nací mujer, no con obligaciones de hacer buenas novelas, sino con muchos deseos de acertar a servirte. (*Novelas amorosas* 23)

> [I offer this book to you, trusting your generosity and knowing that if it displeases you, you will excuse me because I was born a woman, with no obligation to write good novellas but a great desire to serve you well. (2)]

Faced with what she obviously anticipates to be a resistant reader, Zayas relies on various rhetorical strategies, including a focus on androgyny and an appeal to chivalry, as a way to lure readers into her texts.[32] In his approbation, the original censor, Josef de Valdivielso, follows the logic presented in Zayas's preface:

> Y cuando a su autor por ilustre emulación de las Corinas, Safos y Aspasias no se le debiera la licencia que pide, por dama y hija de Madrid, me parece que no se le puede negar. (*Novelas* 4)

> [And when the author, on account of her wonderful emulation of the Corinas, Sapphos, and Aspasias of the world is not owed the sought-out permission, it seems to me that it cannot be denied her, since she is a lady and a daughter of Madrid.]

---

[32] Not all early modern women writing on the woman question accommodated male characters or readers in the direct manner seen in Zayas. Marie de Gournay specifically excludes men as possible readers from *L'ombre: ouvre composé de méslanges* (1626), saying in the "Advìs au lecteur": "I realize that we will get along best if we separate. Is it not an act of charity to put distance between two irritable characters [deux esprits scabreux] before they actually quarrel?" (qtd. in Jordan 285).

The rhetorical overlap between these two excerpts points to Zayas's awareness of the codes of behavior dictating gender relations and, more precisely, to her exploitation of these codes for her own self-authorization.

Throughout the preface, Zayas appropriates the logic used by male cultural authorities to denigrate women. This appropriation allows her to derive a conclusion that legitimates her intellectual and political endeavors. She inverts the dominant models of bodily rhetoric and thereby demonstrates the slippery nature of "scientific" discourses that make truth claims about the "natural" order of things. In the course of this sophisticated argumentation, which is rhetorically similar to other feminist texts of the period, she points to the body as the site of exploration for the issues of social, juridical, and individual reform that will dominate in her novellas. With such references to bodies, writing, and resistance, the preface immediately refers to the culturally constructed boundaries placed on feminine behavior. Zayas's concern for legitimizing herself as an author communicates her awareness of the daring enterprise she undertakes as a woman offering up her intellectual efforts for public scrutiny.

Men are figured as integral to the texts in "Al que leyere" and in the frame tale itself, and the insistence on drawing in the male audience suggests that something larger than merely selling books is at stake. The superficial equilibrium between men and women manifests itself in the soiree through the matching of women's costumes with men's and in the equal division of labor for the narration of the tales.[33] The frame tale and the novellas themselves focus on the complexities of male-female relationships. At both levels of narration, something is amiss between men and women. Lisis learns of Juan's interest in Lisarda in the first scene of the first soiree, for example, when he enters wearing Lisarda's colors rather than her own. This shock propels her into the role of avenger, and she

---

[33] El Saffar has argued in "Ana/Lysis and Zayas" that the equity of narrative distribution corresponds to the dynamics of courtship present in the frame tale of the *Novelas amorosas*. El Saffar suggests that the balance between men and women in the frame tale carries over to the family structure as well, for all of the female frame characters have only mothers while the men have only fathers. El Saffar's careful reading correctly points out that the "redoubling of the separation of the sexes to the second generation" emphasizes "the rigidity of the barrier separating the sexes" (201).

spends the rest of the soiree dealing with Juan's rejection as she entertains Diego's advances. Several of the tales in the *Novelas amorosas* address deep problems between the sexes, showing the physical and emotional risks of courtship and marriage. The risks facing women are made explicit in the politically charged *Desengaños amorosos*, which aims to correct men's behavior and to teach women to look out for themselves.

Zayas seems to weave men into her texts with a certain degree of self-consciousness. The collection reaches out to male readers explicitly–in the preface–and implicitly–through the male characters. These inclusionary strategies recognize men's potential to modify their own behavior and to improve society's treatment of women. Zayas's inclusion of men bolsters her larger political aim of engaging men and women in a plan for social change, but it also requires a balancing act throughout the texts. If the rhetorically manipulative "Al que leyere" manages to capture the resistant reader's attention, this attention must be held throughout the novellas themselves.[34]

The inclusionary strategies used throughout the first volume can be read, then, as an effort to maintain the interest of all readers. In addition to the gender equity and the structure of shared narration in the frame tale, for instance, men's and women's bodies are portrayed as endangered in this first volume. Through various acts of violence and many characters' verbal protests, the human body is shown to be in danger within a cultural system that places exaggerated importance on honor. Periodic protests against women's oppression and the honor code surface in the *Novelas amorosas*, prefiguring the *Desengaños amorosos'* indictment of the practices that victimize women. In spite of these resistant comments, the compar-

---

[34] Given the difficulties of tracing literacy, book buying, and other relevant factors, we cannot know precisely who was reading Zayas's books. Beverley, Cruickshank, and Nalle have discussed the impact of rising literacy on early modern Spanish culture, however. While it is difficult to fix literacy rates for the period –anywhere from 20 percent to 50 percent has been suggested–Nalle's overview of scholarship on this topic concludes that regardless of what documents we use, evidence points to the fact that "more Castilians than ever before were learning to read," and many more women were reading than ever before (76). In the "Prólogo de un desapasionado" in the *Novelas amorosas*, the appeal made actually to buy the book suggests that booksellers worried that few books would be bought, possibly since most people would have heard Zayas's texts read aloud. See Ife's *Reading and Fiction in Golden Age Spain* for more on the transition from public to private reading in the seventeenth century.

atively idyllic *Novelas amorosas* does not forge the close relationship among women's body, voice, and text that is abundantly evident in the second volume, which focuses almost exclusively on the female body.

From the discussion of humors in "Al que leyere" to representations of rape and abuse in the novellas, the first volume sets the stage for corporeal discourse. Highlighting the importance of the body, Lisis's illnesses introduce both volumes. She is recovering from a fever at the start of the *Novelas*, and in the *Desengaños amorosos* we discover her on her deathbed, driven to sickness by tumultuous love relationships. The narrator mentions the possibility that Lisis's bad experiences with men are to blame for her illness: "o que fuese alguna desorden . . . o el pesar de considerarse Lisis ya en poder de extraño dueño" (*Desengaños* 115) [The malaise might have been caused by some general disorder . . . or by Lisis's sorrow at seeing herself in the power of a new and different master (35)]. The institutions of courtship and marriage lead to women's physical danger, in other words, and Lisis is a living example of this correlation. Although medical treatment and attention from men fail to cure her, Lisis recovers with the nurturing assistance of her slave, Zelima. And it is Zelima who best represents the merging of body, voice, and text in Zayas's fiction, so we turn to her in order to explain the success with which Zayas fuses woman with body.

Articulated by Lisis in the introduction to the *Desengaños amorosos*, the rules of narration of this second publication exchange the general didacticism of the *Novelas amorosas* for a gynocentric exemplarity that speaks on behalf of women (*Desengaños* 118). Responding to the masculine literary tradition that portrays women negatively, these texts are meant to free women's voices and to tell their side of the story. As seen in "Al que leyere" and the introduction to the second volume, Zayas's indictment of dominant literary traditions coincides with Hélène Cixous's comments in "Laugh of the Medusa":

> I maintain unequivocally that there is such a thing as marked writing; that, until now, far more extensively and repressively than is ever suspected or admitted, writing has been run by a libidinal and cultural–hence political, typically masculine–economy. (249)

Zayas writes against this "typically masculine" discursive tradition.

Specifically, Zayas creates a fictional world that redresses the exclusion of women by issuing a new set of rules for literary production. Lisis grants Zelima the privilege of being the first narrator to tell a "true" tale of men's deceit. Similar to María de Zayas's position as a woman author breaking masculine barriers, Zelima is the first character in the *Desengaños* to speak against the manipulation, objectification, and commodification of women in discursive and cultural traditions. This intriguing character occupies the uneasy position of a woman speaking out against men in their presence. Zelima's performance as storyteller–as *desengañadora*–is tempered by the intriguing manipulation of her ethnic and class difference throughout the novella.

As the first narrator of the *Desengaños amorosos*, this slave represents an exotic presence in the otherwise homogeneous groups of Catholic aristocrats who populate the frame tale and whose counterparts are the protagonists of the novellas proper. Presented as a gift to Lisis, Zelima has physical markings of slavery on her face. An iron brand in the shape of an "s" with a bar through it has a metaphoric capacity not lost on the reader: "la S y clavo" clearly serve as a fragmented representation of the word "esclavo." With slavery thus written upon her body, the outward declaration of her identity seems fixed as well. The first to express interest in Zelima's life, her owner and friend Lisis shows curiosity that is deflected when Zelima promises to tell her amazing story: "A su tiempo, señora mía, la sabrás, y te admirarás de ella" (*Desengaños* 117) [In due time, my lady, you will hear and you will be amazed to know (37)]. The mystery surrounding this unusually beautiful woman intensifies when she enters the soiree on the first night.

Figured as the outsider *par excellence*, Zelima is presented as a body that immediately attracts attention. Zelima's otherness functions as a means to hook the reader; she represents the "off-center, non-hegemonic identity" described by Sidonie Smith in "Identity's Body" as inviting the gaze (269). Zelima's unique identity (as an impressively dressed, branded slave) grabs the onlookers' gaze, and then a process begins that rapidly converts her into a member of the dominant group. This undifferentiation encourages an identification between Zelima and the reader. In turn, this identification diminishes the triple threat posed by a non-Christian female slave.

The first motion toward the homogenization of Zelima occurs when she tells Lisis that she wants to become a Christian (*Desengaños* 117). This initial indication of Zelima's possible assimilation into the aristocratic, Christian environment of the frame tale minimizes the threat her religious difference might pose. Zelima's physical appearance refers to this mixture of religious identities. As Kaminsky has discussed in "Dress and Redress," Zelima's breathtaking blue and white costume of European and Moorish markings "proclaims her rank but only hints at her nationality and religion" (382). Focusing our attention on the body, the narration carefully describes the details of Zelima's clothing, allowing us to read her for clues of her true identity. The guests respond by variously interpreting her as "una princesa de Argel, una reina de Fez o Marruecos, o una sultana de Constantinopla" and "una ninfa o diosa de las antiguas fábulas" (*Desengaños* 124) [a princess of Algiers, a queen of Fez or Morocco, a sultana of Constantinople (and) a nymph or a goddess from some ancient tale (42)]. These attempts at defining Zelima based on her outward appearance belie a desire to decipher the meanings of her body. This willingness to seek meaning in the body relates to the conditioning provided by long-standing literary, artistic, and philosophical traditions that define woman as body and hold her up to be read. As in "Al que leyere," the exploitation of this conditioning captures and maintains our attention.

Once the audience is at Zelima's mercy, with the women envious of her beauty and the men "in her sway" (*Desengaños* 124), she launches into a vituperation about misogyny that echoes the invective in "Al que leyere." Here, Zelima remarks on the need for women's voices and stories to be heard "pues ni comedia se representa, ni libro se imprime que no sea todo en ofensa de las mujeres" (*Desengaños* 124) [Without a single exception, there is no play staged or any book printed that is not a total offense against women (42)]. Having defined the macrocosmic scope of the storytelling project, Zelima secures the connection between body and text by announcing that, although she could tell many tales of disenchantment, she has chosen to tell her own.

Zelima thus adopts the personal voice, described by Susan Lanser as "indistinguishable from autobiography" in that it consists of "a personal narrator [who] claims only the validity of one person's right to interpret her experience" (19). Lanser points out that, in comparison to other narrative voices, the authority of the personal voice is limited because it must establish its own credibility with the reader. It is, therefore, "less formidable for women than authorial voice, since an authorial narrator claims broad powers of knowledge and judgment" (19-20). Such concern for lack of female authority can be detected in the male characters' reluctance to listen to women in the opening pages of the *Desengaños*. However, Zayas's clever use of the personal narrative voice poses a challenge to Lanser's assertions about uneasy credibility.[35] Indeed, it can be argued that Zelima's autobiographical discourse constitutes the most powerful narrative voice in the *Desengaños amorosos*.

Zelima sets the important precedent of the telling of autobiographical stories of victimization. Of course, for a woman to speak out in early modern Spain required her to take into account the limitations on her speech. Zayas confronts these issues in the preface and portrays Zelima confronting them as well. In spite of literary, philosophical, and cultural traditions disparaging women's intellect, Zelima resorts to autobiography, to the creation and narration of her own experience, as a way to free herself and to free other women's stories and bodies. Zelima's telling of an autobiographical story should also be read, as Mireya Pérez-Erdelyi points out, as an example that all women have their own disenchantment to tell (69). Emphasizing the body, Zelima's autobiography solidifies the relationship between female subjectivity and corporeality that provides the cornerstone for the political agenda of the texts.

Underscoring the multiplicity of her identity, Zelima immediately unravels her initial self-representation. After occupying the narrator's seat, Zelima undermines the assumptions made about her in one fell swoop:

> Mi nombre es doña Isabel Fajardo, no Zelima, ni mora, como pensáis, sino cristiana, y hija de padres católicos, y de los más principales de la ciudad de Murcia [. . .]. (*Desengaños* 127)
>
> [My name is doña Isabel Fajardo, not Zelima, and I am not Moorish, as you think, but Christian, the daughter of Catholic

---

[35] Correspondingly, in "La retórica del yo-mujer en tres escritoras españolas," Redondo Goicoechea has argued that the use of the feminine first person functions to strengthen the didacticism and lend an air of truth to the writing of Zayas, Teresa de Cartagena, and Teresa de Jesús (49).

parents who belong to one of the most prominent families in the city of Murcia. (43, mod.)]

In search of self-authorization, Isabel reinforces her assertion that she is indeed like the other guests by removing the self-fashioned brand from her face so that the audience will be more inclined to believe her ("para que deis más crédito" [*Desengaños* 127]) [so that you will give me more credit (43, mod.)]. In these transformative actions, Isabel reveals herself to be a living example of the baroque conceit of deceptive appearances. With her many identities, she becomes a perfect example of the "elusive subjectivity" that Brownlee has identified as a significant feature of Zayas's discourse.[36]

These performative transformations turn Zelima, the Moorish female slave triply representative of the Other, into Isabel, a Christian aristocrat whose only marker of difference is that she is a speaking woman, willing to perform and give voice to her many identities in a public forum. Zelima/Isabel thus integrates herself into the mainstream, stripping away the layers separating her from the audience as she makes her body a text and encourages the reader to equate textuality with corporeality.[37] Yet the others, expressing a strange combination of joy and alienation, do not accept this transformation easily. After Zelima/Isabel removes the brand from her face, the guests try to imagine "si estaba mejor con hierros o sin hierros, y casi se determinaban a sentir viéndola sin ellos" (*Desen-*

---

[36] Zelima/Isabel's self-representation coincides with the multiplicity of the autobiographical subject's capacity for transformation. Both topics are discussed in Gilmore's *Autobiographics* (introduction) and S. Smith's *A Poetics of Women's Autobiography* (ch. 1). Brownlee and Otero-Torres deal with the issue of subjectivity in Zayas.

[37] The detailed revelation of Zelima's true identity flattens her exoticism. With the notable exception of having been raped, Zelima becomes like the other frame tale characters when she becomes Isabel. This homogenization relates to a general tendency in Zayas's prose to overcategorize in order to maintain the integrity of her aristocratic feminist agenda. Within Zayas's narrative economy and, perhaps by extension, her society, a Moorish slave might not evoke the same level of sympathy from an aristocratic audience as a fellow aristocrat. This neglect of the diversity of the feminine experience corresponds to what Butler would call "colonizing gestures" or "totalizing discourse" (*Gender Trouble* 13). I discuss the aristocratic nature of Zayas's feminism in my conclusion. Also see Suelzer's dissertation, "The Representation of the Noble Subject."

gaños 127) [whether she was more beautiful with the brand or without, and they almost regretted seeing her without it (43, mod.)]. Accustomed to looking at Zelima as a visibly marked slave, the guests experience a discomfort that raises questions about class and ethnicity that the text does not follow up on, but that we as modern readers certainly note. The characters' mixed reaction to Zelima/Isabel's transformation–to seeing her without the brands of slavery on her body–suggests two explanations. In terms of gender, perhaps they find her mutability disturbing. Or, in terms of religious and class difference, perhaps they preferred having an exotic slave in their midst. In either case, the threat posed by this woman's changeability provides the basis for many of her own troubles within her tale, including her rapist's view that she is too undesirable to be reintegrated into the sexual economy.

Isabel continues to upset identity categories as she recounts her autobiographical story. Contrary to usual associations with slavery, Isabel had chosen her identity as Zelima by fashioning herself into a slave in order to represent on the surface of her body the spiritual enslavement that resulted from her rape. To add insult to injury, the rapist professed his love, then subsequently rejected her. As Kaminsky states of Zelima/Isabel,

> She makes material the metaphor of the lover's abiding presence within her and determines to advertise his base and unchristian behavior by wearing outwardly the marks of estrangement from Christian society (Muslim dress) and enslavement (the brand on her face) which his actions have occasioned. (383)

Isabel's transformative act has implications that range from the practical to the political. Ironically, slavery affords her unusual flexibility in that, once sold, she secures a freedom of movement that otherwise would not have been possible. And, in keeping with the bodily aesthetic and feminist didacticism of the *Desengaños amorosos*, her discourse positions the violated female body at the center of the texts.

Through Zelima/Isabel, Zayas authorizes women's creativity just as she does when addressing the reader in "Al que leyere." Announcing that she is a talented poet, Isabel pauses her narration to defend women's right to create, their right to write. She demands that men acknowledge women's creative talents rather than feel threatened by them. She also assesses her own talents without modesty: "Yo fuí en todo extremada, y más en hacer versos, que era el espanto de aquel reino" (*Desengaños* 128) [While I was gifted in everything, I was especially good at writing poetry. I became the wonder of the whole region (44)]. Isabel's defense of her creativity and narration of her journey corresponds to Sidonie Smith's observations about women's autobiography, in which the speaking subject (the I of autobiography) seeks "to pursue her own desires, to shatter the portrait of herself she sees hanging in the textual frames of patriarchy" (*A Poetics* 59). Isabel's claims about her poetic abilities indicate that she is aware of her ability to create, to pursue her own desires. Her personal voice is a poet's voice, and it is with corporeal, creative, Christian, aristocratic authority that she presents herself and her story as texts meant to shatter negative discursive representations and actual mistreatment of women.

It is not coincidental that the only autobiographical tale in the collection appears at the beginning of the *Desengaños*. Isabel's tale of deception, danger, and desire lays out the principle elements of the other nine tales in this volume. Structured around female victimization, all of the *desengaños* portray masculine violence and the victims' frustrated interaction with men. Repeatedly betrayed and violated, the female protagonists either wind up dead (in six stories) or, for four of the fortunate ones, in a convent. That Isabel gives voice to her own suffering sets a precedent that the other female narrators (and women outside the texts) can follow.

At the beginning of her story, Isabel portrays herself as occupying the typical position of a female: objectified by men, she used to react only to other's wishes for her rather than define her own desires. When she was younger, she tells us, she had many suitors and resisted them all, insisting that she would never defy her father's plans for her (*Desengaños* 131). The lack of articulation of her desire at the start becomes increasingly ironic, however. As the tale proceeds, Isabel turns into a woman in control of her identity and in search for justice.

The trauma of rape propels Isabel toward independence and agency. Once she falls victim to this sexual crime, Isabel must come to terms with women's precarious position in a society that emphasizes, even fetishizes, women's sexual purity and physical integrity to such a degree that victimization makes women corrupt. Violently forced out of passivity, she repeatedly articulates her desires. Both in words and in actions, she seeks to repair the loss of self that she feels as a result of being raped. The description of Isabel's painful realization of the rape highlights the profound repercussions of the event while also legitimizing her anger and frustration.

After Manuel locks her in a room and rapes her, Isabel recovers consciousness and realizes what has been done to her. Using what Lynn Higgins and Brenda Silver call the "rhetoric of elision," Isabel gives voice to rape through silence.[38] The silencing of the violent act appears in this description of her experience:

> Pues pasada poco más de media hora, volví en mí, y me hallé, mal digo, no me hallé, pues me hallé perdida, y tan perdida, que no me supe ni pude volver ni podré ganarme jamás y infundiendo en mí mi agravio una mortífera rabia, lo que en otra mujer pudiera causar lágrimas y desesperaciones, en mí fue un furor diabólico, con el cual, desasiéndome de sus infames lazos, arremetí a la espada que tenía a la cabecera de la cama, . . . se la fui a envainar en el cuerpo; hurtóle el golpe . . . me quitó la espada, que me la iba a entrar por el cuerpo por haber errado el del infame [. . .]. (*Desengaños* 137)

> [After about half an hour, I did come to my senses and I found myself–no, I'm wrong, I did not find myself–I saw that I was ruined, so ruined that I did not know myself then nor would I ever again: I shall never recover myself. That affront filled me with mortal rage; what might have caused tears and despair in another woman filled me with a demonic fury. . . . I grabbed his sword, which was lying beside the bed. I tried to sheath it in his body, but he evaded the blow . . . . He wrested the sword from me since I was going to plunge it into my own body [. . .]. (52-53, mod.)]

Reacting with fury to the rape, Isabel first tries to kill the offender and, when this fails, to kill herself. She expresses her rage through the equation of bodily integrity (i.e. virginity) with psychical integrity. Consequently, she interprets this violation as an erasure of self ("no me hallé").

This abrupt change, the erasure of the narrator's core identity, calls into question Isabel's very existence and leaves the reader ask-

---

[38] Entitled "Rhetoric of Elision" (77-78), part two of Higgins and Silver's *Rape and Representation* explores the technique of figuring rape as a textual gap in literary representations of sexual crimes.

ing, "Where is the subject of this autobiography?" Yet at this point we already have a partial answer to this question. In the process of unveiling her identity, Zelima/Isabel already has begun to reveal the multiplicity of self that has been the key to her survival. The rest of the story, including Isabel's unsuccessful attempt to kill Manuel and then herself, revolves around a search for the self lost in the moment of violation. Through this process, Isabel overcomes the position of object in which she found herself in her younger years and the position of victim in which she found herself after the rape. Eventually, she becomes an autonomous subject, an agent of self-invention.

This subject-object interplay is problematized throughout Isabel's story. When she leaves her house and takes on the identity of a slave and, with the help of an ex-servant, is sold for one hundred ducats, she enacts a self-commodification that appears to undermine her newfound independence. In effect, she has chosen to become an object of exchange. However, as Lou Charnon-Deutsch states, Isabel uses slavery to control her destiny, thereby gaining an independence generally unavailable to women (119-22). Isabel's decision to leave her house in search of justice results in her father's immediate death and her mother's rancor over the entire incident. Faced with sudden solitude, Isabel sets out alone to seek retribution for the rape.

In her six-year quest to restore her honor by obliging Manuel to marry her, Isabel lives as the slave Zelima. Critical of the performativity that affords Zelima/Isabel independence of movement, Manuel interprets her masquerade as a sign of dangerous instability. Here he denigrates her mutability when he finally recognizes her:

> ¿Qué disfraz es éste, doña Isabel? ¿O cómo las mujeres de tus obligaciones, y que han tenido deseos y pensamientos de ser mía, se ponen en semejantes bajezas? (*Desengaños* 157)
>
> [What kind of a disguise is this, doña Isabel? How can a lady of your standing, who has wanted and hoped to be my wife, degrade herself thus? (71)].

Later, he again tries to use her costume as a psychological weapon to discredit her. Toward the end of the story, Manuel admits that perhaps he might have been obligated to marry Isabel at one point.

But now he definitively disavows her because he could never trust a vulgar woman who disguises herself and follows him (*Desengaños* 163). From the male perspective, Isabel's agency spills over the boundaries of female decorum, and allows Manuel (a rapist) to indict her for such outrageous actions.

Excessive in its breaking down of boundaries of gender, class, ethnicity, religion, and space, Isabel's slave identity disrupts every basic element of the social order. Manuel's criticism of Isabel's many masks bespeaks a culturally coded fear of the feminine as that which threatens to destabilize and de-center patriarchal order.[39] In this sense, Isabel's agency and autonomy are anomalous. In terms of gender, she is a threat to the social order. In terms of difference, she remains the Other.

The resolution of Isabel's autobiographical tale provides the thematic and didactic framework for the rest of the *Desengaños amorosos*. In spite of her impressive capacity for action, Isabel does not act in response to Manuel's final rejection of her as a debased woman. Rather, another man steps in to resolve the situation. Isabel's suitor Felipe, who has followed her in his own extended masquerade, exacts revenge by killing Manuel. While the death of her offender should mark a moment of release, Isabel is in fact newly obligated to yet another man: she feels that she must marry Felipe to repay him for avenging her honor.

While hiding from the authorities, she contemplates her options and wavers between fulfilling her obligation to Felipe through marriage and returning to her mother in Murcia. Significantly, Isabel sets an example for all women when she liberates herself from these gender-bound social obligations by deciding not to take on the prescribed role of wife dictated by the economies of marriage and honor and made available to her (as an impure woman) only through a man's generosity. Instead, she creates a new option by taking on the identity of a slave again, preferring this self-commodification to the culturally imposed identification of woman as commodity.[40]

---

[39] Like much of Zayas's discourse, this novella can be read in terms of the analysis done on classical and un-classical bodies in Stallybrass and White's *The Politics and Poetics of Transgression*. The tale serves as a clear example of woman as antithetical to the classical body: she is an open body that poses a threat to the stability of the phallocentric, classical, unchanging body of man.

[40] For provocative discussions of the commodification of women, see Irigaray's "Commodities among Themselves" in *This Sex which Is not One* and Sedgwick's *Between Men*.

Later, at the end of her story, Isabel announces her intention to enter a convent to become a slave to God, the lover who will never mistreat her (*Desengaños* 167). In keeping with her creative capacity for writing poetry, telling a tale, and inventing the self, Isabel once again seeks out a cultural space in which she may determine, to the greatest extent possible within patriarchy, control over her life.[41] Isabel finally settles on an option available to women seen as sexually impure by the society. In spite of what might be read as a predictable ending, the persistent exploration of female agency in Isabel's autobiographical tale challenges traditional notions of female sexuality and subjectivity.

Having assumed the identity of a slave devoted to God, Isabel ends her story, leaving all who have heard her "tiernos y lastimados" (*Desengaños* 167) [moved and sorrowful (81)]. This reaction seems to respond as much to the highly personal nature of the discourse as to the content of the narration. In a gesture that communicates the power of Isabel's tale, Lisis offers her jewels for Isabel's convent dowry.[42] The reactions of the frame characters on both a general and a gendered level thus mirror the desired reading of the entire novella collection.

The embedding of the desired effect of the texts within the frame tale is repeated at the end of the frame tale in the *Desengaños amorosos*. Recalling the fate of the various female protagonists, Lisis refuses to marry Diego. She decidedly links herself with Isabel when she mentions that her own doubts about survival in the sexual economy began with Isabel's story:

> no es justo que yo me fíe de mi dicha, porque no me siento más firme que la hermosa doña Isabel, a quien no le aprovecharon tantos trabajos como en el discurso de su desengaño nos refirió, de que mis temores han tenido principio. (*Desengaños* 508)

---

[41] As scholarship on convents has shown, nuns enjoyed a large degree of autonomy within communities that, ultimately, were controlled by male church authorities (see Arenal and Schlau's *Untold Sisters* and Brown's *Immodest Acts*).

[42] By offering her jewels and all that she is worth to help Isabel enter the convent, Lisis implicitly imitates Isabel's subversion of the role of commodity assigned to women by the dominant culture. For a materialist analysis of Isabel's use of money, see Charnon-Deutsch (119-22).

> [it isn't right for me to trust in my good fortune because I feel no more steadfast than the beautiful doña Isabel whose many trials did her no good, as she told us in her own disenchantment, which is when all of my fears began. (402, mod.)]

For purposes of Lisis's interest in self-preservation, Isabel's tale becomes the quintessential example of peril and survival. With the female body figured as text, a female first-person voice, and a story of rape and rejection, Isabel's identification as "slave to her own lover" pointedly responds to the cultural positioning of women as objects in a phallocentric sexual economy.

If the *Desengaños amorosos* aspires to set women's voices free, Isabel initiates the project in a tale in which the female voice carries dramatic weight. Her autobiography connects the female voice with the body, objectivity with subjectivity. The self-conscious fashioning of narrative authority on the part of this, the first narrator in the *Desengaños amorosos*, responds to the narrative gender exclusivity by validating the collective female narrative voice and the collective feminine experience. By negating distance between self and text, "La esclava de su amante" invites us to read women's bodies as texts of violation and injustice throughout the remaining novellas. Declaring her *self* lost after being raped, Isabel demonstrates a strong sense of integrity in her search to make her rapist follow through on his obligation to her. In the end, she chooses to become a nun–a slave to God–in order to protect her emotional and bodily integrity. Given the emphasis on women's community and friendship, Isabel's final choice allows her to assert control over her body and her story. This new life also will allow her to reinvent herself in the gynocentric image of religious women.

Structurally and thematically, Isabel's tale paves the way for the other women narrators. Isabel's personal voice contributes to the collective protest, encouraging other women to speak of their victimization. The remaining nine narrators of the *Desengaños amorosos* take up this task on behalf of their victimized sisters. Yet none will speak from the "I" as she does. Only in the last story, "Estragos que causa el vicio," will a female character speak from her body in a way that recalls Isabel's discourse. In the intervening stories, other women's violated bodies are described with great detail. Yet, as narrator of the final tale, Lisis gives over the narration to her protagonist, Florentina, and thus the collection ends as it began, with a woman speaking for herself.

Even the frame tale ends with an act of bodily protest: Lisis shows control over her own body when she refuses to marry Diego. Speaking in the first person, Lisis hints at her impending announcement that she will bow out of her marriage agreement. Lisis's words follow up on an initial clue about her final intentions given only to the reader, and not the frame characters, at the beginning of the *Desengaños*. Before the start of the soiree, the principal narrator gives us a glimpse into Lisis's private thoughts:

> tuvo lugar en su divino entendimiento de obrar en su alma nuevos propósitos, si bien a nadie lo daba a entender, guardando para su tiempo la disposición de su deseo. (*Desengaños* 116)

> [her sublime intelligence began to forge a new purpose in her soul, even if she never let on to anyone, and saved the revelation of her new desire until the right moment. (36, mod.)]

During the soiree, Lisis has plenty of time to mull over these new intentions. With Isabel's and other women's tales reinforcing her disinclination to marry, she begins her turn at narration with an allusion to feeling overwhelmed by the tales of victimization and injustice. She then creates an air of mystery that anticipates her unconventional decision by referring to herself as a text that we are all invited to read.

The plot twist is explained using corporeal language, thereby concluding the collection with an affirmation of women's connection to the body:

> De manera que, aquí me he puesto a hablar sin engaño, *y yo misma he de ser el mayor desengaño*, porque sería morir del engaño y no vivir del aviso, si desengañando a todas, me dejase yo engañar. (*Desengaños* 470, emphasis added)

> [And so I shall speak without deception, *and I myself shall be the greatest disenchantment*, because it would be equal to dying of deception and not living according to the warnings if, seeking to un-deceive all women, I let myself be deceived. (368, mod.)]

Describing herself as a text–for we must remember that the tales themselves are called *desengaños*–Lisis offers herself up as the greatest disenchantment of all. Tied closely to the body, this turn of phrase refers us back to the corporeal discourse of the novellas. The power of this bodily example confronts the reader as three frame tale characters–Lisis, Isabel, and Estefanía–exit the soiree holding hands. The final act drives home the political statement made by women who refuse to expose themselves to the dangers of male-female relationships. Rather than marry, they free themselves from the cultural practices exposed and criticized throughout the *Desengaños amorosos*.

Building on the various cultural and social deployments of the body in her society, Zayas exploits corporeality throughout her fiction. Framed by narrative that connects women to their bodies, Zayas's *Novelas amorosas* and *Desengaños amorosos* feminize corporeal discourse. With a preface written in the first person and a strategically placed autobiographical tale, both volumes begin with language that speaks from the body.

As can be seen through the rich variations on representations of the body, Zayas's novellas claim the female body as a truly contested site, as a flesh and blood text whose violation is produced by institutionalized misogyny. Writing against a long cultural tradition that uses women's biology against them, Zayas seems to appreciate the difficulty of the task she has set for herself. Seeking to valorize and authorize women's experiences and voices, she chooses the body as the vehicle through which to make her readers invest in the feminine.

Chapter Two

VIOLENCE DENATURALIZED:
FEMINIST READINGS OF THE BODY IMPERILED

Discourse of man is the metaphor of woman.
Gayatri Spivak

THE intellectual history of the West is brimming with seemingly endless metaphors that claim to capture "Woman's" essence. According to Aristotle, woman is an impotent, deficient man. To Freud and Lacan, she is lack; to Derrida, intangible truth. Some of these associations are familiar to us in even broader terms: woman as nature in opposition to man's culture; woman as body to man's head.[1] Thanks to feminist scholarship of the past few decades, this impulse to define "Woman" now seems a transparent attempt to contain women's difference. Like feminists of our own period, Zayas combats and deconstructs metaphors of woman. She challenges conventional constructions of femininity in her representations of assertive female characters and in her virulently pro-woman didacticism.

One metaphor that might be interpreted as being replicated in her fiction, however, is that of woman as body. Frequently portrayed as body only, women often are associated with the devalued aspects of culture and society. As Moira Gatens indicates in *Imaginary Bodies*, "Significantly, both women and corporeality are often negative and function conceptually as the underside to culturally valued terms such as reason, civilization, and progress" (49-50).

---

[1] As Bronfen summarizes based on previous feminist work of Carolyn Merchant, Simone de Beauvoir, and others: "In the equation with nature, earth, body, the Woman was construed [in European culture] as Other to culture, as object of intense curiosity to be explored, dissected, conquered, domesticated and, if necessary, eliminated" (66). I deal with the implications of this equation of woman with nature in chapter three.

Given Zayas's emphasis on female corporeality, what should we make of the potentially problematic association between woman and body in her texts?

Since Scripture has long been one of the major sources of authority called on to justify men's superiority, the problem of woman as body becomes more delicate in the context of a society ideologically and politically tied to the Catholic church. Jordan's discussion of authoritative religious texts (in this case the Pauline epistles) addresses the issue of gender hierarchy:

> The opposition here between flesh and spirit is uncompromising and it is not surprising that woman, who instances man's fleshliness, is ordered to remain in subjection. Man is both the head to her body and also, as Christ is to his church, a figure of the eternal in relation to her as an image of the faithful on earth. (25)

In Spain's early modern period, this discourse of subservience—of woman as flesh subordinated to man's reason—reached feverish heights. As evidenced by different cultural phenomena (such as sumptuary laws, behavior manuals, and legal codes), early modern intellectuals, clerics, and politicians were preoccupied, indeed, obsessed, with containing women's "fleshliness."

Spain's literature reflects this mentality as well: frequently women are portrayed as fickle, devious, unreliable, and lustful. One overdrawn case of these constructions arises in Tirso's *El burlador de Sevilla* (*Don Juan of Seville*), in which women are blamed for provoking men's dishonor and misfortune. After don Juan tricks the duchess, Isabela, into having sex, for example, the king laments the scandal using familiar terminology about women's fickle behavior:

> ¡Ah, pobre honor! Si eres alma
> del hombre, ¿por qué te dejan
> en la mujer inconstante,
> si es la misma ligereza?
> (l. 154-57)[2]

> [Alas, poor honor! If you are man's very soul, why do they leave you in fickle woman's hand, if she is flightiness itself?]

---

[2] At the beginning of Act III in *El Burlador de Sevilla*, Batricio uses similar language to lament women's inconstancy and infidelity.

As anyone who reads male-authored literature of the period knows, women are portrayed as the keepers of masculine honor, as a metaphor for sexual purity and social harmony.

Zayas's fiction directly challenges these negative depictions of women in literature and the metaphors of woman in intellectual discourse. Like pro-woman writers in other parts of western Europe, Zayas fills a discursive and political void by representing women's stories from women's perspectives. Her texts critique systemic misogyny by rewriting traditional literary scripts and retelling them through the female narrative voice.

With men relegated to narrative silence in the *Desengaños*, the principal narrator informs us that the primary purpose of this volume relates to the displacement of highly misogynist male discourse. This feminist intervention is articulated as a response to men's monopoly on discursive power:

> Y como son los hombres los que presiden en todo, jamás cuentan los malos pagos que dan, sino los que les dan; y si bien lo miran, ellos cometen la culpa, y ellas siguen tras su opinión, pensando que aciertan [. . .]. (*Desengaños* 118)

> [Because men preside over everything, they never tell about the evil deeds they do, they tell only about the ones done to them. If you think about it, men are really the ones at fault and women go along with them, thinking they must be right. (37-38)]

This message echoes the outline of Zayas's project given in the preface: as a writer, Zayas is committed to correcting the cultural script that portrays women negatively. She inscribes this commitment into the structure of the texts by showing female characters speaking about women. Williamsen has indicated that this stated intention of redressing a masculinist tradition confirms that the soiree enacts "women's usurpation of a previously male dominated sphere" ("Engendering" 643).[3] Zayas endorses the need to dismantle and correct the vilification of women prevalent in the spheres of intellectual production and consumption.

---

[3] On Zayas's response to dominant literary tradition, also see Yllera (48-52). Zayas's intervention into male discourse is closely related to Christine de Pizan's explanation in *The Book of the City of Ladies* (1405) of her frustration with the antifeminist sentiments frequently expressed by male authors: "It seems they all speak from one and the same mouth" (3).

While the revisionist intent of Zayas's texts is clear, the focus on women's corporeality as a means to convince readers of the legitimacy of a political agenda requires further inquiry. With women figured as flesh in Western teleologies, what can we make of Zayas's reliance on female corporeality in her purportedly feminist fiction? Does this connection undermine her revisionist intent by repeating a cultural pattern that figures women as body only?

The interconnectedness of violence and gender relations in Zayas's texts provides a point of entry into the political implications of the author's use of corporeality. In a very fundamental sense, Zayas's reliance on bodies exposes the impulse to control women in the culture at large. The corporeal examples in her texts force readers to recognize the reality that feminists still want to overcome and that Grosz expresses succinctly: "Women have been objectified and alienated as social subjects partly through the denigration and containment of the female body" (*Volatile Bodies* xiv).

The privileging of corporeal discourse in Zayas also has an experiential component that should not be overlooked. Since most of her female protagonists experience some sort of injustice, and female bodies appear in different stages of violation and decay, empathetic readings are encouraged to help place the reader in the position of woman. In essence, the body-based texts encourage psychological identification which, in the end, reinforces Grosz's assertion that "being a body is something that we must come to accommodate psychically, something that we must live" (*Volatile Bodies* xiii). Zayas's texts put readers in the position of woman; they work to make readers understand the position of women whose bodily integrity is violated.

Implicit in this interpretation of Zayas's politicized aesthetic is a reading of the violated bodies as one of the primary means to encourage identification with women. This marriage of politics and aesthetics differentiates the texts from pornography, sensationalism, and voyeurism, all of which depend on the exploitation of (female) sexuality and corporeality. Such exploitation involves the naturalization of sexual violence and objectification. To the extent that Zayas's politics rely on the display of the body, she seems to count on the reader to be voyeuristic, to be conditioned to the contact with women's bodies, and even their violated bodies, in art. In this sense, it would be absurd to deny that the texts do not use the body manipulatively. However, this manipulation has a political purpose, for Zayas displays the body as part of a concerted effort to convince readers to sign on to her feminist agenda.

The *Novelas amorosas* and the *Desengaños amorosos* intervene in the culture of violence by exposing the misogyny inherent in the polity, in gender relations, and in the family. Unlike many debased deployments of the female body in art, Zayas emphasizes a pro-woman political agenda. Unlike texts engaged in rhetorical violence–texts that subordinate the woman's suffering and victimization "to notions of artistic ability and aesthetic effect" (Bronfen 50)–Zayas's novellas do not ignore characters' pain.[4] As the following analyses of the dynamics of violence suggest, Zayas's aesthetic depends on a denaturalization of violence that deconstructs the metaphor of woman and replaces it with humanized representations of individual women's lives and of the lived body.

I. CIRCULATING VIOLENCE

In *Over her Dead Body*, Elisabeth Bronfen discusses the options available to the spectator of images of dead and dying women in art. Grappling with the centuries-long tradition of the aestheticization of dead and dying female bodies, Bronfen wonders about the possible positions one can adopt when taking in such images:

> Should one assume the position of a morally involved spectator, treating the represented body as though it were the same as the material body it refers to, focusing, that is, on the question of reference and in so doing denying the representational aspect? . . . Or should one assume the position of the aesthetically involved spectator, distanced, disinterested, treating the representation of a

---

[4] Bronfen is working here with de Lauretis's explanation of "The Violence of Rhetoric," a concept that overlaps with Zayas's connection of violence with gender. Defining the technology of gender as the "techniques and discursive categories by which gender is constructed," de Lauretis argues in *Technologies of Gender* that the construction of gender implicitly involves the "en-gendering" of violence (38). While de Lauretis deconstructs male discourse to reveal the associations between women and violence, Zayas makes explicit the motivations for masculine violence. With regard to the representation of pain in Zayas, see Routt's application of Scarry's *The Body in Pain* in "El cuerpo femenino y la creación literaria."

dying body only as a signifier pointing to many other signifiers . . . foreclosing the question of the real? (44-45)[5]

In discussing the reactions to aestheticized death, dying, and decay as a choice between moral and aesthetic involvement, Bronfen imagines a spectator who consciously chooses which position to occupy when "reading" an imperiled female body. This imaginary, idealized spectator is necessarily sympathetic to the possible connections between art and reality, and is aware of the metaphoric capacities of representation.

Even though one might argue that most spectators do not engage in such complex thinking when taking in an image of a violated body, it is true that most were and are accustomed to reading woman as metaphor—looking to her (and her violated body) as a signifier of disorder. This conditioning translates into a tendency to read aesthetically, to search representations for their metaphorical implications. Bronfen's articulation of two potentially conflicting positions occupied by consumers of images of violated women points to the referential and representational techniques that converge in Zayas to encourage a morally involved reading from those who otherwise would tend to read aesthetically.

Like the series of paintings of a dying woman referred to by Bronfen, Zayas's texts also place "us as spectators in the interstice between an aesthetic and an empathetic response" (44). Looking at the various manifestations of violence and its consequences in the texts, it might seem that the sheer abundance of violence licenses or favors a purely aesthetic response to the plights of the female characters. Yet the insistence on the materiality of individual women's bodies challenges and, if successful, denaturalizes the reader's conditioning to read violence aesthetically. This individuation and didacticism encourage readers to eschew purely aesthetic readings of the violated bodily text.

Zayas's texts ease the reader into this moral dilemma. The first novella of the collection, for example, presents a relatively aes-

---

[5] While Bronfen specifically discusses artistic representations of real women, the issues of the body's materiality pertain to Zayas's fictional representations of women as well. By citing Bronfen, however, I do not mean to suggest any association between realism and Zayas's own texts. For another book-length consideration of the traditional association of women with death, see Bassein's *Women and Death: Linkages in Western Thought and Literature*.

theticized treatment of violence. "Aventurarse perdiendo" draws on a rhetoric of violence to introduce the disruptive force of love relationships into the texts. In one of many confirmations of the close relationship between Zayas's texts and the literary canon, Cervantes's *Novelas ejemplares* and Zayas's *Novelas amorosas* both open by referring to the popular genre of the pastoral novel. Cervantes's first exemplary novella, "La gitanilla" ("The Gypsy Girl"), explores idyllic gypsy life and Zayas's "Aventurarse perdiendo" positions the tranquility of nature against the perils of human relationships.

When Fabio discovers the crossdressed Jacinta in the mountains near Montserrat (a scene in "Aventurarse perdiendo" that is closely related to the sighting of Dorotea in *Don Quijote*), he finds her working as a shepherd boy (*zagal*), resting by a fountain and lamenting her misfortune.[6] Jacinta's language directly contrasts with the pastoral setting. In a song that leads Fabio to her, she sings:

> matadme, penas, matadme,
> pues por lo menos dirán:
> murió, pero sin mudarse.
> ¡Ay bien sentidos males,
> poderosos seréis para matarme,
> mas no podréis hacer que amor se acabe!
>
> (*Novelas* 40)

> [kill me, sorrows, kill me, for then at least it can be said she died without ever changing. Alas, heartfelt woes, you are powerful enough to kill me but not powerful enough to end my love! (14)]

In this song, the first speech act of a female character in the novellas proper, Jacinta introduces violence into the texts by equating love with death. In addition to drawing attention to her body–she is, after all, willing to sacrifice herself–Jacinta also proclaims herself to be an anomalous woman in that, unlike many, she is resolutely dedicated to love.

The commonplace equation between love and death in this song depends on a metaphoric, and thus symbolic, treatment of vi-

---

[6] Dorotea's and Jacinta's discovery scenes are highly voyeuristic. While the male onlookers in *Don Quijote* (I, 28) fixate on Dorotea's white feet, Fabio stares at Jacinta's white hands.

olence.[7] The majority of the first novella sustains the initial equation of love with death put forth by Jacinta. Love seems to kill Ariadna, who dies rather melodramatically upon hearing that she has been spurned by her lover, and Félix is nearly killed by Jacinta's dishonored brother, who dies in the scuffle. For Jacinta, however, the violence of love remains purely symbolic, relegated to the conventions of amorous discourse. She expresses violence in her song and experiences it in a dream in which a man stabs her in the heart. Obsessed with this dreamworld man, who later appears and betrays her, Jacinta comes to realize that love is, indeed, treacherous. While she escapes real physical injury and eventually enters a convent, her personal experience locates violence in the rhetorical realm of song and in the subconscious, symbolic dreamworld.

"Aventurarse perdiendo" sets the stage for the relatively subdued violence of the *Novelas amorosas*. Compared to the *Desengaños*, this first volume downplays violence in favor of lighter fare.[8] With men and women sharing the role of narrator and with the purpose of entertaining Lisis, the *Novelas amorosas* contains less violence and gives less attention to violent acts than the *Desengaños*. Yet this pattern is shattered in the *Desengaños*, a volume in which violence comes to the fore as the primary signifier of women's oppression. The contrast between the dream-state violence of "Aventurarse perdiendo" and the detailed account of Isabel's trauma in the first tale of the *Desengaños* captures this shift in purpose and content. If there is anything symbolic about the rapes, murders, and other crimes against women in the second volume, it is that the violence represents profound social dysfunction.

By the final tale of the *Desengaños amorosos*, violence has spread to such an extent that a man erupts into an explosion of aggression and destroys his household. In "Estragos que causa el vicio," the adulterous Dionís's reaction to his wife's alleged adultery sends him into a state of unfettered rage. Lisis narrates "Estragos,"

---

[7] Jacinta's amorous discourse and dream images echo the conventions of courtly love seen in a large group of texts and genres including medieval lyric poetry, Boccaccio's *Elegy of Lady Fiammetta*, and the Spanish *novela sentimental*.

[8] In *Feminismo y forma narrativa*, Foa correctly criticizes readings that see the *Novelas amorosas* as purely diversionary, pointing out the several unhappy endings and the presence of violence and death in the *Novelas* (73). While violence appears in these first ten tales, and while love relations are tumultuous, the overall tone of the first volume is less violent and incisive than the second.

a tale of savage violence that incorporates the issues of injustice, hypocrisy, and masculine violence addressed to varying degrees throughout the collection. Warning of the dangers of men's control over female bodies, the tale contains the collection's last wave of violence, which is precipitated by a fatal act of misreading an innocent body. This mistaken reading of the body results in the massacre of an entire household.

"Estragos que causa el vicio" tells the story of Florentina, a woman who has had a four-year affair with her brother-in-law while living with him and her sister. A misguided female servant suggests a trick by which the brother-in-law, Dionís, will come to believe that his innocent wife Magdalena is having an affair with a young servant. Dionís will then kill Magdalena, thus freeing him to marry his lover, Florentina. The plan proceeds without a glitch: when Dionís sees the young man leaving his wife's room, he automatically assumes his wife to be guilty of impropriety. Despite his own long-standing sexual relationship with his sister-in-law, he flies into a rage that leads him to murder everyone in his house, including himself and excepting Florentina, who barely escapes with her life.

The description of the ill-fated wife Magdalena underscores the hypocrisy and cruelty of the uxoricide. Here we have Florentina, the victim's sister, describing the murderous scene:

> En tanto, don Dionís, ya de todo punto ciego con su agravio, entró adonde estaba su inocente esposa, que se había vuelto a quedar dormida con los brazos sobre la cabeza, y llegando a su puro y casto lecho, a sus airados ojos y engañada imaginación sucio, deshonesto y violado con la mancha de su deshonor, le dijo:
> "¡Ah, traidora, y cómo descansas en mi ofensa!"
> Y sacando la daga, la dio tantas puñaladas, cuantas su indignada cólera le pedía. Sin que pudiese ni aun formar un ¡ay!, desamparó aquella alma santa el más hermoso y honesto cuerpo que conoció el reino de Portugal. (*Desengaños* 496)

[Meanwhile, don Dionís, by now totally blinded by the affront to his honor, entered his innocent wife's room. She had gone back to sleep with her arms raised over her head. He approached her pure, chaste bed with angry eyes, his deceived imagination seeing it soiled, dishonored, and violated by the stain of his dishonor. He said: "You traitor, and how comfortably you sleep in my dishonor!" Drawing his dagger, he stabbed her as many times as his blind rage required. She couldn't even utter "alas!" before her saintly soul abandoned the most beautiful and chaste body the kingdom of Portugal had ever known. (392, mod.)]

In this passage, the husband clearly misreads his wife's body. He sees her in bed and interprets her innocent slumber as an added offense to his honor.[9]

Yet Florentina, who narrates at this point, immediately re-reads the woman for us, emphasizing not only the saintliness of the soul but the chastity and beauty of the innocent body. This narrative intervention highlights the disparity between masculine and feminine readings of the female body. This feminization of bodily discourse (for we hear a woman narrating another woman's dead body) also discourages the reading of the body on purely aesthetic terms and encourages, in Bronfen's terminology, a morally involved reading. The intervention also makes explicit the danger of men reading women, a dynamic expressed throughout the novellas as men act out their anxieties about sexuality and honor. Rather than condemn Florentina for her adultery and her complicity in the plan to get her sister murdered, the tale glosses over her guilt; church and state officials absolve the protagonist. Lisis later repeats this pattern by blaming the 'evil' servant who conjured the plan in the first place (*Desengaños* 508). By exonerating Florentina and highlighting Dionís's rage, "Estragos que causa el vicio" suggests that the larger issue at stake is men's control over women's bodies. Dionís's participation in a sexual double standard underscores once again the obsession with controlling female sexuality and corporeality.

With this stark comparison, we see that the initially subdued, symbolic violence in the first novella of the *Novelas amorosas* progresses in the *Desengaños* to irrational homicide and suicide. The narration reflects the shift by first contrasting Dionís's rage with Magdalena's innocence, then by lingering on the final violent act. In fact, Florentina's reconstruction of these events for the benefit of her male rescuer causes her such strife that she faints merely from

---

[9] Ordóñez uses similar language to discuss Zayas's representation of gender relations in the collection: "Women in the 'novelas' of María de Zayas are repeatedly victims of the misunderstanding of men: husbands, brothers, and women acting in collusion with men *misread* wives, sisters, mistresses, and even friends" (4, emphasis added).

relating the lengthy (three-page) account of the murders.[10] Even her rescuer, guiding the reader's reaction, is left "suspenso y espantado de lo que había oído" (*Desengaños* 499) [shocked and stunned by what he'd heard (395)]. Thus the tales come full circle: a far cry from Jacinta's pastoral setting, in which the violence of love first is expressed rhetorically, the twentieth tale leads the reader through horrific scenes of bloodshed. Both Jacinta's and Florentina's stories find resolution in the sanctity of the convent, signaling that all violence is unacceptable and that women are safe only when removed from relationships with men.

The contrast between Jacinta's dreamed violence and Florentina's testimony of a bloody massacre highlights one of the most striking aspects of Zayas's portrayal of female victimization: the texts elucidate an entire spectrum of women's suffering that ranges from depression and frustration to physical pain and torture. Through these interwoven representations of oppression, fear, and danger, Zayas fashions her cultural commentaries to include such issues as psychological abuse and conjugal violence which, until recently, have not figured into contemporary discussions of violence against women. If we pause to consider that domestic violence did not enter the realm of public discussion and study until the 1970s, we see that Zayas's layered treatment of this phenomenon comes early in the history of advocacy for women's rights. Commenting on the near absence of a written record of violence against women, Jan Horsfall writes, "Patriarchies have no doubt produced a long and mostly unwritten history of wife battering" (18). Yet Zayas provides us with a literary treatment of violence against women that takes into account psychological as well as physical impacts of violence.[11]

---

[10] Clamurro has suggested that "Estragos" is "one of the texts that most vividly illustrates how the complexity of narrative structure reflects both the madness and delirium of carnal love and also the decadence of the social order" ("Madness" 220). This analysis describes the tale's narrative structure (with its plurality of narrative voices and its repetition of violent events) as enhancing "the sense of frenzy and derangement essential to the psychological and ideological goals of the text" (222).

[11] Hélisenne de Crenne's *The Torments of Love* should be considered a predecessor to Zayas's texts. This sixteenth-century sentimental novel is told from a female perspective and includes descriptions of the protagonist being beaten by her husband. Over time, there have been highly public protests against wife battery, among which Frances Power Cobbe's 1878 "Wife Torture in England" stands out as a notable example. G. Walker discusses domestic violence as a public issue in contemporary society in *Family Violence and the Women's Movement* (22-23). For

The use of violence, particularly in the *Desengaños*, again brings us to the question of purpose and motivation. Since the focus on violence is synonymous with a focus on the female body, we should consider not only possible pornographic content, but also issues regarding marketing and sensationalism. Like much male-authored literature, Zayas's novellas display the violated female body. Yet this is not the violence of male-authored texts: unlike the space left for many readings of Mencía's violated body at the end of *El médico de su honra*, Zayas relies on overt criticism and narrative strategies to construct pro-woman didacticism and guide the reader to pro-reform readings. By putting the spotlight on women's bodies and stories, Zayas's fiction forces the reader into a reflective, if not empathetic, position. As Ruth Nadelhaft has suggested, literature with sympathetic treatments of domestic violence involves readers by forcing them to consider their views on the subject and asking them to take a moral stand (247).[12] These are the demands placed on the reader of Zayas's tales. Regardless of the degree or the type of violence carried out against the female characters, both the frame characters as listeners and we as readers come away with an acute sense of compassion for the victimized women who struggle, protest, and sometimes survive as they suffer abuses at the hands of their abductors, lovers, and family members, including, in some cases, women.

As can be seen in these, the first and last, novellas, Zayas shifts violence from the metaphoric to the material level, politicizing and feminizing bodily discourse prevalent in her culture and in the literary tradition against which she was writing. That the seeds of violence are introduced at the outset of the first novella, appear regularly throughout both volumes, and culminate in the bloody "Es-

---

a brief discussion of domestic violence and its general treatment in literature, see Deats and Lenker's "Introduction" to *The Aching Hearth: Family Violence in Life and Literature*.

[12] Specifically, Nadelhaft suggests a series of questions that sympathetic treatments of domestic violence in literature ask of the reader: "Where are you on this issue? Are you there for me? Will you intervene?" (247). The humanized treatment of women's suffering in Zayas make clear that her texts avoid "rhetorical violence" and, more pointedly, eschew pornographic (e.g., objectifying and often violent) representations of women's bodies. For a historicized discussion of the rise of pornography in seventeenth-century Europe and the difficulties of defining the battleground of porn, see Hunt's introduction to *The Invention of Pornography*, "Obscenity and the Origins of Modernity, 1500-1800."

tragos que causa el vicio" points to violence as a central element of the texts. Relying on representations of violence to bring the message to the fore, Zayas's texts deconstruct the metaphor of woman. With the scales tipped toward the feminine–both in corporeal and narrative terms–the collection rewrites the symbolic value of the violated female body and humanizes the plight of women.

Faithful to their differing purposes, the *Novelas amorosas* and the *Desengaños* emphasize distinct aspects of violence. The entertainment-oriented first volume deals primarily with the threat of violence, while the pro-woman *Desengaños amorosos*, with its emphasis on bettering women's situation, denaturalizes violence through individualized, detailed accounts of violent acts. The emphasis on violence in the second volume also stifles the broad range of female agency seen in the *Novelas amorosas*: comparatively free from the rampant bloodshed of the *Desengaños amorosos*, the female characters of the *Novelas amorosas* seek and often find varying degrees of empowerment. In contrast, the women of the second volume routinely encounter frustration, pain, and death. They exert definitive control only when they escape to convents. As the quantity and severity of the violence increases, the moralism increases. And as the focus on didacticism mounts, so does the pressure on the frame tale audience and the reader to comply with Lisis's gendered mandate for social change, which tells men to "respect and honor women" and demands that women raise their consciousness about the treacheries of men (*Desengaños* 506). In effect, the texts force us to accommodate ourselves to the position of woman in a particular historical and cultural moment. By "living" the body of woman, readers are expected to modify or even radically change their awareness of the cultural scripts that contain and define women narrowly and, in Zayas's eyes, perilously.

II. *Novelas Amorosas*: Violence Contained

In spite of the tranquility of the first scene of "Aventurarse perdiendo," when Fabio realizes Jacinta is a woman, he expresses dismay over her dangerous life. Quick to point out the peril of her situation, he vows to accompany Jacinta to a "más descansada y menos peligrosa vida" (*Novelas* 43) [a more restful and less perilous life (17, mod.)]. Later, Jacinta reveals that she has been working as a shepherd for four months, living peacefully in spite of the beasts and bandits mentioned by her rescuer. Although Jacinta eventually agrees to follow Fabio's suggestion and enter a convent, the diametrically opposed conceptions of female safety as communicated by the two characters subtly underscore a fundamental aspect of Zayas's representation of the gender gap. The man, who presents himself as a chivalric rescuer, perceives living in the uncivilized mountains as threatening to the woman's well-being. Yet, as Jacinta narrates her story, she shows that she has suffered not from her adventures in the wild but from the physical and psychological damage wrought by her relationships with men.[13]

Women's awareness of the dangers of sexual relationships permeates the first novella. Compared to the misfortune Jacinta encountered in her relationships with one lover who died and another who abandoned her, the threat of physical harm while working as a shepherd boy is not as marked as Fabio presumes. The juxtaposed tale of female vengeance, "La burlada Aminta," demonstrates the dangers of sexuality even more graphically. In this tale, the protagonist Aminta endures the physical and emotional violation of having sex with a man who reneges on his marriage promise to her. The high stakes of the honor code are made clear in the three murders that occur in the tale.

From the beginning of the *Novelas amorosas*, the threat of violence is cast as a primary concern for women. While Jacinta finds refuge in crossdressing and, later, in a convent, other female characters also attempt to protect, avenge, and/or save themselves from men's treachery and brutality. As can be seen in table 1, which details the violence in the *Novelas amorosas*, many of the women succeed in escaping or punishing male violence and betrayal. This success, marked by the survival and the happy endings of all of the female protagonists, reinforces the overriding theme of female empowerment in this volume. The sporadic and often devastating presence of violence throughout creates a threatening subtext of violence; yet many times violence is only hinted at or unsuccessfully attempted, and often is not carried out. While exploring women's varied responses to betrayal and violence, the *Novelas amorosas* generally figures women as independently minded, resourceful, and in control of their own subjectivity.

---

[13] With regard to Jacinta's life in the hills outside of Barcelona, Greer explains in "The (M)Other Plot" that Montserrat has been variously associated with Christian, pre-Christian, and Catalan nationalist ideals (97).

VIOLENCE DENATURALIZED 97

Table 1. Violence in the *Novelas amorosas*

Novella	Violence	Description	Outcome
Aventurarse perdiendo (#1)	1) Stabbing (dream) 2) Suicide 3) Murder	1) Jacinta dreams of man stabbing her in heart 2) Ariadna drinks poison 3) Félix stabs Jacinta's brother	1) She falls in love, is betrayed, and later enters convent 2-3) Ariadna and Jacinta's brother die
La burlada Aminta (#2)	1) Murder 2) Murder	1) Jacinto shoots female neighbor 2) Aminta stabs ex-lover and his mistress	1) Innocent man wrongly accused, jailed 2) Aminta changes name, marries; her victims die
El castigo de la miseria (#3) [original ending in brackets]	1) Abuse [2) Suicide]	1) Marcos beats his wife [2) Marcos hangs self]	1) Wife leaves him [2) Marcos buried in holy ground]
El prevenido, engañado (#4)	1) Child abandonment 2) Murder 3) Murder 4) Abuse	1) Woman abandons infant 2) Woman kills black lover 3) Woman drowns husband 4) Fadrique beats his lover	1) Fadrique rescues the child, later marries her 1-4) Fadrique flees from all of these women
La fuerza del amor (#5)	1) Abuse 2) Attempted murder	Adulterous husband beats Laura then tries to stab her	Viceroy allows Laura to enter convent
El desengaño amando (#6)	1) Suicide	Lucrecia kills herself	Cadaver is publicly burned
Al fin se paga todo (#7)	1) Intent to murder 2) Rape 3) Murder 4) Abuse 5) Murder	1) Gaspar almost stabs Hipólita's husband 2-3) Hipólita kills rapist brother-in-law 4-5) Gaspar beats her, robs jewels	1-3) King pardons Hipólita; she temporarily enters convent, then marries Gaspar later killed for stolen jewels
El imposible vencido (#8)	No violent acts		
El juez de su causa (#9)	1) Abuse 2) Attempted rape	1-2) Estela beaten then almost raped by kidnapper	1-2) Estela rescued; kidnapper and accomplice executed; Estela temporarily becomes soldier and viceroy
El jardín engañoso (#10)	1) Murder	Motivated by a lie, Jorge kills his brother	Jorge marries woman who lied; neither is punished

The *Novelas amorosas*, concerned with entertainment and exemplarity, presents the threat and possibility of violence while limiting its realization. This containment of violence makes possible the portrayals of empowered women in the first volume. In contrast, women in the *Desengaños amorosos* are so concerned with their survival and so constrained by misogyny that little room remains for deeper explorations of women's independence and empowerment. As table 1 indicates, the *Novelas amorosas* is limited to seventeen violent acts and five attempted (failed or aborted) acts of violence. Many other incidents are treated with a certain degree of levity, particularly in the satirical "El prevenido, engañado." Much of the violence relates to intent rather than action, with several unsuccessful attempts at violent crime involving characters who wish to kill but do not act on their urges. These empty threats and abandoned attempts at murder and rape reinforce the textual limitations on violence in the *Novelas amorosas*, especially since they pale in comparison to the bloodshed of the *Desengaños amorosos*. From the abandonment of an infant (who is immediately rescued) in "El prevenido, engañado" to the death of a woman who dies of heartbreak (and is resuscitated by her lover) in "El imposible vencido," some potentially heartwrenching, yet not overtly violent, incidents are treated with a relatively light touch. One clear example of this disparity between the *Novelas amorosas* and the *Desengaños amorosos* can be found in the different endings in the two volumes. With the exception of "El castigo de la miseria" (which ends with the miser's suicide in the first edition or, in later editions, with his solitude), the tales of the *Novelas amorosas* seek resolution not in violence, but in marriage (as is the case in six of the tales) and the convent. Only four novellas ("La burlada Aminta," "El prevenido," "Al fin se paga todo," and "El jardín engañoso") involve murder, and none of the female heroes dies.[14]

---

[14] The suicide ending was included only in the first edition of the *Novelas*, and does not appear subsequently; even the twentieth-century editions (e.g. Amezúa, Portal, and Redondo Goicoechea) do not include the suicide. In his edition, Olivares does include the ending in a footnote, however. In the alternative ending, Marcos simply dies from a fever developed after reading his wife's reprobatory letter. No evidence (regarding censorship, for example) has been found to explain this change in the text. As to the overall quantification of violence in the collection, it should be noted that other acts could have been included in this chart. Like the catalogue of violence in the *Desengaños*, this list includes only official executions when they are imposed in response to violent criminal behavior. I do, how-

Introduced in the first tale of the *Novelas amorosas*, violence circulates throughout the volume: Jacinta dreams of being stabbed, various characters are murdered, and four women are beaten by men. Helping establish the feminist overtones of the entire collection, the most graphic depictions of violence in these tales involve violence against women. Some passages allude to women's suffering and pain, as in the beating scene of Isidora in "El castigo de la miseria": "[él] llegó a las manos con su señora . . . no con poco dolor de su señora" (*Novelas* 154) [he beat his wife . . . she suffered no little pain (102)]. Laura's and Hipólita's beatings are related in detail, for example, and Hipólita literally offers her body as proof of the violence inflicted on her when she indicates that her lover tore off her clothes and beat her with his belt (*Novelas* 323). The delicacy with which she then unveils her wounds contrasts with the inscription of rage on her body. The attention given to processes and results of violence in Hipólita's tale echoes the scene in which a flow of blood covers Laura's white teeth in "La fuerza del amor." These are just some of many examples that elicit empathetic readings of the body in the texts.

In addition to the steady stream of violence carried out almost exclusively against women in the *Desengaños amorosos*, violence against men arises on several occasions in the *Novelas amorosas*.[15] The two most salient examples of this occur in the tales of women avengers, "La burlada Aminta" and "Al fin se paga todo." Other men are subjected to similarly violent acts, but neither the acts nor the violated bodies are described in detail. Nevertheless, the presentation of violence as a destructive force underscores a crucial element of this first volume: violence affects and threatens both sexes.

---

ever, include suicide because this is a violent, albeit self-inflicted, act. All of the suicides relate to the characters' own *desengaños amorosos* and, in this sense, reinforce the connection between desire and death in the collection. For the record, the death penalty is imposed in the *Novelas amorosas* (cf. "El imposible vencido" and "El juez de su causa") and in the *Desengaños* (cf. "La inocencia castigada" and "El traidor contra su sangre").

[15] Although some men fall victim to violence in the *Desengaños*, none of these is a main character. Notably, this violence receives comparatively little narrative attention. With the exception of the murdered rapist in "La esclava de su amante," Pedro's nearly-murdered best friend in "El verdugo de su esposa," the murdered homicidal in-laws in "Mal presagio casar lejos," and the suicide "victim" Dionís in "Estragos que causa el vicio," other male victims (servants, pages, and rival lovers) figure only marginally in the tales.

The threat posed to men and women figures the human body to be endangered in amorous interactions.

While disparate in their content and themes, many of the tales comprising the *Novelas amorosas* portray the different ways women threaten the social order and, more specifically, how women's sexuality and intelligence–their bodies *and* minds–threaten individual men. While far from being three-dimensional characters (this is more of an episodic than a psychologically profound genre, after all), men often perceive women as a threat in this volume. In a certain sense, some of the women do threaten men's monopoly on power: the avengers (Aminta and Hipólita) transgress the borders of prescribed feminine behavior, and "El juez de su causa" portrays a woman who lives as a male soldier and viceroy before reclaiming her female identity.

The two satirical tales of the *Novelas amorosas* provide a good framework for examining the strategies used by Zayas to expose the cultural figuration of woman as a threat. Narrated by male characters, "El castigo de la miseria" and "El prevenido, engañado" follow two male protagonists through their sexual and amorous adventures. Closely related to Cervantes's novella, "El casamiento engañoso" ("The Deceitful Marriage"), "El castigo de la miseria" describes the life of the miserly hero Marcos, who marries a woman strictly for her money, only to find out later that things are not as they had appeared. On the first morning of the marriage, Marcos discovers that Isidora is not the woman he had thought her to be:

> no halló sino una fantasma, o imagen de la muerte, porque la buena señora mostró las arrugas de la cara por entero, las que les encubría con el afeite, que tal vez suele ser encubridor de años, que a la cuenta estaban más cerca de cincuenta y cinco que de treinta y seis, como había puesto en la carta de dote [. . .]. (*Novelas* 151)
>
> [. . . what he saw was a phantom, a deathly ghost. The good woman's face showed each and every wrinkle she had so carefully covered with makeup, which usually can disguise one's age, which, in her case, was closer to fifty-five than the thirty-six she'd declared on her dowry agreement. (100, mod.)]

The woman's aged body–perceived by Marcos as ghostly and deathlike–shocks the protagonist. Little does he know that this corporeal degradation signals larger trouble ahead.

The miserly man, who had hoped to make a good marriage by presenting himself as wealthy, has had the tables turned on him by a woman who beat him at his own game. But if Cervantes's hero admits that he set out to trick someone else and was deceived (*Novelas ejemplares* II, 292), Zayas's protagonist less readily accepts his fate. Trying to avenge himself, Marcos allows another woman to dupe him before the tale ends: the servant Marcela concocts a ruse to take him to a false sorcerer, promising to fix his problems and, in the meantime, taking a percentage of the fee. Repeatedly caught in the spokes of the fortune-hunting wheel, Marcos falls victim to his own shortcomings in his dealings with clever women.

A doubly masculine perspective frames the next tale, in which the frame character Alonso narrates a man's sexual adventures. "El prevenido, engañado," which centers on women's duplicitous and confounding behavior, relies on sexuality as the overarching rubric. Introducing his tale, Alonso says he will tell everyone about Fadrique's search for a marriageable woman

> . . . para que ninguno se confíe en su entendimiento, ni se atreva a probar a las mujeres, sino que teman lo que les puede suceder; estimando y poniendo en su lugar a cada una; pues, al fin, una mujer discreta no es manjar de un necio, ni una necia empleo de un discreto [. . .]. (*Novelas* 166)
>
> [A man shouldn't rely solely on his own judgment, let alone dare to test a woman. He should watch out for himself and esteem each woman and accept her as she is. In the final analysis, an intelligent woman is no match for a foolish man, nor is a foolish woman right for an intelligent man [. . .]. (114, mod.)]

Alonso's introductory remarks suggest that men cannot be trusted to understand women's elusive nature. Alonso's connection between men's fear and the multiplicity of possible female identities prepares readers for the variety of feminine characterizations found in the novella itself.

Much to the protagonist Fadrique's dismay, all of the women he encounters embrace sexuality as a key aspect of their individuality. Their sexual activities and astute minds repeatedly confound and deter him. Threatened by their intelligence and sexual agency, Fadrique collapses the women into one category: ". . . temo a las mujeres que son tan sabias más que a la muerte . . . (y) me tienen tan escarmentado las discretas, que deseo tener batalla con una boba" (*Novelas* 191-92) [I fear women who know so much, more than I fear death itself. I'd like to find a woman who's as ignorant of the ways of the world as this one is wise in them (133)]. Ultimately, he changes his mind and comes to prefer educated, discreet women.

As in "El castigo de la miseria," the joke in this tale is always on the male protagonist. In his search for the perfect wife, Fadrique's encounters with various independent women lead him to the wrongheaded conclusion that uneducated women are those most inclined to protect men's honor and to maintain their own "purity." In this strange, episodic story, Fadrique spends sixteen years in relationships with women who constantly surprise him with their behavior in all sexual matters. Fadrique has one lover who leaves her newborn baby for dead; another who kills her black lover with her sexual appetite; another who poses as a man and makes sexual advances in bed toward Fadrique; one who kills her husband for Fadrique's sake; and yet another who locks Fadrique in a trunk when her husband unexpectedly returns home.

Even when he settles down and marries, Fadrique's troubles do not end. Having recovered his first lover's abandoned baby and placed the child in a convent, Fadrique later marries the grown girl and instructs her to keep vigil over their bed. In giving his wife a lance, Fadrique masculinizes her, essentially outfitting her with a phallus with which to protect the sexual integrity of the marriage. Dressed nightly in armor, the naive (and eventually exhausted) Gracia stays awake, watching over her sleeping husband as if she were his guard. Finally, her luck improves when Fadrique is out of town and a new man, who realizes her naivete, poses as her "other" husband. After learning a more enjoyable way to spend her nights (having sex, obviously), Gracia resists reverting to the old ways when Fadrique returns. When he learns of this transformation, Fadrique finally admits to the impossibility of controlling women. Repeatedly turned off by previous lovers' clever manipulations, he had grown increasingly attached to the notion that the perfect wife is a stupid, uneducated woman. In the end, he realizes his mistake:

> Y todo el tiempo que vivió, alababa las discretas que son virtuosas, porque no hay comparación, ni estimación para ellas; y si no lo son, hacen sus cosas con recato y prudencia. (*Novelas* 216)

[For the rest of his life, don Fadrique praised discreet women who are virtuous, saying that they are priceless and beyond comparison; and, if they're not virtuous, at least they know how to behave prudently and modestly. (152, mod.)]

Before coming to terms with this logic, however, Fadrique confronts women who operate as subjects and refuse to be contained by his desire for them. As Brownlee has noted about this tale, "What is important extradiegetically is Zayas's ability to represent the diversity of female subjectivity" ("Elusive" 168). In "El prevenido," this diversity revolves around women's sexuality; each of the female characters encountered by Fadrique articulates her desire in ways that he finds shocking.

At one point, for example, Fadrique loses his temper with a lover when he finds her in bed with another man. Here we find an example of Zayas's portrayal of the threat that women's intelligence and sexuality pose to men. Fadrique freezes when the naked young lover takes a shoe in his hand as if it were a gun. As the man backs out of the room, he threatens to kill Fadrique with his "pistol." Violante then laughs uncontrollably, and the twice insulted hero reacts with violence:

> Desto más ofendido el granadino que de lo demás, no pudo la pasión dexar de darle atrevimiento, y llegándose a Violante la dió de bofetadas, que la bañó en sangre, y ella perdida de enojo le dixo que se fuese con Dios, que llamaría a su cuñado, y le haría que le costase caro. (*Novelas* 203)

[The gentleman from Granada felt more humiliated by her laughter than by anything else, he could not contain his passion. He rushed over to doña Violante and struck her in the face, bathing it in blood. Furious, she told him to get out, she would call her brother-in-law, she would make don Fadrique pay dearly. (143, mod.)]

Rather than stop beating Violante when she threatens to call for help, Fadrique continues to take out his aggression–plausibly his pent up hostility toward women in general–on her: "El, que no reparaba en amenazas prosiguió, en su determinada cólera, asiéndola de los cabellos y trayéndola a mal traer, tanto, que la obligó a dar gritos" (*Novelas* 203) [Heedless of her threats, his rage increased. He grabbed her by the hair and beat her until she was forced to scream (143)]. Finally, Fadrique recognizes that he could be punished for his behavior, so he flees before the authorities arrive.

Later depictions of violence against women in the *Novelas amorosas* (in "La fuerza del amor" and "Al fin se paga todo," for example) similarly portray masculine violence as motivated by retaliation and containment. These later tales continue to emphasize the connection between sexuality and violence. While the scene with Violante begins with a comical, phallic premise–a naked lover protecting himself with a substitute sword–the retaliatory violence keeps the humor in check. Fadrique unsuccessfully tries to keep women's sexuality in check as well. This violent episode is followed by a series of brief descriptions of odd affairs, including one in which his lover throws her husband in the river so she can be with Fadrique.[16] In spite of its presence in the *Novelas amorosas*, violence still does not provide fodder for extensive moralism as it does in the *Desengaños*.

Isidora's deception of the miser and Violante's sexual liberation speak to the thread of female empowerment that runs through the *Novelas amorosas*. As seen in Jacinta's independence, in Laura's plea to the "vain legislators of the world," and in the tales of violent women avengers, female characters influence men and determine the paths of their own lives in the first volume. Other female protagonists in the *Novelas amorosas* also enjoy independence and power. Abandoned by her father and husband, Clara, in "El desengaño amando," takes great risks to free her lover from a spell cast by another woman, for example. And while the two novellas involving miracles, "El imposible vencido" and "El jardín engañoso," comply with the conventions of medieval miracle tales, both of the female heroes achieve their goals in the end.

---

[16] Brownlee's discussion of Zayas's literary technique in this tale highlights the murder of the unnamed husband. Focusing on the humorous aspect of the young lover holding a shoe up as a weapon, Brownlee contrasts the episode of Violante's infidelity with the homicide that comes later: "This jarring contrast of levity followed by such grotesque behavior . . . is clearly meant to arouse the reader's *admiratio*, to keep the reader on the edge of his or her seat" ("Elusive" 170).

As the only violence-free tale of the entire collection, "El imposible vencido" tells the story of Leonor, a woman who suffers so much from love sickness that she dies, only to be revived by her lover. Constanza, the protagonist of "El jardín engañoso," maintains her integrity when she is released from her obligation to have sex with a bothersome suitor. The road to a happy ending for both women is rocky: Leonor has to overcome death and Constanza has to get out of a deal she unwittingly made with the devil. Moreover, both face social pressure regarding marriage. Leonor's father tricks her into marrying a man she does not love, and Constanza marries a man because he manipulates her into thinking he is lovesick. With their link to miracle tales, these novellas rank among the most conventional of the collection. The female characters, who might be read as responding to male desire rather than acting of their own accord, add a further dimension to the representations of women in the *Novelas amorosas*.

In contrast to these women, most of the other female protagonists in the *Novelas amorosas* outmaneuver, outwit, or overpower men. These characterizations expand the options open to women. This liberal portrayal of female subjectivity coincides with the desire to impress and *maravillar* the audience: what better way to "enchant" the reader than by upsetting expectations about gender relations and sexuality? The limited role of violence in this volume also fits the stated goal of the soiree: the novellas concern themselves more with entertainment than persuasion, and the containment of violence helps maintain a certain levity. Although it is present in most of the novellas, violence simply receives less narrative space, less attention, than in the *Desengaños amorosos*. The containment of violence–particularly the minimal focus on violence against women– makes possible the complex exploration of female subjectivity in the *Novelas amorosas*. Inasmuch as women live merely with the threat, but not the constant realization, of male brutality, there is still room for female subjects to maneuver. Subverting prescribed gender roles for women, depicting women as sexually and intellectually autonomous subjects, Zayas reveals a multiplicity of interesting and often positive female subjectivities that are possible when violence is contained.

III. Systemic Violence in the *Desengaños amorosos*

The empowered role of women in the *Novelas amorosas* differs significantly from the emphasis on victimization in the subsequent volume. Speaking of the collection on the whole, Elizabeth Ordóñez correctly indicates that Zayas "inscribes power into the plots of women, making women agents and subjects, even if only temporarily or surreptitiously" (6). While the *Novelas amorosas* explores women's agency, the *Desengaños amorosos* highlights the impermanence and even the impossibility of women's safety. The gap between male and female experience is, in some respects, always already present in this collection. Similar to the beginning of the *Novelas amorosas*, the theme of the endangered female body appears in the introduction to the *Desengaños amorosos*. Lisis's illness has mysterious origins linked with love, and she lies on her deathbed for nearly a year before regaining her strength. No longer able to put off her marriage to Diego, Lisis agrees (out of obedience to her mother) to move ahead with the union and, in honor of the upcoming occasion, convenes the soiree, with the wedding planned for the third night of the celebration.

In spite of the apparent compliance with a standard patriarchal narrative, Lisis sets strict storytelling guidelines that rebel against masculine hegemony. Reinforcing this rebellious impulse, the tales in the *Desengaños amorosos* purportedly are grounded in reality and doused with didactic rhetoric. B. W. Ife explains the standard baroque trope of connecting fiction with reality in *Reading and Fiction in Golden Age Spain*:

> Spanish Golden Age writers and intellectuals held the view that in an important, powerful, and inexplicable way a well-wrought fiction commands attention and demands acceptance of what it says; in short, it makes us believe in it. (49)

With this intent made explicit through the insistence that the tales, now called *desengaños* rather than *maravillas*, relate "true" stories of masculine deception, Zayas effectively politicizes the texts by forging a fictionalized link with reality.[17] The volume then plunges

---

[17] Among others, Foa has highlighted Zayas's insistence on the veracity of the

the reader into various violent incidents that, when considered together, function to protest patriarchal gender relations.

Through this indictment of a cultural system in which men are not held accountable for their behavior and are free to enact violence as they please, the question of personal politics is posed implicitly to frame characters and readers alike. The texts seem to ask us what we will do to stop the violence. As the principal narrator of the *Desengaños amorosos* indicates, the tales are meant "desengañar a las damas de los engaños en que viven" and "tratar con rigor las costumbres de los hombres" (258) [to disenchant the ladies about the deception in which they live (and) to deal harshly with men's customs (167)]. With these intentions, the volume purposefully excludes men from the narrative act and, in essence, effects a certain liberation for women's voices. Complying with the mandate to tell true tales of masculine deception, the female narrators release in graphic detail the terror of violence that, more often than not, results in the death of the female protagonist. Within this didactic framework, each tale describes at least two acts of violence, with some incorporating a half dozen or even a dozen deaths. Violence here focuses even more sharply on victimization of women, many of whose violated and decaying bodies are described in graphic detail. Just as Isabel lives with the devastating effects of sexual assault, violence determines other women's fate.

From Lisis's discourse of illness to the final massacre in "Estragos que causa el vicio," Zayas pushes the boundaries of violence in these tales of women's *desengaño*. The different manifestations of violence against women portrayed throughout the novellas share certain characteristics. The perpetrators, whose relationships to the victims vary, either seek to destroy the objects of their desire–wives, lovers, and others–or to avenge themselves of women perceived as offending men's honor. The motivations behind the violent acts of

---

tales, indicating that it confirms Zayas's moralist intent (*Feminismo* 103). Foa, however, views this moralizing impulse as glorifying women at the expense of men (*Feminismo* 132). A more comprehensive view of Zayas's uses of exemplarity explores her denunciation of systemic cultural problems. For an excellent cluster of articles on exemplarity in the Renaissance, see Rigolot ("The Renaissance Crisis of Exemplarity"), Jeannert ("The Vagaries of Exemplarity"), Stierle ("Three Moments in the Crisis"), Hampton ("Examples, Stories, and Subjects"), and Cornilliat's response ("Exemplarities") in *The Journal of the History of Ideas* (October 1998).

these texts overlap with Liz Kelly and Jill Radford's description of male sexual violence in "The Problem of Men":

> [Sexual violence is] one of the defining characteristics of a patriarchal society. It is used by men, and often condoned by the state, for a number of specific purposes: to punish women who are seen to be resisting male control; to police women, make them behave or not behave in particular ways; to claim rights of sexual, emotional and domestic servicing; and through all these maintain the relations of patriarchy, male domination and female subordination. (238-39) [18]

All of these motivations for sexual violence appear in the *Desengaños amorosos*. As shown in table 2, which details the violence in the *Desengaños*, the flow of spilled blood in these novellas identifies men as the victors in the power struggle between the sexes. Gone are the pastoral settings and the unquestionably empowered female characters of the *Novelas amorosas*. The balance of power definitively tips toward the masculine in the *Desengaños amorosos* as women are confined, maimed, and killed at every turn.

Table 2. Violence in the *Desengaños amorosos*

Novella	Violent Act	Description	Outcome
La esclava de su amante (#1)	1) Abuse	1) Isabel's servant beaten by another woman	—
	2) Rape	2) Isabel raped when unconscious	2) Disguised as slave, Isabel follows rapist
	3) Murder	3) Her new suitor kills rapist	3) She decides to enter convent
La más infame venganza (#2)	1) Murder	1) Juan kills man	1) Juan flees, his sister enters convent
	2) Rape	2) Juan rapes Camila	2-3) Camila placed in convent; dies at home six months after poisoning
	3) Murder	3) Camila poisoned by husband	

---

[18] Kelly and Radford rely here on J. Hanmer's discussion of male sexual violence in "Male Violence and the Social Control of Women," published in Littlejohn et al.'s *Power and the State*.

Table 2. (Continued)

Novella	Violent Act	Description	Outcome
El verdugo de su esposa (#3)	1) Attempted murder 2) Murder	1) Wronged husband tries to kill friend 2) Innocent wife bled to death by husband	1) Friend saved by divine intervention 2) Husband and lover move in together
Tarde llega el desengaño (#4)	1) Attempted murder 2) Murder/Torture 3) Murder	1) Jaime stabbed 22 times 2) He burns his wife's cousin to death; terrorizes wife 3) He stabs slave	1) Jaime flees 2) Wife dies 3) Slave dies, Jaime goes insane
La inocencia castigada (#5)	1) Rape 2) Torture/ Attempted murder	1) In trance, Inés raped nightly by Diego for 1 month 2) Husband, brother, and sister-in-law trap her behind wall	1) Inés exonerated; Diego punished 2) Inés rescued by female neighbor; relatives executed; Inés to convent
Amar sólo por vencer (#6)	1) Abuse 2) Murder	1) Aunt beats Laurela 2) Assisted by aunt, Laurela's father and uncle push wall over onto her and handmaid	Laurela and handmaid die; Laurela's sisters enter convent out of fear; mother to convent upon father's death
Mal presagio casar lejos (#7)	1) Murder 2) Murder 3) Abuse 4) Murder 5) Murder 6) Murder	1) Mayor and her page stabbed to death by her husband; sister María escapes 2) Leonor and son killed by her husband 3) Blanca beaten by husband 4) Marieta murdered by her husband and father 5) Blanca's father-in-law and husband have her bled to death 6) Blanca's brother kills in-laws	All die immediately except María, who eventually dies from injuries sustained when jumping out window Blanca buried in Spain; Duque de Alba scourges the Low Countries

Table 2. (Continued)

Novella	Violent Act	Description	Outcome
El traidor contra su sangre (#8)	1) Murder 2) Attempted murder 3) Murder	1) Alonso stabs sister 2) Alonso and friend stab sister's suspected lover 22 times 3) Alonso decapitates new wife with assistance of friend	1) Sister dies 2) Alonso's father incarcerated then set free; helps son flee 3) Alonso and friend executed
La perseguida triunfante (#9)	1) Torture 2) Attempted rape and murder 3) Murder	1) Beatriz's eyes gouged on husband's orders 2) Beatriz almost raped and killed by brother-in-law 3) Beatriz blamed for Prince's death	1) Beatriz's sight restored by Virgin Mary 2) Brother-in-law mauled by lion 3) Prince resuscitated; Beatriz pardoned
Estragos que causa el vicio (#10)	1) Assault and murder	Dionís kills 11, beats and stabs Florentina, commits suicide	King pardons Florentina; she enters convent

In contrast to the conventional "happy ending" marriages in the *Novelas amorosas*, the *Desengaños amorosos* communicates an emphatically anti-marriage message in both the frame tale and the novellas proper. In fact, matrimony here is shown as utterly dangerous for women, and resolution is found in either femicide (in six novellas) or in the convent (in the remaining four). No surviving female character chooses marriage. Instead, convent life offers the sole alternative for women: in this safe, feminine space, women find protection from the violence that permeates the stories of courtship and marriage in the second volume. The violence of the ten *desengaños* presents the violated female body as testimony to the injustices of the patriarchy. Frustrated in their attempts at self-protection, speech, and even survival, the female characters are, on the whole, denied the empowerment achieved by their counterparts in the *Novelas amorosas*. On this topic, Jordan indicates that, in spite of similarities between male- and female-authored feminist texts in the early modern period,

> Treatises signed by women differ only (although not consistently) in showing no enthusiasm for marriage; their criticisms of the

married state are frequently expressed in utopian visions of a purely female society. (19)

Abandoning the more celebratory view of marriage seen in the *Novelas amorosas*, Zayas portrays male-female relationships as oppressive, unjust, and dangerous to women's physical safety in the *Desengaños*.

Predictably, men's paranoia regarding female sexuality motivates femicide in the *Desengaños*. Camila, Roseleta, Ana, Blanca, Magdalena, and three other wives die at the hands of their husbands, while the unwed Laurela and Mencía fall victim to their father and brother, respectively. Enraged by women's sexual impurity, men also torture their female relatives in "Tarde llega el desengaño" and "La inocencia castigada." Some women facilitate these actions by either falsely presenting other women as adulterers (e.g. "Tarde llega el desengaño" and "Estragos que causa el vicio") or by actively offering up others for victimization (e.g. "La inocencia castigada" and "Amar sólo por vencer"). This complicity on the part of a minority of female characters complicates what otherwise might be seen as overly simplified depictions of women's innocence in the face of men's sadism. In contrast to the sword-wielding Aminta in the *Novelas amorosas*, none of the female characters in the *Desengaños* actually kills another woman, but their acts of betrayal do not go unremarked, either. Almost all of the women who set up their sisters for victimization are killed and, with the exception of Florentina, all are judged harshly by the female narrators.[19]

The acts of betrayal and violence in the *Desengaños amorosos* respond to a generalized devaluation of women, to cultural codes that objectify women and justify violence in cases of "suspect" sexuality. The fearful attitude toward women's sexuality coincides with

---

[19] The sister-in-law in "La inocencia castigada" assists with walling Inés into her torture chamber. Along with the father and brother, the sister-in-law is executed. The nameless black slave in "Tarde llega el desengaño" falsely accuses Jaime's wife of adultery. When she admits her wrongdoing two years later, Jaime stabs her to death. The aunt in "Amar sólo por vencer" beats Laurela and, later, leads Laurela and her handmaid to their death. Unlike other female characters who betray women in the *Desengaños*, the aunt receives no punishment. Finally, the maid in "Estragos que causa el vicio" devises the plan that sets the massacre into motion; she dies during the flurry of violence. While clear to the reader, Florentina's complicity in this plan goes unremarked by the narrators; yet she is subjected to Dionís's violence and barely escapes with her life.

Margo Wilson and Martin Daly's assessment of male sexual proprietariness as a primary motive for wife murder:

> In every society for which we have been able to find a sample of spousal homicides, the story is basically the same: most cases arise out of the husband's jealous, proprietary, violent response to his wife's (real or imagined) infidelity or desertion. (90)

The sociologists then conclude that "the motives in wife-killing exhibit a dreary consistency across cultures and across centuries" (96). Zayas's texts also "exhibit a dreary consistency" in that the motives for femicide ultimately relate to proprietary attitudes toward women.

The massacre in the final tale, "Estragos que causa el vicio," epitomizes this critique of a culture that allows men sexual freedom while sanctioning the murder of women merely suspected of sexual improprieties. This last tale serves as a guide to masculine logic and exposes the ideologies that give men rights over women's bodies and minds. Regardless of women's varying degrees of innocence and guilt, male protectors consciously decide to end the women's lives for different, yet ultimately proprietary, reasons.

A closer look at the dynamics of violence as they relate to male proprietariness exposes a logic that threatens to do away with women entirely. If it weren't for the option of the convent, the female characters would have no place in which to seek refuge from violence. Interestingly, the violence against women proliferated in the *Desengaños* incorporates many of the characteristics of violent relationships laid out by Lenore Walker in *The Battered Woman*: initial surprise, unpredictability of battering incidents, overwhelming jealousy, unusual male sexuality, concealment, extreme psychological abuse, family threats, extraordinary terror, perceived omnipotence of the batterer, and the victim's awareness of death potential (73-75). In explaining the cycle of violence in battering relationships, Walker has identified a three-phase abuse cycle. The "tension building phase," constituted by minor incidents of battering and general psychological abuse, is followed by the "acute battering phase," in which a violent discharge of the residual tensions occurs." Finally, the third phase, that of "kindness and contrite behavior," involves a kind attitude on the part of the batterer as he attempts to gain back the favor of the abused woman (55-70).[20] Zayas's portrayal of these dynamics of violence against women underscores for us, as readers in the twenty-first century, the behavioral patterns associated with violence against women and the consistency of such violence over time.

With their proprietary motivations for femicide, the seventh and eighth *desengaños* exemplify many characteristics of violence as identified by Walker.[21] As powerful critiques of patriarchy, "Mal presagio casar lejos" and "El traidor contra su sangre" attack the supremacy of male authority in domestic, social, and political affairs. Both tales exploit the absolute power of the father figure. This insistence on the father's power criticizes the very basis of a social structure that perpetuates male rule by relegating women to the underclass. The sons in these two novellas blindly follow their fathers' orders, attempting to please their fathers at the expense of women's lives. The father's law stands strong here, as do misogynist and proprietary attitudes. These factors work in tandem to violently erase the feminine, and the texts exemplify the dangers of unchecked paternal law. These juxtaposed tales issue a wake-up call for readers to take heed of Zayas's proposed reforms.

Coinciding with Walker's three-phase cycle of violence, "Mal presagio" intertwines a misogynist subtext with the politics of Philip II's reign. The murders of Blanca and her sisters by foreign royalty distance the reader from the atrocities by locating the violence in other countries, attributing the brutality to political tensions elsewhere in the Spanish empire. Yet the perverse creativity and precise execution of the murders transcend the political framework, particularly since the murder of a Flemish woman by her father leaves no doubt as to the misogyny behind the violence. The Portuguese husband goes to great lengths to fake a love letter in his wife's handwriting in order to "justifiably" stab her to death. The Italian husband actually uses his wife's body against her, strangling her with her own hair, ostensibly because she praised a Spanish man. Both of these uxoricides are framed in terms of falsified sex-

---

[20] Overviews of violence against women can be found in Caputi and Russell's "Femicide: Sexist Terrorism against Women"; Breines and Gordon's "The New Scholarship"; Dobash and Dobash's *Violence against Wives*; and Wilson and Daly's "Till Death Do Us Part."

[21] Dobash and Dobash's *Violence against Wives* offers similar theories on the issue of wife abuse and murder.

ual impropriety, with the husbands using this legally sanctioned justification to kill their wives. In straightforward scenarios of misogynist acts, these wife murders expose the problem of giving men power over women's bodies.

Furthermore, the protagonist's own marriage is framed in terms of paternal control. Agreeing to marry "(p)or conveniencias a la real corona y gusto de su hermano" (*Desengaños* 339) [at the pleasure of the king and to please her brother (245)], the orphaned Blanca demands that her Flemish suitor court her in Spain. The Flemish prince agrees and departs for Spain, even though this trip displeases his father immensely (*Desengaños* 340). Cast in terms of duty to empire and patriarchy, this matrimony is conceded to under the umbrage of paternal power. With the father-in-law's ire directed toward her, Blanca receives an anti-Spanish tongue-lashing upon her arrival in Flanders, and here begins the psychological abuse and tension building that characterize the first phase of the cycle of violence. In spite of her initial uneasiness with her new husband, Blanca is surprised by the harsh treatment she receives.

The acute battering of the second phase of violence occurs when the prince and his father interrupt Blanca's lament. An argument ensues, and the prince beats her. In spite of the painful memory of the beating that surges every time she sees him, Blanca, like many modern-day abused women, still "amaba ternísimamente a su esposo" (*Desengaños* 356) [loved her husband deeply (261)]. Soon Blanca's brother- and father-in-law garrote her sister-in-law Marieta to death, whereupon Blanca's husband enters the phase of kindness. When Blanca asks him about his father's malevolence, the prince distances himself, claiming that Marieta's murder must have been justified.

Terrorized and helpless, Blanca foresees her own death and makes the proper arrangements. This practical behavior indicates that she perceives the danger of living in a house where the father's wish is the sons' command. Meanwhile, she discovers her husband having sex with his (male) page, an act that is represented here as aberrant and evil, and therefore easily falls under Walker's category of "unusual sexuality."[22] The cycle of battery begins again; this

---

[22] Perry discusses the harsh policies against male homosexuality in "The 'Nefarious Sin' in Early Modern Seville." Also see Haliczer (*Inquisition and Society*, esp. 302-05), Herrera Puga, and Monter (*Frontiers*, 276-99).

time, however, she will not survive. Tensions build when Blanca orders the servants to burn the bed. Later, she is bled to death under the watchful eye of the father-in-law, with her husband pleading for her salvation only when the blood flows from her veins. Ultimately the father has the last word, sending his son out of the room and triumphantly crying, "Así tuviera a todas las de su nación como tengo a ésta" (*Desengaños* 363) [I only wish I had all Spanish women in the same position I have her in (268)]. So ends the life of this protagonist, whose marriage and victimization are motivated by the desire to please the paternal. Masked in political tensions, the violence of this novella transcends national concerns and demonstrates a deep-rooted misogyny that knows no borders.

The juxtaposed eighth novella, "El traidor contra su sangre," builds on the father-pleasing femicide of "Mal presagio casar lejos." This plot turns on a son's quest to please his father at the cost of two women's lives. Here, the female perspective diminishes and our contemporary understanding of the phases and characteristics of abusive relationships no longer plays a significant role. Instead, the novella rests on the misogyny of a father and his son, who leave two women's cadavers as evidence of men's proprietary attitudes. Perceiving his daughter as a financial liability akin to a bad investment, Pedro wants her to lead a religious life, potentially enabling him to leave his entire fortune to his only son, Alonso.[23] In defiance of her father's wishes, Mencía entertains the advances of her suitor, Enrique. This backfires, however, as it results in her death and in the attempted murder of her lover. Importantly, the father consents to and assists with the act of vengeance against Mencía. Society's complicity in the murder of women is implied in an encounter that Alonso has with a priest, whom he tells about the murder and forces to take his sister's confession. Such is the priest's fear about the upcoming violence that he merely hears Mencía's confession and leaves, not daring to tell anyone until the murder is made public.

---

[23] Pedro's relationship with his daughter is based on material concerns: he wants to invest in his son's future and not his daughter's. This treatment of family relations is in line with M. King's description of a daughter in early modern Western society as a liability: "From the instant of her birth, the prospect of a dowry loomed large over the female: she represented potential loss rather than potential gain" (26).

Proceeding to Naples with his father's financial backing, Alonso defies his father's wishes by marrying a woman of modest station. Eventually disowned for his actions, he blames his resultant poverty on his wife and turns against her when his father expresses displeasure over the match. In an effort to regain favor, Alonso enlists a male friend to assist him in decapitating his wife, an action accomplished in a dinner table scene similar to the murder of Marieta in the previous tale. The men are executed for their crimes, but this news fills Pedro with pride: "Más quiero tener un hijo degollado que mal casado" (*Desengaños* 398) [Better a son beheaded than one ill wedded (300)]. With these words, the father–now made grotesque with misogyny–yet again condones femicide, applauding his son's efforts to please him and privileging masculinity over women's lives.

As in the rest of the *Desengaños amorosos*, Zayas exploits the dangers that male authority poses for women in these two novellas. The paternally imposed mindset serves as a metaphor for the patriarchy and its abuses of women, abuses depicted in the other eight novellas of the *Desengaños amorosos* and in several stories in the *Novelas amorosas*. These male characters, who kill to please their fathers, exhibit dehumanized, proprietary attitudes toward their female relatives and freely attack the female body whenever the rule of the father is violated or threatened. "Mal presagio casar lejos," which involves psychological and physical abuse as well as many other characteristics of wife abuse, demonstrates the startling parallels between Walker's observations about violent relationships and Zayas's representations of this phenomenon. The portrayal of the fathers as causing and condoning their sons' abusive behavior also coincides with contemporary theories on the intergenerational effects of violent behavior. As Bonnie Yegidis has stated, many researchers now perceive modeling or imitative behavior as the number one factor contributing to family violence (26). The sons in these novellas obediently carry out violent acts, using violence against women as a strategy for maintaining patriarchal order and for pleasing their fathers.

Most of the violence against women in the *Novelas amorosas* and the *Desengaños amorosos* is motivated either by men's struggle to contain women's perceived sexual impurity or to punish women for challenging male authority. Yet, given the different circumstances of each novella–women's varying degrees of guilt in their perceived transgressions and the hatred expressed in some of the tales–it becomes clear that the violence is not situational, but systemic. Through these stories of violence and victimization, the frame characters explicitly turn the personal into the political. The inscription of social ills onto the female body registers a protest against the treatment of women in society.[24] Through representations of violence and victimization, Zayas's texts expose the oppression and abuse of women as phenomena related to the cultural investment in preserving masculine authority and rule.

IV. READING THE BODY

Zayas presents the violated female body as a literal and figurative embodiment of the power imbalance between the sexes. The repetition of violent acts in these texts portrays a dysfunctional social body dependent on violence to maintain the phallocratic social order.[25] The hyper-masculinized discourse of the two tales analyzed above speaks to the ways in which corporeal discourse provides a key to understanding Zayas's critique. "Mal presagio" and "El traidor" rely on detailed, repeated violence against women as a plot device that marks out the tenets of a misogynist cult of masculinity: long-suffering female characters are described variously as beautiful, virtuous, and innocent as they lie bleeding, dying, and even dead. With this feminization of victimization in the *Desengaños amorosos*, women no longer enjoy the freedom of action or movement seen in the *Novelas amorosas*. The conflation of the aesthetic with the moral brings us back to a consideration of Bronfen's theory of spectatorship vis-à-vis the violated body.

To articulate the tensions between the moral and the aesthetic in readings of Zayas, I would like to return for a moment to the last

---

[24] The sympathetic nature of Zayas's depictions of violence against women is consonant with the observation, made by Radford and Russell in *Femicide: The Politics of Woman Killing*, that "(t)he very act of speaking out against femicide is itself an act of resistance" (303).

[25] Levine's analysis of Shakespeare's *A Midsummer Night's Dream* captures the potential for social criticism that can be found in similarly graphic representations of violence. Levine indicates that the repetition of sexual violence by Theseus "suggests that sexual violence is somehow larger and more comprehensive than Theseus himself, that it is built into, virtually the given of, life in Athens, the *polis*, itself" ("Rape, Repetition" 211).

aestheticized body of the collection. In the description of Magdalena's death in "Estragos que causa el vicio," the husband's excessive violence is contrasted with the saintly purity of the murdered wife. The female narrator quotes the husband's cry for revenge, but then redresses the man's mistaken ideas about his wife's affair. Florentina corrects the male misperception when she describes Magdalena as having the most beautiful and chaste body in the history of Portugal. When the innocent woman dies from repeated blows from her husband's dagger, the narrator makes the connection between masculine aggression (the man's blind rage) and the unjust act (*Desengaños* 496). Told by a female narrator implicated in the crime–for Florentina agreed to the maid's plan to incite this murder in the first place–the narrative provides a vivid description of the violent masculine excess that results from the fear of female sexual impropriety.

The narrative actually frames our reading for us in that it focuses not on Florentina's role in her sister's predicament, but, rather, on the ways the excesses of masculinity lead Dionís to mark an innocent woman's body with his wrath. The repetition, sexual anxiety, and aestheticization of this scene encapsulate crucial aspects of Zayas's representations of male violence. The narration of Magdalena's death leads us to read Dionís as overly protective, hypocritical, and, finally, irrationally aggressive in his reaction to Magdalena's perceived adultery. Through the detailed, repetitive account of one man's rage, the tale deconstructs the cultural codes of sexuality and power distribution. Again, the dysfunction of cultural codes informing masculinity and sexuality is written onto the woman, whose violated body elicits sympathy and challenges cultural practices.

The aestheticization of the body in Zayas's novellas works in tandem with the didactic aspect of the texts to deconstruct the projection of male sexual anxiety onto women. Predictably, given this critical stance toward the figuration of woman as receptacle for men's anxieties, the texts repeatedly linger on the violent act and its consequences to help elicit the desired moral response. The violence against Blanca in "Mal presagio casar lejos" exemplifies this narrative treatment. The first time Blanca's husband beats her, it is because he has become exasperated with her complaints (*Desengaños* 356). This description, like the tale itself, emphasizes the motivations for violence (i.e., the containment of women) and the brutality of the act. Violence against women escalates in the tale, as seen in the subsequent murder of the sister-in-law Marieta:

> Y fue que, a lo que después se vio, tenían atado al espaldar de una silla un palo, y haciéndola sentar en ella, su *propio marido*, delante de su padre, la dio garrote; que esta tan *cruel sentencia* contra la *hermosa y desgraciada señora* salió de acuerdo de los dos, suegro y yerno. (*Desengaños* 356-57, emphasis added)

> [What must have happened, from what people could tell later, was that they'd tied a stake to the back of a chair, then they made Lady Marieta sit down and *her own husband*, in the presence of her father, garroted her. This *cruel sentence* against the *beautiful and unfortunate lady* came from some agreement between the two men, son-in-law and father-in-law [. . .]. (261, mod.)]

As in the previous description, the narration uses various adjectives and turns of phrase to elicit sympathy for the female perspective. The female narrator highlights the aspects of betrayal (i.e., the woman's husband kills her with the approval of her father) and of male control (i.e., the men agree to sacrifice the unsuspecting woman). Like most of the other descriptions of violence in Zayas, this passage unequivocally condemns the men's violent behavior.

Finally, Blanca's death is represented in terms of the sacrifice of an innocent victim. Bled to death at the behest of her father-in-law, Blanca's body receives detailed attention:

> A poco rato que la sangre comenzó a salir, doña Blanca se desmayó, tan hermosamente, que diera lástima a quien más la aborreciera, y quedó tan linda, que el príncipe, su esposo, que la estaba mirando, o enternecido de ver la deshojada azucena, o enamorado de tan bella muerte, volviéndose a su padre con algunas señales piadosas en los ojos, le dijo:
> "¡Ay, señor, por Dios, que no pase adelante esta crueldad! . . . Porque os doy palabra que, cuanto ha que conozco a Blanca, no me ha parecido más linda que ahora." (*Desengaños* 363)

> [The moment the blood began to flow, doña Blanca fainted. She was so beautiful the sight would have filled her worst enemy with pity. She looked so lovely that the prince, her husband,

could only stare at her. Perhaps he felt affected by the sight of the stripped lily, perhaps he was enchanted by such a beautiful death, he turned to his father with tears of compassion in his eyes and said: "I swear to you that as long as I've known Blanca, she has never looked lovelier than she does now." (267-68, mod.)]

Two dynamics arise here: the narration strives for a wholly empathetic reading of the woman's death; and the death provokes a disturbing response in Blanca's husband, who finds his wife more appealing in death than in life. Williamsen has analyzed this scene and the prince's reaction in terms of the perversely seductive appeal of a powerless (dead) woman, for Blanca has been reduced to a purely corporeal, yet undoubtedly contained, stasis ("Death Becomes Her" 622).[26] Like Magdalena and Marieta, this dead female character no longer poses a threat to the men around her because her difference has been irrevocably contained. The disparity between the cruelty of the murder and the beauty of the corpses further emphasizes the women's victimization.

In addition to the aestheticization of bodies in the act of being murdered, the aestheticization of corpses reintegrates the dead women into the narration and reinforces the moralistic reading elicited by the violence. Ever aware of the body's power to signify, Zayas portrays dead women who defy corporeal disintegration. Blanca's cadaver remains intact and fresh long after her death, for example. With its integrity serving as a sign of the soul's glory in the narrator's words (*Desengaños* 365), Blanca's bodily purity in death confirms the vitality of her spirit. Both of the cadavers of women in the next tale, "El traidor contra su sangre," also maintain lifelike qualities long after the murders. When Mencía's lover finds her several hours after her brother killed her, the wounds flow with fresh blood and her beauty confirms the woman's spiritual transcendence of physical victimization (*Desengaños* 382). Like many of these descriptions, the scene recalls medieval miracle tales when the already

---

[26] Bronfen uses a disturbing quote from Edgar Allen Poe as a focal point for her analyses of the conflation of women, death, and beauty: "the death of a beautiful woman is, unquestionably, the most poetical topic in the world." In dealing with the connection between death and femininity, she summarizes Eugénie Lemoine-Luccioni's *Partages de femmes* in stating that "beauty arouses sexual desire at the same time that it forbids it, because it is intangible" (Bronfen 64).

dead Mencía warns her lover of impending danger. Later, when Mencía's brother decapitates his wife, he buries the head. After his capture, Alonso reveals the location of the head to the authorities, who find it "tan fresca y hermosa como si no hubiera seis meses que estaba debajo de tierra" (*Desengaños* 398) [as fresh and beautiful as if it hadn't lain buried for over six months (299)]. Calling upon paradigms of martyrdom, these specific scenes invoke the incorruptibility of saints' bodies, equating the bodily defiance exhibited by virtuous Christians with the virtue (and defiance) of women victimized by men.

Moreover, in defiance of men's impulse to contain women, many female characters are represented as empowered in the face of death. Made explicit in the miracle tale "La perseguida triunfante," in which the innocent female protagonist is punished for various alleged crimes and healed by the Virgin Mary, these depictions of corporeal integrity in the face of injustice translate into an indictment of misogynist behavior. Contrary to the disempowerment of the dead subject, Zayas's images of violated bodies and corpses with varying degrees of life still left in them defy, if only temporarily and fantastically, the irrefutable success with which men contain women through violence in these texts.

Grieve's insightful interpretation of Zayas's use of such images concludes that the author "dismantles hagiography" by "exhorting women to resist emulation that leads to their detriment and downfall" (104). As the rich, varied descriptions of violence against women suggest, Zayas takes this dismantling of hagiography one step further: she also lays bare the cultural underpinnings that sanction the perpetration of violence against women and that make it nearly impossible for women to defend themselves. This deconstructive process is realized through texts that personalize women's suffering and narrate the dynamics, as well as the consequences, of violence.

Through its focus on violence, this novella collection exposes the misplaced cultural codes that construct woman as a metaphor for man's sexual anxiety and gender identity. The dynamics of violence revolve around sexual proprietariness and, at a more general level, systemic misogyny, both of which are resolved through violent containment of the feminine. If we think of representations of dead and dying women as locating the reader, in Bronfen's terms, "in the interstice between an aesthetic and an empathetic response," we can see that Zayas's narration encourages the reader to take a morally involved position. Zayas humanizes the violent scenarios by couching her corporeal aesthetic in a didactic, woman-centered framework. Drawing the reader in through aestheticized bodies, the texts guide us toward an empathetic reading of the body imperiled.

Part Two

THE BOUNDARIES OF GENDER

CHAPTER THREE

WOMEN'S PLACE IN THE SOCIAL ORDER: PUBLIC, PRIVATE, AND CONVENT LIFE

> *Catch it. Put it in a pumpkin, in a high tower, in a compound, in a chamber, in a house, in a room. Quick, stick a leash on it, a lock, a chain, some pain, settle it down, so it can never get away from you again.*
>
> Margaret Atwood

THE early modern period has been understood traditionally as marking the birth of the modern subject and of the modern nation state. On the Spanish front, the project of nation building was initiated by the Catholic monarchs in the fifteenth century, reaching heights of grandeur in the sixteenth century, and, finally, declining during the following one hundred years. Influenced by the politics of conquest and the impulse toward unity, the formation of the nation affected the formation of the emerging modern subject in Spain. The project of unification depended on the regulation of a comprehensive range of human endeavors, including intellectual production, religious identity, and sexual behavior. In *Feminist Readings of Early Modern Culture*, Traub, Kaplan, and Callaghan address the implications of such shifting cultural norms throughout Europe: ". . . just as the subject emerged as an increasingly bounded, private self, various social mechanisms arose which also compelled its subjection" (4). As can be inferred from behavior manuals, religious doctrine, philosophy, art, scientific discourse, and political dicta, the relationship of individuals to the self changed tremendously during the period.[1]

---

[1] Gatens similarly describes the changes in the seventeenth century: "The seventeenth century was witness to at least two births of interest to us here. First, the

Zayas's portrayal of the individual (woman) struggling to survive echoes the experience of emerging subjects whose identity formation depended, to a certain degree, on negotiating their relationship with the mechanisms of control of the patriarchal state. The tension between obedience and resistance, between homogeneity and individuality, plays out on the woman's body in Zayas's novellas. Her representations of violence dramatize the tension between the impulse to individuality and the push toward conformity. Familial, national, and gender loyalties, such as those established in "Mal presagio casar lejos," become the sources of dissension and interrogation throughout the texts, for example. Zayas's depiction of the female subject in crisis also casts doubt on the institutional practices that helped create and discipline the modern subject. Specifically, Zayas uses myriad wounded and dead bodies to protest the masculinist practices of containing women's bodies. This concern for women's place in society implicitly critiques the privilege of the male subject and the denial of more inclusive gendered subjectivities in early modern culture.

Zayas's texts portray men as acutely threatened by women, and even compliant and acquiescent women often are perceived by men as disruptive to the social order. This order, defined and upheld by patriarchal ideology, was enforced partially in early modern Spain through the maintenance of outward appearance: the desire to protect one's honor and *fama* helped keep individual behavior aligned with the prescribed morals and laws of the state.[2] By connecting

---

birth of the human *subject* who is both the subject *of* governance . . . and one subject *to* governance. Second, the birth of the modern body politic, which is represented as a product of reason, designed to govern, manage and administer the needs and desires of its subjects" (50). Traub and her co-editors bring nuance to the traditional, overdetermined notion of the "birth" of the subject by emphasizing the process of subject formation with the term "emerging subjects," which they use both in the title and the introduction. Equally nuanced in the treatment of subject-formation, Cascardi analyzes what he sees as the unique Spanish case of early modern society in "The Subject of Control in Counter-Reformation Spain" in *Ideologies of History* (105-31). In addition to the essays in Traub's anthology, the question of female subjectivity and women's role in Renaissance culture also are dealt with in: Davis (*Society and Culture in Early Modern Europe*, especially "Women on Top" [124-51]), Kelly ("Did Women Have a Renaissance?"), Perry (*Gender and Disorder*), Sánchez Ortega ("Woman as Source of Evil"), and Vigil (*La vida de las mujeres*).

[2] The repeated bankruptcies and political blunders of Philip IV's reign reveal the emphasis on outward appearance and the commitment to a "golden age" rhetoric that led to bad policies and decisions. As Elliott indicates, Philip's was a

women's behavior to men's honor, the value system raised the stakes in the control of women's sexuality. The body-based aesthetic of Zayas's texts protests this and other cultural realities. Nonetheless, the novellas do not express dissatisfaction with the political and cultural systems per se, and they do not call for revolution. Instead, the violence and didacticism in the *Novelas amorosas* and the *Desengaños amorosos* decry institutionalized injustice in a social order that refuses to fully acknowledge women as subjects.

In his essay "Patriarchal Territories," Peter Stallybrass engages the import of bodily discourse in relation to cultural practices. Incorporating gender into a Bakhtinian analysis of the body, Stallybrass observes that "there can be no simple opposition between language and the body because the body maps out the cultural terrain and is in turn mapped out by it" (138). With great attention paid to violence and its consequences, Zayas's novellas inscribe hyperbolized cultural norms onto women's bodies. Her violence-filled, woman-focused narrative maps out a fundamental problem of the early modern condition: the masculinist hegemony of the emerging nation fails to account for difference, particularly women's difference.

In privileging the feminine as *the* neglected category of difference, the texts explore the detrimental (and deadly) effects of the exclusion of women from the body politic. Philosopher Moira Gatens describes this exclusionary system in terms of the perpetual identification of woman with nature in opposition to man's culture and politics:

> This division between nature and culture, between the reproduction of mere biological life as against the production and regulation of social life, is reflected in the distinction between the private and the public spheres, the family and the state. These divisions are conceptually and historically sexualized, with woman remaining mere nature, mere body, reproducing in the private familial sphere. (51)

Historically, in other words, the connection between biology and society has been made patent in the materialization of gendered

---

highly ceremonious state that "attempted to extend the range of its power by resorting to ceremony, propaganda, and image making" (164). Never mind that the crown had to declare bankruptcy several times during his reign–what mattered most was to preserve one's reputation (Elliott 124). As to Zayas's own commentary on the political situation, see Clamurro's "Ideological Contradiction."

spatial spheres. While men have access to the public sphere, women are consigned to domestic space. The boundaries that result from these spatial differences uphold the divisions between the sexes by affording men freedom of movement and by controlling women's access to non-domestic spaces. As a consequence of such insistent regulation and discipline, many aspects of the social order–including the justice system, sexual norms, marriage, and education–have operated to the exclusion of the feminine.

The spatial discourse in Zayas's novellas mimics and, at times, subverts cultural practices related to the containment of women. With domestic and public space gendered throughout the novellas, Zayas's representation of the physical boundaries of gender calls attention to the detrimental effects of enclosure. The phenomenon of obedient wives (Camila, Roseleta, Blanca, etc.) killed in their homes by their husbands in the *Desengaños amorosos* speaks to a fundamental dynamic in Zayas's texts: confinement fails to provide a safe space even for compliant women. The collection leaves us with the impression that women have no space of their own: women cannot count on any bodily or spatial integrity at home or in public. Writers such as Fray Luis de León proclaim during this period that a wife "ha de entender que su casa es un cuerpo, y que ella es el alma dél" (171) [must understand that her house is a body, and that she is the very soul of the house]. Zayas reproduces this equation of the domestic sphere with femininity, then exposes the myth that women are safe at home.[3]

While Zayas's texts denounce women's lack of access to *letras y armas*, the politics of bodies and space convey a layered critique of the containment of women and of female subjectivity. In addition to the violence that occurs in every private space imaginable, the uneven application of justice in Zayas's texts also locates women on the margin of society's concerns. Negotiating society's expectations for women, many of Zayas's female characters come face to face

---

[3] It should be noted that research on the Renaissance has suggested that our contemporary conception of public and private spheres does not translate precisely to the early modern period. The blurring of public and private manifests itself most obviously in the many components of Renaissance print culture (cf. Goldsmith and Goodman's *Going Public*, and Wall's *The Imprint of Gender*). When discussing gender in Spanish culture, however, the insistence on women's relegation to domestic duties and the prohibitions on women's public access justify an analysis of Zayas's own responses to the many spatially bound mandates of the period.

with a doubly-layered justice system in which individuals (e.g., husbands and fathers) and state officials make decisions regarding the limits of women's behavior. Yet, in reality and in fiction, justice during this period was often compromised by the obsession with (individual) honor. As the novellas make apparent, the connection of women's bodies to men's honor is fraught with danger.

The double standard applied to male and female sexuality played out both formally and informally during the period. As Perry indicates, economic and gender factors influenced access to justice, since men were able "to buy the silence of sexual partners or victims and to keep concubines because they could afford them" (*Gender and Disorder* 121). Women, on the other hand, had to maintain the highest standards (and appearances) of chastity in order to protect themselves from suspicion and possible retribution. Zayas represents these values in depictions of obsessively proprietary men and of women who are marginal to the social order. As women are violated in their homes, many male characters keep women from having reliable access to either a private or a public justice system. Meted out indiscriminately, individual characters' punishment for perceived sexual improprieties reinforces male sovereignty over women.

The efforts by Zayas's male characters to silence and control women reiterate cultural practices of the period. As alluded to in chapter one, the inclusion in the *Nueva Recopilación* of the medieval secular law granting men the right to kill adulterous wives speaks volumes for the precarious position of women at the time. Vigil intelligently addresses the significance of this law, saying that in spite of the extremely low rate of its official, documented implementation (less than five known cases in two hundred years), we should not minimize the fact that a death penalty was associated with women's adultery (154). The mere existence of the law highlights the institutionalized nature of men's control of women's bodies.

One telling point of comparison between fictional and historical accounts of women arises in a seventeenth-century case involving a man named Cosme who wanted to kill his adulterous wife. In 1629, the man's wife and her lover were found guilty of adultery by the authorities and were turned over to the husband for punishment. A group of friars and commoners formed a circle around Cosme, attempting to convince him not to exact vengeance. Although Cosme was said to make wild gestures showing his disagreement, the friars whisked the wife off to the convent and helped the lover escape before Cosme could stop them. The incident is memorialized in the *copla*: "Todos le ruegan a Cosme que perdone a su mujer; y él responde con el dedo: señores, no puede ser" [Everyone begs Cosme to set his dear wife free; and he responds with his finger, Dear sirs, it cannot be].[4]

This incident raises the issue of men's social responsibilities and their power: even as Cosme planned to kill his wife in a legally justified execution, society intervened on moral grounds. The case also makes manifest the sexual politics of the period as they were inscribed into the honor code and, to a lesser extent, into the written legal code. Heavily imbricated in the false dichotomy between public and private, this story epitomizes the honor code's dependence on the appearance of one's intact honor as well as on the desire to keep individual behavior in line with dominant ideology.

This example of thwarted wife-murder provides yet another way to read the conflation of body and gender politics in the early modern period. Entrusted to protect the integrity of the female body and sanctioned by the legal system to act as agents of justice, men had access to all facets of women's lives. As we have seen in the catalogues of violent acts, Zayas's texts criticize the marginalization of women from the body politic by exposing the injustice of the dually-conceived public/private justice system.

Both the historical record and Zayas's texts tell us that women's bodies functioned in the early modern period as an extension of male identity and sexuality. This conceptualization of the feminine coincides with Gatens's general observations about the West: "The female body, in our culture, is seen and no doubt often 'lived' as an *envelope, vessel,* or *receptacle*" (41). Zayas's representations of violence against women offer a biting critique of the conceptualization of woman as a vessel of the male ego. Imbued with enclosure imagery and examples of injustice, the collection uses the body to map out the boundaries of behavior and to interrogate dominant ideologies of gender. The dialectic between space and violence questions the limitations of the nascent social order.

---

[4] Cosme's story and this couplet appear in Vigil (*La vida* 150-51).

I. BODIES AND SPACE

The spatial dimension of Zayas's texts explores architectural, geographical, psychological, and behavioral borders. It also draws attention to the universal lack of safe boundaries within which women can seek refuge from masculine domination. Equated with the domestic sphere in many novellas, women are victimized in the purportedly safe space of the home. The spaces of violence take on multiple meanings as characters are trapped behind walls, bled to death in their beds, killed in their homes, and left for dead in the wild. The interplay of space, bodies, and gender shows women's subjectivity to be circumscribed by men's violence and control.

Historical and anthropological feminist research has put into relief the importance of space as a factor in social interaction and organization. As Susan Reverby and Dorothy Helly explain, the concept of space as gendered became a popular topic of study and debate in the 1970s. Advocating a shift in the study of space in the early 1970s, Michelle Rosaldo proposed to examine the split between the public and the private domains as a means of providing "a universal framework for conceptualizing the activities of the sexes" (23-24). Much of the research on gendered space relates to the division of labor in the postindustrialized world, but Rosaldo, Nancy Chodorow, Sherry Ortner, and others also have pinpointed several ways to think about gender relations. As Rosaldo explains,

> (I)n all human societies sexual asymmetry might be seen to correspond to a rough institutional division between domestic and public spheres of activity, the one built around reproduction, affective, and familial bonds, and particularly constraining to women; the other, providing for collectivity, jural order, and social cooperation, organized primarily by men. (397)

This simply stated theory has been criticized (even by Rosaldo herself) as being too narrowly conceived and as too pessimistic in its view of gender relations.[5] Nonetheless, the attention given to space

---

[5] Feminists certainly are not the first group to take up the discussion of separate, gendered spheres. As Kerber points out in "Separate Spheres, Female Worlds," Alexis de Tocqueville and Friedrich Engels both discuss such spatial separation. Laying the groundwork for later feminist work in this area, Engels argued

and spatial divisions in women's lives is instructive for understanding the boundaries placed on women's behavior in certain cultural contexts. A gendered consideration of space foregrounds the crucial observation that power, in Rosaldo's terms, often is constrained by "spatial range" (398): individuals' power often relates to their ability to assert themselves in different spaces, including the public square, the master bedroom, and the courtroom.

Throughout Zayas's texts, the female characters' experiences intimately are tied to the spaces they inhabit. In this regard we should remember that women in Golden Age Spain had limited access to public spaces: they had to be accompanied in public and were excluded from most official positions of power, for example.[6] Believing that "women were a part of a divine plan reaffirming male power" (Cruz, "Studying Gender" 196), Fray Luis, in *La perfecta casada*, emphasized women's duty to stay home and stay silent: ". . . la naturaleza, como dijimos y diremos, hizo a las mujeres para que encerradas guardasen la casa, así las obligó a que cerrasen la boca" (154) [nature, as we have said and will say again, made women to stay inside at home, and so they are obliged to close their mouths as well]. Like other fictional creations of the period, Zayas's female characters often venture into situations and spaces that would not have been considered proper for women. The transgressive women –those who blatantly challenge spatial and behavioral limits–often succeed in their endeavors in the *Novelas amorosas*. Representations of women who cross boundaries of gender and space create a cogent message of defiance in this first volume.

Striking examples of transgression in the *Novelas amorosas* can be found in the crossdressed female protagonists (Jacinta, Aminta, and Estela), all of whom gain access to the public sphere; the female avengers (Aminta and Hipólita), who appropriate violence and honor; and the sexually active women in "El prevenido, engañado," who defy sexual mores and act as agents in the private sphere. The treatment of spatial and gender boundaries throughout

---

that the home was controlled by men (Kerber 13). Reverby and Helly give an overview of the evolution of the public/private debate, in their introduction to *Gendered Domains: Rethinking Public and Private in Women's History*. For recent discussions on the social construction of space and its relation to gender, see Spain (*Gendered Spaces*, esp. 1-29) and Rose (*Feminism and Geography*, esp. 41-62).

[6] Perry's "In the Hands of Women" (ch. 1, *Gender and Disorder*), addresses women's limited access to public commerce.

this volume delineates the conventions dictating proper feminine behavior. At the same time, these boundaries suggest that women, when not constrained by masculine violence, can circumvent restrictive conventions, protecting or even liberating themselves from male dominance.

The use of space to demarcate gender boundaries in the *Novelas amorosas* maps out some of the cultural, behavioral, and spatial limitations placed on women. In many cases, however, spatial discourse in this volume relates to behavior that subverts conventional gender roles and challenges the impulse to contain women. Taken as a whole, the first volume depicts and subverts spatial constraints that correspond to real limitations placed on women in society. Zayas juxtaposes women's lack of freedom with examples of freedom of movement. This juxtaposition confronts readers with the various practices that keep women in check and shows women to be intellectually and physically capable of great mobility.

Zayas's own journey into the realm of publication announced in "Al que leyere" and Jacinta's foray into the mountains introduce the importance of spatial discourse at the outset of the *Novelas amorosas*. Like the avengers, Aminta and Hipólita, these first two women who cross boundaries challenge taboos about women behaving as agents of action. Domestic space also figures prominently, something that comes as little surprise in texts that explore issues of marriage, love, and desire. Like Calderón's *La dama duende* (*The Phantom Lady*), in which Angela's phantasmagoric movements enable her to seek a husband within the confines of her home, the female characters of the *Novelas amorosas* often exert influence in the private sphere.

Lisis's apartment provides an example of women's control over space in the *Novelas amorosas*. Inhabited by the female guests of the soiree, the apartment provides an intimate domestic framework. The lavish domestic details of Lisis's home feminize both soirees: "Coronaba la sala un rico estrado, con almohadas de terciopelo verde, a quien las borlas y guarniciones de plata hermoseaban" (*Novelas* 31) [The room was crowned by a rich dais piled high with mountains of green velvet cushions ornamented with splendid silver embroidery and tassels (9)]. Within this atmosphere, Lisis banters with her ex-lover Juan, takes on a new lover to spite the old, and, in the *Desengaños*, exerts power over men by excluding them from the task of narration. This assertion of female power is counterbalanced, however, by the tensions between the sexes. These tensions carry great weight in the frame tale, as they lead to Lisis's lengthy illness and contribute to her eventual withdrawal from marriage. In addition to the strained relations between the sexes in the domestic frame tale setting, the home emerges as a site of power struggle between men and women in several novellas, suggesting that women are at risk even within space gendered as feminine.

Strengthening the impact of this depiction of a violated private sphere, the *Novelas amorosas* explicitly equates the feminine with domestic space in two novellas. Alvaro, the frame narrator of the satirical "El castigo de la miseria," explains the protagonist's stupefaction upon entering the house of the woman he quickly decides to marry. This passage, in which Marcos defines the woman in terms of her house, captures the synonymity between women and domestic space that loomed large in Zayas's culture:

> Entró don Marcos en casa de doña Isidora, casi admirado de ver la casa, tantos cuartos, tan bien labrada y con tanta hermosura; y miróla con atención, porque le dixeron que era su dueña la misma que lo había de ser de su alma. (*Novelas* 129)

> [When don Marcos entered doña Isidora's apartment, he was nearly thunderstruck to see it, with so many rooms, so well and even beautifully arranged. He examined everything very carefully because he'd been told that the woman who was about to become the mistress of his heart was mistress of all this. (83, mod.)]

Blinded by greed, Marcos cannot see through the charade of Isidora's contrived beauty and wealth. Following Fray Luis's dictum, he conflates the house with the female body, trusting that one's beauty and integrity stand for the other's. Only after the marriage does he discover that both have been misrepresented to him. He has seen what he wanted to see–a richly decorated house and a youthful bride–and has failed to see the ruse. Isidora, on the other hand, manipulates Marcos's conflation of women with material goods, for she clearly mobilizes the "property" value of women in her plan to trick the miser. Like "El prevenido, engañado," in which the domestic sphere is the site of female sexual excess, "El castigo de la miseria" subverts the idealization of the private sphere's capacity to contain women.

Several empowered female characters in the *Novelas amorosas* communicate the possibility of women's successful navigation of public and private space. Variously empowered through crossdressing, sexual freedom, witchcraft, violence, and sheer wit, female characters in this collection often break with the standard codes of behavior and act on their own desire. Yet the violence against women shatters the presumed tranquility of the feminized private sphere, issuing a reminder of men's control of women's bodies and spaces.

Even in this brief overview, we can see that the multifaceted treatment of public and private space in the *Novelas amorosas* both replicates and subverts cultural norms regarding space and gender. Introducing violence in the home, the texts also begin to suggest what later becomes obvious in the *Desengaños amorosos*: women are subject to the whims of masculine aggression and control in every space imaginable. That several characters, including the physically assaulted protagonists in "La fuerza del amor" and "Al fin se paga todo," choose to leave their husbands opens up the liminal space of the convent as part of the geography of women's existence. In fact, the convent figures as the only permanently safe space for women in the entire collection. The various cultural meanings of this space are explored in the *Novelas amorosas*, where women enter and are placed in the convent for different reasons.

The motif of the convent runs through the entire collection and serves as a counterpoint to men's hegemony over women's bodies. The convent also epitomizes the gendering of space in the *Novelas amorosas*.[7] While Jacinta ("Aventurarse perdiendo") and Gracia ("El prevenido, engañado") enter convents at the behest of men, Laura ("La fuerza del amor") chooses the convent over returning to her abusive husband. In contrast to the women, male protagonists in these tales view the convent as a space of containment, meant either to protect women from the outside world or to protect the world from corrupt women.

---

[7] See chapter three of Cushing's 1996 dissertation, "The Novellas of María de Zayas y Sotomayor" (126-71), for another analysis of the function of the convent.

In a last-ditch effort to win back his long suffering wife, for example, Diego tries to turn his lover over to the authorities in "La fuerza del amor":

> para que [su Excelencia] la metiese en un convento, porque apartado della, y agradeciendo a Laura los extremos de su amor, la adorase y sirviese eternamente. (*Novelas* 246)

> [so that (His Excellency) could place Nise in a convent; because, separated from Nise forever and eternally grateful to Laura for her extreme love, he would adore his wife and serve her always. (179, mod.)]

Here Diego offers one woman in exchange for another, presenting the convent option as a punitive measure aimed at containing his lover's 'disruptive' sexuality. The suggestion of Nise's removal to a contained space relates closely to early modern "conversion houses." As Perry discusses in "Magdalens and Jezebels," the enclosure of women in the three major institutions of brothels, Magdalen houses, and prisons provided a tripartite structure of containment for unchaste women as well as for those perceived as deserving of pity. Similar to the Italian *convertite* houses, which were asylums for reformed/reforming prostitutes, the Magdalen houses (*casas de recogidas*) in Spain provided an institutionalized space for penitence and reform.[8] Perry indicates that these houses of penitents accepted women "placed there for correction" by men (which would be the case of Nise, for example), and women fleeing from husbands and lovers who entered of their own accord (e.g., Laura in "La fuerza") (133). For men, the convent offered the possibility of removing dangerous feminine elements from society; for women with means, it could provide safety and self-protection.[9]

---

[8] Cohen describes the rise of the *convertite* houses in terms of the emphasis on reform during the period: "Indeed, conversion became a leitmotif of the entire Counter Reformation, with a rising call to purify corrupt clergy and to recruit to the faith apostates to Protestantism and the unlearned poor" (169). As Penyak discusses in "Safe Harbors and Compulsory Custody," *casas de depósito* existed in Mexico during the colonial period as well, functioning "as one of a broad sweep of protective and punitive institutions for adolescent and adult women" (84). See Pérez Baltasar's *Mujeres marginadas: Las casas de recogidas en Madrid* for an analysis of these institutions in Spain.

[9] Given the hierarchy of gender in the Catholic church, it is logical that the convent is a contested site. Research has shown that nuns have found ways to overcome

Women's concern for safety explains Laura's decision. Fearful of her husband's violence and tired of his disrespect, Laura sees God as a faithful and appreciative lover (*Novelas* 246). The woman's emphasis on security directly contrasts with Diego's intention of punishing Nise by removing her from sexual circulation. Thus, like Hipólita in "Al fin se paga todo," Laura looks to the convent as a nurturing space. In contrast, Diego and other male characters see it as a mechanism of punishment and control.

This dual conceptualization of convents underscores the psychological distance between men's and women's perceptions of gender relations and sexuality. Similar views of space arise in "El desengaño amando," a story that involves a complex chain of women's emotional attachments to one man. Fernando has sex with Juana after promising to marry her, gets distracted when he falls under a spell cast by Lucrecia, abandons Juana (who enters a convent), marries and abandons Clara, and finally dies after Clara breaks a spell cast on him. Toward the beginning of the tale, the spurned Juana falls ill and decides to devote her life to God. Although Fernando makes the initial suggestion that Juana enter the convent, she couches her decision to become a nun in assertive rhetoric:

> Y no penséis que por estar defraudada de ser vuestra mujer escojo este estado, que os doy mi palabra que aunque con gusto vuestro y de vuestra madre quisiérades que lo fuera, no acetara tal, porque . . . propuse de ser esposa de Dios y no vuestra, y así lo he prometido. (*Novelas* 269)
>
> [Do not think I have chosen this path because I've been cheated of being your wife; I promise you that, even if you now were to try to marry me with all your heart and your mother's blessing, I wouldn't accept . . . . I made up my mind to become Christ's bride and not yours, and this I have vowed. (196)]

Juana's impassioned speech rejects Fernando's power over her and presents religious life as a positive option.

As in "La fuerza del amor," the man in "El desengaño amando" views the convent as a removal mechanism. Fernando eagerly pro-

---

or circumvent male power (cf. Arenal and Schlau; Weber). In *Immodest Acts*, for example, Brown tells the story of the Italian Benedetta Carlini, a nun who gained so much power in her convent that she became a threat to church authorities.

vides Juana with a dowry because he is happy to free himself from the obligation to marry her (*Novelas* 270). From his point of view, the convent presents an easy way to warehouse women, to take them out of circulation when they are no longer needed or wanted. Fiercely independent, Juana rejects Fernando's masculinist view and embraces the convent's protective function.

Women's perception of the convent's nurturing power arises several times in this novella. Juana recovers from her illness in the convent, for example, and she lives to take care of Fernando and Clara's two daughters while Clara searches for her wandering husband. After gaining entrance into the house in which Lucrecia has cast a spell on Fernando, Clara bides her time until she can release Fernando from the spell. When Fernando dies two months after the spell is lifted, Clara remarries but her daughters choose to remain in the convent. Following Juana's example, the girls become nuns, leaving the reader to speculate about their motivations. Do they fear that the new father-figure will also abandon them or are they responding to a positive experience in the convent? In either case, the daughters' decision validates the feminine conception of the convent as a safe, familial space for women.

The female characters of the *Novelas amorosas* tend to view convents as offering safety and refuge to women variously motivated by fear, religion, and desire for community. The convent represents a site of struggle as well: it has the seemingly paradoxical characteristic of being a feminized space controlled by the male-dominated church. In this sense, it seems appropriate that, in the culture and in Zayas's fiction, many men see it as a space of enclosure serving to control female sexuality. Through this disparate gendering of space, Zayas adds yet another layer to her discussion of men's and women's struggles for control.

Zayas's representation of the gendered perceptions of the convent is in keeping with Cruz and Perry's observations about women in early modern Spain: "The enclosure of women, either through marriage or in convents, did not guarantee their control, whether real or fictional" (xix). In fact, Zayas rejects the notions of containment and punishment. Instead, the convent emerges as the space *outside the narrative* that may be entered only by female characters and that remains inaccessible even to the reader. Lisis's final decision to reject Diego specifically de-emphasizes religiosity in favor of feminine safety. Similarly, the novellas dealing with the theme in the

Novelas amorosas downplay religiosity and emphasize protection: only Juana in "El desengaño amando" specifically expresses religious conviction as her motivation for entering the convent.[10] By refusing to consistently cast the characters' choices in religious terms, Zayas's texts present a secularized depiction of the convent as the only inviolable space for women.

Figured as beyond the reach of men, the convent represents an alternative space for women in these novellas. The multilayered interplay between public and private spheres in the *Novelas amorosas* introduces issues dealt with more extensively in the *Desengaños*, in which the violation of private space and of the female body reaches crisis levels. Nonetheless, the *Novelas amorosas* touches on issues of enclosure and violence, while also examining the various functions of the convent. Representations of violence, female sexuality, empowered women, and masculine control portray the private sphere as a contested site between men and women. Through these spatially bound battles, Zayas plants the seeds for the depiction of the domestic sphere as a war zone in which men fight to control women, and women struggle to survive.

II. The Boundaries of Violence: The *Desengaños Amorosos*

The cultural ideologies mapped out through the body gain clarity and definition in the *Desengaños amorosos*. Tensions between the sexes run high and the didacticism increasingly focuses on women's endangered position in society. Masculinist constructions of woman –as body to be conquered, as vessel of men's honor, as wantonness to be contained– are portrayed in the *Desengaños* as engendering and legitimizing violence against women. While Fray Luis and other cultural authorities insisted on equating the sanctity of the house

---

[10] Jacinta ("Aventurarse perdiendo") seems reluctant to enter the convent, but says she will do so even though she will not take vows–hence her statement, "aventuraréme perdiendo" (*Novelas* 78) [I will venture everything (44, mod.)]. Laura in "La fuerza del amor" goes to the convent when fleeing an abusive relationship. Gracia is placed in the convent in "El prevenido, engañado," and returns to take vows and be with her mother after becoming a widow. Clara's daughters take vows in the same convent as their surrogate mother, Juana, in "El desengaño amando." Hipólita enters the convent only temporarily before marrying García in "Al fin se paga todo." Juana is the only character who indicates that her religious beliefs dictate her choice to enter the convent.

with the integrity of the female body (e.g., "her house is a body"), Zayas represents an absolute violability of both the house and the body. In the final analysis, Zayas criticizes the enclosure of women, using representations of violence to expose the negative effects of the culture's unexamined complicity in the control of women.

The subversive elements of Zayas's bodily and spatial aesthetics can be better understood through Stallybrass's analysis. Elaborating on Bakhtin's typology of the classical versus the grotesque body, Stallybrass suggests that the chaste, homogeneous, culturally constructed woman has a classical body: "her [cultural] signs are the enclosed body, the closed mouth, the locked house" (127). Made synonymous with the domestic sphere, this woman is enclosable, relegated to silence. Zayas's descriptions of violated female bodies in the *Desengaños amorosos* forcefully challenge the metaphorical, ideological, and physical containment of women by portraying violated female bodies as bleeding, rotting, and dying. The violation of the domestic sphere functions as a metaphor for the violation of women, and the female body exemplifies the problems attending enclosure and control.

Throughout the tales, female characters' bodies are open and gaping, and their flesh speaks for the injustices of unchecked male privilege and control. Like many hagiographic representations, the violated body expands beyond itself in Zayas's texts.[11] This aesthetic, explored at length in the following pages, corresponds to Stallybrass's summary of

> the Renaissance *topos* that presents woman as that treasure which, however locked up, always escapes. She is the gaping mouth, the open window, the body that [in Bakhtin's terms] "transgresses its own limits" and negates all those boundaries without which property could not be constituted. (128)

The tension between the impulse to contain woman and woman's perceived openness is figured in this trope in terms of woman's un-

---

[11] The descriptions of swelling and decaying bodies suggest that another possible source for these occasionally grotesque representations of corporeality might be found in the rituals and ceremonies surrounding death in early modern Spain. See, for example, Orso's *Art and Death at the Spanish Habsburg Court* and Eire's *From Madrid to Purgatory: The Art and Craft of Dying in Sixteenth-Century Spain*.

manageable physicality. Zayas leads the reader through image after image of open, bleeding bodies. By framing these images with critical commentary, she encourages the reader to recognize men's responsibility for the problems caused by the containment of women.

Unlike the female body that "always escapes" and "transgresses its own limits," Zayas portrays women who cannot escape violence. Women's bodily excesses in these texts result from men's violent impulses to control the "gaping mouth, the open window" that is the female body. Representations of female victimization reach excessive levels in Zayas's prose. Like the representations of lifelike corpses, the seeping and wounded bodies function to protest the masculinist practices that give men power over women and that fail to consider the consequences of such a system. Zayas's language seeks to puncture the cultural myths that link masculinity to women's chastity and to the practices that make women dependent on men for their survival. Like the nineteenth- and twentieth-century writers discussed by Gilbert and Gubar in *The Madwoman in the Attic*, Zayas vivifies the fact that cultural pressures and practices make their mark on women's bodies.[12]

Male-female relations reach full-fledged battle proportions in the *Desengaños*. Emphasizing this crisis, violence permeates the novellas and the frame characters employ an abundance of military rhetoric. Lisis's introduction to "Estragos que causa el vicio" expresses militaristic attitudes about love and desire. Declaring war against men, she states, ". . . porque como todos están ya declarados por enemigos de las mujeres, contra todos he publicado la guerra" (*Desengaños* 470) [because all men are declared enemies of women, I have declared my war against all men (367)]. She then encourages women to rise to the occasion of fending off men's deception and men to respond accordingly:

> ¡Ánimo, hermosas damas, que hemos de salir vencedoras! ¡Paciencia, discretos caballeros, que habéis de quedar vencidos y habéis de juzgar a favor que las damas os venzan! Este es desafío

---

[12] In chapter one, "The Queen's Looking Glass," Gilbert and Gubar trace manifestations of illness, such as anorexia and hysteria, in women's writing. Likewise, chapter two, "Infection in the Sentence: The Woman Writer and the Anxiety of Authorship," has served as a guideline for feminist scholars' considerations of women's relationship to writing and to their bodies since the publication of *The Madwoman in the Attic*.

> de una a todos; y de cortesía, por lo menos, me habéis de dar la victoria, pues tal vencimiento es quedar más vencedores. (*Desengaños* 470)
>
> [Courage, beautiful ladies, for we shall overcome! Patience, discreet gentlemen, for you shall be overcome and shall have to rule in favor of the ladies who vanquish you! This is one woman's challenge to all men. If just from courtesy, you must grant me victory and by being conquered, you too shall win. (368)]

Couched in the vocabulary of competition and war, Lisis's rhetoric manipulates men into only one choice: they must allow themselves to be vanquished by women in order to wipe out violence and distrust in gender relations. This turn of logic, effected through a play on words that equates surrender with conquest and emphasizes the imperative to resolve the war between the sexes.

The domestic sphere comes to the fore as the logical locus of this war of desire and dominance in the *Desengaños amorosos*. Part two in *Femicide: The Politics of Woman Killing* zeroes in on an issue that emerges as one of the fundamental messages of Zayas's texts. Calling the patriarchal home "the most lethal place for women," Radford and Russell make an observation about modern life that applies to Zayas's representation of domestic space:

> It is ironic that the place where women should expect to feel safest–their own home–is the place where they are least safe from lethal sexual violence when they share that home with a man. Also ironic is the fact that it is those men whom women are encouraged to trust and look to for love and protection who pose the greatest risk, be they husbands, lovers, or former husbands or lovers. (77) [13]

---

[13] Dolan's *Dangerous Familiars* similarly concludes that representations of domestic violence in early modern England portray the home as the most common place for violence, with "familiars" being those most likely to commit violent acts against each other (cf. introduction, esp. 4, 31). Dolan's superb study provides marked points of contrast between Zayas and male-oriented and authored representations of violence (in broadsides, ballads, dramas, pamphlets, etc.). Dolan explains that the English texts she discusses almost universally represent outspoken women as a threat to the social order, while violent men were not as strongly condemned: "Even when pamphlets or ballads present husbandly excesses as irresponsible and analogous to tyranny, they do not represent this petty tyranny as threatening social order in the same ways that petty treason [i.e., the legal category for murder of husband or master] did" (90).

As the incidence of violence and violation increases in the second volume, women's control over the domestic sphere lessens. In almost direct opposition to the portrayal of empowered women in the *Novelas amorosas*, the female characters lose ground in the *Desengaños amorosos* as their bodies are violated in countless ways both in and out of the home. The hints in the *Novelas amorosas* about women's lack of sovereignty in the domestic sphere become an integral part of the spatial discourse of the second volume.

In the *Desengaños amorosos*, the home immediately is marked as unsafe in that Lisis suffers even more when reminded of her amorous problems. In spite of, or perhaps because of, the frequent visits by Juan, Diego, and Lisis's rival, Lisarda, Lisis's condition worsens. She begins her recovery only when the slave Zelima comes onto the scene. This dynamic imprints the frame with the importance of female solidarity.[14] Moreover, the healing process in these introductory pages establishes the crucial connection between mind and body as Lisis seeks relief from her physical and psychological problems.

Recurring entrapment imagery in the *Desengaños* is one of the most salient manifestations of woman's lack of sovereignty over self in these texts.[15] Anxiety about confinement arises in the *Desengaños* not only in private spheres such as Lisis's bedroom, but also in public spaces. Highly conscious of multifaceted oppression of women, the *Desengaños* depicts female characters as continually frustrated in their attempts at empowerment and escape. Such frustration arises both within the home and without, within marriage and without, as numerous female characters are battered and killed. Any semblance of justice that had previously existed in the *Novelas amorosas* diminishes, leaving women exposed to violence.

The excesses of violence in the *Desengaños amorosos* are made manifest through at least two acts of violence in every tale and

---

[14] Another aspect of the process of recovery that I do not consider here is that Zelima poses no threat to Lisis precisely because of her status as a Moorish slave. Even though the texts emphasize the curative effects of female companionship, given the complex and often dismissive treatment of the Other throughout the collection, we might speculate that Zelima's presumed difference (of status, ethnicity, and religion) obviates any threat that she might pose to Lisis. For another perspective on Zelima's tale, see Oltra's "Zelima o el arte narrativo de María de Zayas."

[15] Ordóñez discusses Zayas's position as a woman writer in terms of spatial discourse: "Anxieties about spatial confinement may encode, then, anxieties about authorship in textual traditions similarly restrictive to women" (6).

through detailed descriptions of women's victimization and suffering. The violence culminates with the massacre in "Estragos que causa el vicio," which forces readers to reckon with uncontrolled male rage. If excess challenges the order that it exceeds, as Grosz indicates (*Volatile* 187), then the excessive violence of these didactic tales must be understood in terms of the social order, in terms of gender relations and power distribution within this order.

With this framework of excess and order in mind, we can look at the import of bodies and space in the *Desengaños*, particularly as the dynamic plays out in the second through fifth tales–"La más infame venganza," "El verdugo de su esposa," "Tarde llega el desengaño," and "La inocencia castigada." The tightly knit relationship between spatial and bodily discourse in this volume, and most notably in these four tales, adds yet another layer to Zayas's critique of women's oppression.

Before turning to these stories of domestic violence, we should consider that two novellas in the *Desengaños*, "La esclava de su amante" and "La perseguida triunfante," assure readers that women are equally unsafe in public and private spheres. The protagonists, Isabel and Beatriz, are thrust into the public sphere as a result of horrible domestic experiences. As discussed in chapter one, Isabel's autobiographical narrative in "La esclava de su amante" introduces the difficulties faced by women who venture into the public sphere. Understanding that she cannot navigate public space safely but determined to do so in order to vindicate herself, Isabel seeks independence in the disguise of a slave. After her sovereignty of self is violated both in the private sphere (when she is raped) and the public sphere (when she is captured by Moors), Isabel eventually refuses to re-enter the sexual economy. Instead, she chooses a convent as her refuge.

As the only other protagonist to venture so boldly into the public sphere, Beatriz in the ninth novella, "La perseguida triunfante," encounters frustration similar to that of Isabel, so it is not surprising that both women choose similar religious paths. Beatriz's brother-in-law, Federico, illicitly courts her in the palace while her husband is away. This violation of a woman in her private space has political implications as well, for the subordinate male subject shows no restraint in his aggressive courtship of the married queen. In a final effort to protect herself, Beatriz inverts the paradigm of men's containment of women: she attempts to contain Federico's aggressive sexuality by locking him in a cage until her husband, King Ladislao, returns. Her authority to invert such strong patriarchal paradigms is dubious, however, and her efforts fail when Ladislao refuses to believe her innocence. He demands that she be taken ten leagues away and that her eyes be gouged. The frame narrator Estefanía describes this last action as emblematic of universal misogyny: the huntsmen gouge Beatriz's eyes "con el oficio de hombres contra esta mujer, como hacen ahora con todas" (*Desengaños* 431) [with the usual habit of men against women, as they now do with all women (330, mod.)]. That is, they engage in the typically masculine behavior of blinding a woman with deceit.

Beatriz finds salvation only in miraculous intervention, as the Virgin Mary intervenes to save her on several occasions. The portrayal of women as being denied access to justice on Earth conveys an extremely pessimistic message about gender relations. The queen's integrity is violated repeatedly, and this connection conflates the public sphere (politics) with the private (home/body). Ultimately, the novella suggests that a lone woman, even a queen, cannot beat a system that denigrates all women. The Virgin must intercede to heal Beatriz's body, prevent her execution, and give her refuge in the sanctity of a cave.[16]

Beatriz reaps the benefits of this soothing, empowering feminine environment, where she recovers by reading the life stories of saints, developing an intense sense of spirituality, and awaiting her re-entry into the world. The Virgin sends Beatriz out into the world years later, dressed as a male healer who will cure those afflicted with the plague. She eventually succeeds in converting her brother-in-law back to goodness and convincing her husband of her innocence. With her personal problems solved, Beatriz chooses a new course for her life. Much to her repentant husband's dismay, she rejects the secular world–in which she has been victimized–and enters a convent to devote herself to a religious life.

While Isabel and Beatriz suffer mental and physical violation, the remaining protagonists of the *Desengaños amorosos* encounter claustrophobic, even deadly, situations exclusively in the private sphere. In most of these novellas, entrapment imagery abounds. Re-

---

[16] Gilbert and Gubar discuss the importance of cave symbolism in women's writing: "the womb-shaped cave is also the place of female power, the *umbilicus mundi*, one of the great antechambers of the mysteries of transformation" (95).

peatedly, women are enclosed and violated in the domestic sphere. Following Isabel's trials in public and private domains, the second through the fifth tales reiterate the connection between violence and enclosure. These novellas depict women who fall victim to their husbands, lovers, and fathers. The repetition of violence–and of its connection to space and containment–exploits the impulse to contain women in a period in which their behavior increasingly was regulated.

An explicit critique of cultural codes of behavior appears in "La más infame venganza," a tale that engages many aspects of spatial confinement. Juan locks up the recently orphaned Octavia so as to prevent his sister from spending their inheritance:

> para que ella no gastase nada, [Juan] la tenía tan encerrada y necesitada de todo, que aunque él no la tuviera así, ella misma se quitara de los ojos de todos, por no parecer en menos porte que el que traía en vida de sus padres [. . .]. (*Desengaños* 179)

> [To prevent her from spending a cent, he kept her totally shut in and deprived of everything. Even if he hadn't kept her cloistered like that she herself would have remained aloof from the eyes of society so people wouldn't see her less elegantly dressed than when her parents were alive. (93)]

The frame narrator Lisarda's description of the enclosure highlights the woman's dependence on her brother for money and supervision. Octavia's needy state and her hypothetical, self-imposed isolation point to both genders' (and society's) use of domestic confinement as a method of maintaining the appearance of chastity and normalcy.

Octavia's brother fails to comply with his obligations as brother and male heir, for he quickly kills a man and leaves town as a fugitive. His absence leaves Octavia totally on her own, and soon thereafter her troubles begin. Her suitor Carlos, who sees both Octavia and the house as unprotected property, freely visits Octavia without concern for her reputation. Lisarda describes the repercussions of this situation from a woman's perspective:

> quedando Carlos con el ausencia de don Juan por dueño de la casa de Octavia, entrando y saliendo en ella sin ningún recato, restaurando los gustos perdidos con tanto exceso, que ya le vinieron a cansar, cuando ya toda la ciudad lo murmuraba, re-

tirándose las señoras de ella de comunicar ni ver a Octavia, por estar su fama tan oscurecida. (*Desengaños* 182)

[Don Juan's absence left Carlos master of Octavia's house. He came and went without the least precaution, making up for lost pleasure with such excess that soon Carlos began to tire of it. By then the whole city was gossiping about their affair and the ladies stopped receiving Octavia, her reputation had become so clouded. (95, mod.)]

Like the house, which passes from one man's control to another's, Octavia's fate also lies in men's power. The criticism directed at Octavia's brother throughout this tale reinforces one of Zayas's recurrent themes–that of men's responsibility to protect women. Interestingly, the narrator's emphasis on the woman's compromised honor in this passage glosses over Octavia's complicity in her sexual relations with Carlos. This feminized narrative strategy emphasizes Carlos's hypocrisy, for he repeatedly seduces Octavia under the false promise of marriage. The equation of Octavia with the unprotected house reiterates the synonymy between women and the private sphere, and establishes the violability of both.

The private sphere remains associated with the female body throughout this novella. Carlos lies to Octavia, promising to marry her when he does not intend to do so. Under false pretenses, he suggests that she enter a convent until his father approves their union. In the meantime, Carlos marries another woman. At Octavia's behest, her brother returns to help his sister, but his revenge takes an insidious form. Seeking to avenge the damage done to his property (his sister), Juan will damage another man's "goods" by having sex with or, if that fails, by raping, Carlos's new wife, Camila.

Juan courts Camila, but she resists his advances and keeps the issue secret so as not to arouse her husband's suspicion. Finally, Juan crossdresses and, posing as a noblewoman in distress, gains access to Camila's private quarters. Then he rapes Camila in her own bedroom. In retribution for this rape, Camila's husband eventually poisons her. Despised for her perceived sexual impurity, Camila finds herself in a similar situation to Octavia; both women are mistreated by the same men and then suffer the consequences of a perceived loss of bodily integrity. Throughout the tale, as in the *Desengaños* as a whole, the lack of safe space for women is highlighted through the depiction of men's control over women's bodies.

The hypermasculinist ideologies that conceive of women as property and as extensions of male honor are inscribed violently onto the female body in this tale. When Juan rapes Camila, he stakes out his territory visually by marking her body with dagger wounds to the chest (*Desengaños* 193). Her husband places her in a convent and lets her out only at the behest of the governor and other noblemen in Milan. Yet Carlos simply cannot get over the fact that his wife's bodily integrity has been compromised. After keeping her cloistered in the house for one year, he poisons her, but the poison does not kill her immediately:

> Y fue el caso que no la quitó el veneno luego la vida, mas hinchóse toda con tanta monstruosidad, que sus brazos y piernas parecían unas gordísimas columnas, y el vientre se apartaba una gran vara de la cintura; sólo el rostro no tenía hinchado. (*Desengaños* 195)

> [It was the case that the poison did not kill her immediately; instead, her whole body swelled so monstrously that her arms and legs looked like huge pillars, and her stomach distended at least a rod from her waistline. Only her face was not swollen. (108, mod.)]

The botched poisoning of Camila reflects Carlos's rage toward her. In a grotesque, expanding state, Camila lives as a martyr for six months before finally succumbing to death. Camila's body literally expands beyond its own limits, transformed by male violence into the threatening, grotesque body that her husband perceives her to be. Through both spatial and bodily discourse, this tale makes a strong statement against the reliance of masculinity on violence as well as against men's failure to live up to their roles as protectors.

The tales that follow criticize men's violent reactions to perceived sexual impropriety just as fervently as "La más infame venganza." The third tale of the collection, "El verdugo de su esposa," provides a counterpoint to "La más infame venganza": the female protagonists in both stories get caught in a web of sexuality and violence. While Camila is raped in retribution for her husband's misconduct and subsequently killed, Roseleta in "El verdugo" is wooed by her husband's best friend and eventually killed by her husband. The moral of the stories, as communicated by the frame narrator Nise, is that women exist in a double bind: if they notify their husbands of other men's advances, they will be punished; if they do not say anything, they will meet the same dreary fate as the other women. Or, as Cruz has stated with regard to Zayas's denunciation of this double standard, women's "innocence is no guard against social retribution" ("Feminism" 46-47).

The frame tale characters repeatedly condemn women's precarious position in the culture, noting that women's behavior and attitudes have little bearing on the treatment they receive from men. As Nise says,

> En el discurso de este desengaño veréis, señoras, cómo a las que nacieron desgraciadas nada les quita de que no lo sean hasta el fin; . . . porque en la estimación de los hombres el mismo lugar tiene la que habla como la que calla. (*Desengaños* 211-12)

> [Now, in the course of this disenchantment, ladies, you'll see how for women who are born to be unfortunate there's no way to prevent their misfortune to the very end . . . because, as far as men are concerned, a woman who speaks is in the same position as one who remains silent. (125, mod.)]

Indeed, many of the women characters are passive and silent, portrayed as complying with the culturally accepted definition of the obedient Christian woman as she is described by Fray Luis and Juan Luis Vives, among others.[17] However, Zayas's texts offer examples that contradict Fray Domingo de Baltanás's typically early modern assertion "que [con] los príncipes y los sacerdotes y las mugeres, no basta que sean buenos sino que lo parezcan" [that with princes and priests and women, it is not enough to be virtuous. One must appear to be so].[18] Zayas shows women as lacking control over men's perceptions of their sexual purity. Predisposed to distrust and even fear the female body, men apply their own versions of individual justice aimed at disciplining women in the *Desengaños amorosos*.

---

[17] Bergmann's "The Exclusion of the Feminine in the Cultural Discourse of the Golden Age" explores the construction and dissemination of ideals of femininity throughout the sixteenth and seventeenth centuries.

[18] Rhodes quotes Baltanás in "Skirting the Man: Gender Roles in Sixteenth-Century Pastoral Books" (144 n. 25).

This message of uneven justice comes out in the interaction between the two men in "El verdugo de su esposa." After his life is saved by miraculous intervention, the suitor in this story confesses to having courted his best friend's wife. He also swears to the wife's innocence before he enters a monastery. Yet the husband, Pedro, refuses to believe the story, which was brought to his attention by his mistress. Pedro continues to feel rancor for what he sees as his wife's sexual improprieties. Eventually, the public knowledge of the case exacerbates the situation and Pedro grows to hate his wife; he cannot bear the humiliation and refuses to indulge the idea of her innocence. Like other male characters in the collection, Pedro resorts to violence. First, he bleeds Roseleta to death in her bed. Then, adding insult to injury and effectively declaring his culpability in the crime, he allows his lover to move in with him the same night he kills Roseleta. The violation of the female body and the home conveys yet again men's ability to disrupt the integrity of a woman's body and space.

The contrast of divine justice (God steps in to save the suitor from his impending death) with the lack of human justice (Pedro is never prosecuted for the uxoricide) suggests that women have no control over their destiny. The parallel situations of Camila and Roseleta in the two stories point to the same conclusion. In spite of their dissimilar reactions to similar situations, both women die at the hands of their husbands. The frame character Nise summarizes this trap when she describes men as wholly predictable in their treatment of women ("para las mujeres todos son unos" [*Desengaños* 222] [as to women, men all act the same (135, mod.)]). This assessment holds true in the frame tale, in which the female characters condemn the violence, and the male characters defend it (*Desengaños* 223). Specifically, the men defend Pedro's right to punish his wife because his honor was compromised by the accusation of adultery. These gendered interpretations of violence add fuel to the fire, exposing the gap between men and women that makes reform a difficult, if not impossible, prospect. And, like Magdalena's death in "Estragos que causa el vicio," the murders of these female protagonists connect male aggression with ideals of masculinity.

Men's obsession with women's sexual purity contributes to equally disturbing scenarios in the fourth novella, "Tarde llega el desengaño." A dark account of one's man's fatal errors in judgment, much of this tale is told in the first person by the interior narrator, Jaime. An inhabitant of the Canary Islands, Jaime has created a topsy-turvy world that he rules with an iron fist. Preceded by Jaime's strange description of a torrid affair with a princess that ended with her attempts to kill him, the story is a variation on the themes of the previous tales. A black slave accuses Jaime's wife, Elena, of an adulterous relationship with her cousin. Like other male characters in the *Desengaños amorosos*, Jaime responds with rage and violence, killing the cousin, and imprisoning and torturing Elena in her own house.

Kept in a small, kennel-like space and made to eat table scraps and drink out of her cousin's skull, Elena is not killed immediately. Jaime keeps her alive "porque una muerte breve es pequeño castigo para quien hizo tal maldad contra un hombre que ... la puso en el alteza ..." (*Desengaños* 249) [because a quick death is small punishment for one who committed such a crime against a man who ... raised her to such heights (158, mod.)]. This calculated dehumanization amounts to a grotesque, concerted effort to contain a woman through deprivation and imprisonment. Jaime also allows the slave to take the wife's place at the table and in her bedroom, thus punishing Elena even further by substituting her with a black slave. Easily threatened by female sexuality–which, from Jaime's experiences with the princess, has strong associations with danger and death–Jaime reacts to the possibility of his wife's impropriety with an elaborate plan to punish her.

The excesses of Jaime's actions take men's efforts to contain women to morbid extremes. As Cristina Enríquez de Salamanca has observed, Jaime reacts perfunctorily, blindly, throughout the tale: he loves the princess without knowing anything about her, he marries Elena because she reminds him of his first lover, and he complies with the honor code without reflection or hesitation.[19] As in most of the tales of the *Desengaños*, a woman suffers because of a man's rigid and excessive assertion of control over women. The emphasis on entrapment imagery in the novella speaks on a symbolic level to the obsession with containing women's open, uncontrollable bodies.

The fifth novella in the *Desengaños amorosos* also exemplifies the closely drawn relationship between spatial and bodily discourse.

---

[19] For more on the motif of blindness, see Enríquez's "Irony, Parody, and the Grotesque in a Baroque Novella."

The complex sexual politics of "La inocencia castigada" engage the concept of justice, showing definitively that women are subject to individualized notions of justice and often are not protected by the official justice system. The narrator, Laura, introduces the story by giving its moral: "En cuanto a la crueldad, no hay duda de que está asentada en el corazón del hombre, y esto nace de la dureza de él" (*Desengaños* 264) [As for cruelty, there's no doubt that it dwells in the hearts of men, that is why they're so hard-hearted (173)].

The odd, sexualized intrigue of "La inocencia castigada" presents a scenario in which all of the male characters act cruelly toward the protagonist, Inés. Diego persistently courts the young, beautiful, married woman. After repeated rejection, he seeks the help of a clever intermediary, who devises a scheme by which another woman will dress in Inés's clothes and stand in for her as Diego's sexual partner. During a two-week period, Diego believes that he is having an affair with Inés, only to find out that he has been deceived. More dogged than ever, he turns to a necromancer, who creates a wax representation of Inés that will make her come to Diego's house whenever he desires her. Diana Álvarez-Amell has assessed the power of this wax image, arguing that it immobilizes Inés's agency and puts her body and mind entirely at the disposal of male desire (29).

For the next month, Diego summons Inés to his bedroom at night, having sex with her even though she has only a vague awareness that something is askew. Although she is tormented by the memories of the nightly sessions, Inés ascribes the thoughts to inexplicable nightmares and tries to continue living normally. Susan Paun de García suggests that these nightly sexual encounters, which I read as rape, can also be read as necrophilia in that Inés seems to be nearly dead when under the spell ("Magia" 50). As Whitenack has indicated in "'Lo que ha menester,'" Zayas uses "most of the conventions of the chivalric motif, whereby seducers use magic in order to satisfy lust, and the victims only give in because they are not themselves" (175). With the discovery of the ruse, Inés's degree of participation and the pronunciation of her innocence receive great attention. The actions of the Corregidor and the brother, who repeatedly test the degree of Inés's complicity before declaring her innocent, belie a need to prove beyond any doubt that she did not go to Diego willingly. They turn Diego over to the Inquisition and proclaim Inés's innocence. Nonetheless, the husband and brother, convinced by the sister-in-law of Inés's complicity, decide to punish Inés for having an affair. So, in spite of her exoneration by the authorities and her own overwhelming feelings of guilt–which include begging her husband for a swift death–Inés is subjected to a secondary justice system based on the honor code.[20]

Inés's punishment amounts to a plan meant to rein in female sexuality and agency. The descriptions of the entrapment epitomize Zayas's critique of women's physical and psychological confinement. Walled into this tiny space, Inés has no contact with the outside world for six years. The emphasis on spatial confinement communicates an obsession with containment on the part of the sister-in-law, husband, and brother. By enclosing Inés in the smallest space possible, her relatives choose a method of torture that symbolically responds to the threat of her "loose" sexuality. The role of the sister-in-law does not go unremarked: the frame characters later condemn the men for their cruelty and the sister-in-law who, as a woman, should have taken pity on Inés (*Desengaños* 282, 289).

The participation of other women in these acts of betrayal and confinement is counterbalanced in the tale only by a neighbor woman's assistance. Saved by God's guiding hand and this woman's intervention, Inés nonetheless has deteriorated during her captivity. Her body has eaten away at itself and she never will regain her sight. Once again, containment literally marks the female body in this tale, as the description of Inés upon her release makes clear:

> [estaba] . . . tan flaca y consumida, que se le señalaban los huesos . . . los vestidos hechos ceniza, que se le veían las más partes de su

---

[20] Suggesting in "'Lo que ha menester'" that "something is going on besides a complaint at the masculine obsession with honor" (184), Whitenack contextualizes Zayas's treatment of witchcraft and concludes that the use of magic in this tale differs significantly from its use in "El desengaño amando," for here it functions "to warn males that a neglected wife might well be vulnerable to seduction" (186). This interpretation, at odds with Stackhouse's theories about the reconciliation of verisimilitude with magic in the tales (cf. "Verisimilitude"), aligns "La inocencia" with the satirical "El prevenido, engañado" in that the latter serves as a warning to men about the dangers of mistreating women. Valbuena's discussion of "Sorceresses, Love Magic, and the Inquisition of Linguistic Sorcery in *Celestina*" provides an interesting point of comparison to Zayas's own presentation of witchcraft.

> cuerpo; descalza de pie y pierna, que de los excrementos de su cuerpo, como no tenía dónde echarlos, no sólo se habían consumido, mas la propia carne comida hasta los muslos de llagas y gusanos, de que estaba lleno el hediondo lugar. (*Desengaños* 287)

> [(she was) . . . so consumed and emaciated that you could count her bones. . . . Her clothing had disintegrated so you could see most of her body through the tatters. Her feet and legs had no covering because her body wastes, which she couldn't dispose of, had consumed the flesh of her legs up to her thighs, which were covered with sores and worms that swarmed in that gross place. (196)]

The image of the body in decay reveals the suffering of a woman who has fallen victim to personal justice that responds to a masculinist honor code. The description builds on the martyrdom paradigm as well. Perry's description of lay religious women in *Gender and Disorder* resonates with the portrayal of Inés's body: "women who became *beatas* were advised to protect themselves from 'unclean thoughts' by thinking of their bodies as corpses, full of worms" (122).[21] As Williamsen indicates, even the house has been used against Inés; in Zayas's texts the "house serves as an instrument of torture employed against women" ("Challenging" 142). With no recourse to justice, this woman, like many of the victims of the tales, is made grotesque by the injustice that grows out of a cultural obsession with women's chastity. The roles of the female intermediary and the sister-in-law suggest that some women's collusion in these obsessive practices puts their sisters at even higher risk, for the innocent have nowhere to turn until, if they are lucky like Inés, they can join the convent.

Representations of Inés's gaping, worm-filled body capture the complexity of Zayas's bodily aesthetic. Thought of as open vessels —as the passive receptacles of men's seed and of men's honor—women were described by male cultural authorities as being in need of enclosure.[22] Zayas explodes these myths by literalizing, even physical-

---

[21] Perry bases her observations on Pérez de Valdivia's *Aviso*.

[22] Cruz elegantly explains the effects of Inés's entrapment: "As cautionary tale, Inés's immuring serves to shield men from both the horror of the Other, of the castrated and castrating female body, and the allure of its generative power" ("Feminism" 47). In Cruz's psychoanalytic discussion, Inés's removal to the convent echoes her torturous entrapment in the wall, thus indicating that the tale itself is

izing, this ideology: women are made grotesque, made to be open bodies, through men's obsession with controlling sexuality. Rigid compliance with the honor code becomes inscribed onto the female body, and Zayas reflects this inscription back to us by exposing (through bones, skin, flesh) the damage wrought by blind acceptance of the honor code.

Functioning to deconstruct the patriarchal order, the excess of violence permeates the *Desengaños amorosos*. Spatial confinement and the disruption of domestic space hyperbolize the impulse to confine women. Broken, bleeding, expanding, and decaying bodies represent a physical, overstated manifestation of the dangers of a social system that has no reliable mechanism to protect women. While the *Novelas amorosas* depicts private and public spheres as accessible to women and as possible spaces of feminine empowerment, the *Desengaños amorosos* rules out the potential for privacy and safety within even a woman's own home. The countless descriptions of women's enclosure, physical pain, and emotional distress reiterate at the spatial level the limitations placed on women at the intellectual, physical, and emotional levels. The desire to control women effectively squeezes women out of their private spaces in the *Desengaños*. The trajectory toward violence taken by the twenty novellas leads to an ever-limited domestic world, one that brims with violence and violation.

As the violence increases in the *Desengaños amorosos*, women lose ground on the domestic front: male characters exert their authority until finally most of the women are, in fact, controlled by violence. The explosive rage of Dionís, the husband who kills his wife and the entire household in the last novella, exemplifies the male fury that arises periodically in many of the other tales. Unlike the real-life Cosme's wife–spared from impending violence by virtue of public intervention–Zayas's characters often are subjected to violence in the domestic realm. This portrayal of women's confinement refers the reader to men's unquestioned dominance over women. The spatial dynamics also map out the ideologies of gender and help to lay bare the practices by which violence is engendered and gender is constructed. In Zayas's texts, the politics of space are inte-

---

trapped by the male social order's rejection of the feminine: "Her subsequent placement by the patriarchy in a convent, where she lives a 'saintly' life, extends her enclosure and denotes her incapacity to come to terms with difference" (47).

gral to gender relations, in which the domestic sphere of the home and the female body both emerge as contested sites between the sexes. This representation of women as dominated, violated, and enclosed in the private sphere leaves the reader wondering what space, what place, is left for women.

The convent is, in fact, the only space represented as a possible safe haven for women. As Lisis's final choice suggests, the convent represents a way to avoid marriage and to express solidarity with women. While gendered perceptions of the convent's function emerge in the *Novelas amorosas*, the *Desengaños* unapologetically presents this as a space to which women may escape after having been victimized by men. This apparently escapist solution coincides with other early modern women's writings: Christine de Pizan imagines a city of women, Moderata Fonte portrays a widow's home as a refuge, and Aurelia Verdella would do away with men if they were not needed for procreation of the race, for example.[23] Notably, the escapism of Zayas's characters in the *Desengaños amorosos* results directly from women's disillusionment with men. Without psychological or physical room to maneuver, the female subject quite literally takes a beating in the *Desengaños*. The only four surviving female protagonists of the novellas–Isabel, Inés, Beatriz, and Florentina–choose convent life. Depicted as a refuge, the convent represents a violence-free zone for women.

Conventual discourse functions as a counterpoint to the relentless violence of the texts. The unfettered anger and violence of the male characters challenge the reader to reflect on the role of violence in constructions of masculinity.[24] Through the seemingly irrational actions of men who violently overreact to allegations of sexual misconduct, Zayas's texts explore the exploitation of women within the social order. While some of these portrayals of angry, aggressive

---

[23] Jordan's chapter on "Sex and Gender" discusses Verdella's (140-41) and other early modern feminists' positions on integrationist and segregationist sexual politics (134-247). For a complementary analysis of other feminist stances taken in the latter part of the seventeenth century, see Stuurman's "Literary Feminism in Seventeenth-Century Southern France: The Case of Antoinette de Salvan de Saliez."

[24] Boyer has noted that Zayas's novellas "stress the *disorder* inherent in masculinist plots that exalt and ritualize the hegemony of the male protagonist and the patriarchal system at the expense of a powerless female victim" ("Toward a Baroque" 69 n. 12). I would agree, adding that the "masculinist plots" criticized in Zayas's texts encompass both literary and cultural norms.

men recall other, male-authored Golden Age texts, Zayas consistently feminizes the plots, emphasizing the female experience and inscribing the effects of dangerous cultural scripts onto the female body.

Through insistent spatial confinement and physical punishment, the texts subvert the notion that women represent instability, that they cannot be contained. As opposed to the culturally constructed threat of women's grotesque bodies, Zayas's violent male characters pose the single greatest threat to domestic tranquillity. The excess of the texts protests the link between masculinity and violence. Finally, by showing that violence has no boundaries, Zayas's connection of bodies with space criticizes the disempowered position of women in the emerging social order.

CHAPTER FOUR

CROSSDRESSERS, AVENGERS, AND THE PERFORMANCE OF GENDER

> *It does not befit a woman like you to carry a sword, nor to do other manly things that men do. Nor is it always and in all places fitting for a woman to do everything that is proper to a woman . . .*
>
> Giannozzo Alberti

GIANNOZZO Alberti's fifteenth-century prescriptions for proper feminine behavior exemplify the concern for controlling women that is apparent in the dominant discourse of the early modern period.[1] Zayas's depiction of the violence and abuse in relations between the sexes reveals the underside of this compulsive concern. Indeed, the analyses of violence in the previous chapters suggest that Zayas portrays a world in which no mechanism–social or political–functions to check men's behavior.

Faced with these representations of women's exclusion from institutions of justice, we come away from the *Novelas amorosas* and the *Desengaños amorosos* feeling pessimistic about women's possibility for survival. While similarly negative overtones permeate baroque discourse, Zayas constructs a politicized aesthetic that centers on deep-seated problems in gender relations. In doing so, she criticizes the fragility of the very foundations of a social order in which women have no guarantees of protection.

Violence in Zayas's fiction leaves few options to women. Victimized in their homes, many female characters forcibly are enclosed and contained by the men around them. Alberti's comments in the epigraph discursively enact this entrapment. First idealizing femi-

---

[1] Giannozzo Alberti's comments appear in Leon Battista Alberti's *Libri della famiglia* (1441) (qtd. in Jordan 53).

ninity and admonishing women not to bear arms, Alberti goes on to dismiss undiscerning femininity, emphasizing that women should not "do everything that is proper to a woman" in all circumstances. As in Alberti's oppressive schema, women cannot win for losing in Zayas's fictional world.

As any reader of Zayas knows, she is an author who infuses her texts with ambiguity and ambivalence. Just when a large pattern emerges, even a pattern as pervasive as her representation of the containment of women or the denunciation of men, examples come to mind that require a reconsideration of the ideologies at work in the texts. Zayas, in other words, invariably presents us with exceptions to the rules. In the case of spatial dynamics, the dismal picture of women's confinement does not tell the whole story of Zayas's representations of women and men. In addition to those survivors who choose the convent as their refuge, there are other characters who elude and defy containment. The women in "El prevenido, engañado," for example, maintain sexual independence in spite of the male protagonist's attempts to impose his own standards of sexual purity on them. Women in other novellas crossdress, commit adultery, and even murder. Treated as comic, brave, independent, and brazen, the female characters who transgress find ways to subvert behavioral norms. By and large, these transgressions amount to an assertion of agency in matters of honor, sexuality, and violence, as women assume the sexual, behavioral, and political privileges afforded to men.

To the extent that many of Zayas's women characters engage in unconventional gender behavior, they defy, if only temporarily, the cultural impulse to define femininity and control female sexuality. Since many of these transgressions challenge mechanisms of social control, I would like to follow up on the previous chapter's analysis of containment by looking at the most dramatic examples of what can be called "gender transgression"–the blatant defiance of gendered codes of behavior. Like its layered treatment of women's emotional and physical confinement, Zayas's novella collection offers many insights into the strategies individuals might adopt in their refusal to conform to social expectations.

The paired stories "La más infame venganza" and "El verdugo de su esposa" discussed in the previous chapter easily lend themselves to this analysis. In these tales, two suspicious husbands kill their innocent wives. The first woman, Camila, does not tell her husband of another man's advances, whereas the second woman, finding herself in the same situation, informs her husband. Both women end up dead. Before telling "El verdugo de su esposa," the frame tale narrator Nise indicates the purpose of the tale:

> porque se vea que, si Camila perdió con su esposo por callar las pretensiones de don Juan, en el engaño que ahora diré no le sirvió a otra dama para asegurar su crédito con su marido avisarle de las pretensiones de otro don Juan, aunque el cielo abonó su causa. (*Desengaños* 201)
>
> [so you can see that if Camila was ruined because she didn't tell her husband about don Juan's courtship. In the disenchantment I'm about to tell it did another lady no good to inform her husband about the pretensions of a different don Juan despite the fact that heaven supported her cause. (115, mod.)]

Camila and Roseleta attempt to escape the compromised situations in which they are courted and, in Camila's case, raped, by men other than their husbands. The similar resolution of the tales dramatizes the impossibility of overcoming husbands' suspicions of sullied honor. Showing women to be trapped by a system that allows them little control over their lives, these tales, and the collection in general, question whether it pays to comply with dominant models of femininity.

With these nuanced treatments of women's powerlessness in the face of men's aggression, Zayas's novellas unequivocally repudiate violence against women. The representations of gender transgression challenge dominant constructions of gender at the same time that they open up space for reconceptualized boundaries of behavior. As we have seen, many of Zayas's female characters act independently. Tiring of men's abuse and of systemic injustice, female characters often take charge of their lives in ways that lead to tragic or, at times, successful outcomes. This assertion of agency is not uncommon; at least one female character rejects passivity and acts on her own desire in each novella. Some women even go so far as to do those "unfeminine" things warned against by Alberti. By carrying swords, participating in battle, dressing as men, and exerting political power, some of Zayas's women engage in what Alberti calls the "manly things that men do."

In laying claim to a plurality of female subjectivities, Zayas's wide-ranging characterizations question the restrictive gender codes of the period. Desirable as well as undesirable masculine and feminine characteristics are presented and commented upon throughout the novellas. Such models of behavior are most obviously present, as we will soon see, in the frame tale. The blurring of boundaries challenges prescriptive gender ideology such as that espoused by Alberti. The violence enacted by the female protagonists of "La burlada Aminta" and "Al fin se paga todo" is emblematic of such problematization. These tales legitimize female-authored violence, yet also ventriloquize this violence through the trope of crossdressing, in Aminta's case, and, to a lesser extent in Hipólita's case, through borrowed weaponry. Women's transgression also offers another opportunity to explore Zayas's responses to her culture's constructions of masculinity and femininity.

Zayas's novellas constitute both an indictment of the cultural system and a highly self-conscious interrogation of the arbitrary nature of narrowly defined gender codes. Over and over, men go unpunished for victimizing women. Combatting this injustice, some female characters break out of traditional roles in attempts to assert individuality and to seek retribution.[2] As seen in the dynamics of violence, bodies, and space, the emphasis on gender and the repetition of certain behaviors lie at the center of Zayas's interrogation of social ills. Like many of the other plot lines, the avenging characters' appropriations of masculinity and femininity relate to sexuality and desire. In this sense, the transgressors engage different aspects of identity politics for the explicit purpose of attaining their goals of vengeance, escape, or sexual conquest. In spite of their varying motives, these transformations can all be read as fundamentally performative representations of gender.

To flesh out this discussion of gender and performance, I would like to turn to Judith Butler's work on gender and discourse. As one of the key tenets in her analyses of sex, gender, and discursivity, Butler insists (correctly, to my mind) on

> the understanding of performativity not as the act by which a subject brings into being what she/he names, but, rather, as that reiterative power of discourse to produce the phenomena that it regulates and constrains. (*Bodies that Matter* 2)

---

[2] In *Dramas of Distinction*, Soufas refers to dramatic plots in which women usurp traditionally masculine roles as plots that express "the counterdiscourse of flexible boundaries between roles" (20).

Linking her initial analysis of gender as performance (cf. *Gender Trouble*) to the concepts of repetition and regulation, Butler wants us to come to terms with the necessary imbrications of compliance and resistance in the (reiterated) performative act. More probing in its treatment of sex *and* gender than *Gender Trouble*, *Bodies that Matter* questions the status of sex as a biological given and considers how cultural imperatives encourage certain identifications (sexual, affective, and other) and, thus, encourage reiterations of dominant gendered behavior. Butler uses this schema of identification and reiteration to explain the entrenchment of dominant ideologies and to point out that the cultural center is defined by means of such identifications. Butler's emphasis on discursivity provides a key to understanding Zayas's representation of gender relations. Through the repetition of certain patterns of behavior and through layered extranarrative commentaries on such behavior, Zayas's texts offer up bodily performance as an exploration of gender and identity politics.

Zayas's fiction directly engages the meanings produced by repetition and performance. In this sense, Butler's assertion that an individual assumes sexed and gendered identities through the acceptance or rejection of cultural norms of behavior is extremely useful in deciphering the underpinnings of Zayas's representations of gender. The dynamic of acting and being acted upon–itself a dialectic of power–is crucial here, for it speaks to the willful participation of the subject and to the ways that cultural discourses impact an individual. Butler suggests that subject formation depends on

> a process by which a bodily norm is assumed, appropriated, taken on as not, strictly speaking, undergone *by a subject*, but rather that the subject, the speaking "I," is formed by virtue of having gone through such a process. (*Bodies that Matter* 3)

Asserting that both sex and gender are performative processes, then, Butler's *Bodies that Matter* explores the implications of "the exclusionary matrix by which subjects are formed" (3).

Identification with the patriarchal and, in Zayas's culture, Catholic center is effected through the repetition of a matrix of codes. Thus, the individual who identifies with the dominant culture tries to create an alliance with the cultural center by reenacting prescribed roles of gender, religion, class, sexuality, and ethnicity, etc. Conversely, the individual who rejects these prescribed roles does so through disidentification, a process resulting in one's displacement to the cultural margins. Useful for its articulation of the ways in which individuals identify with the center, this framework also leads us to examine the consequences of such identification. Like the forceful critique of access to education, arms, and justice present in Zayas's texts, the consideration of gendered codes of behavior causes us to question who, indeed, has access to inclusion in the cultural center.[3]

Through representations of violence and injustice, Zayas's collection protests the exclusion of women from the center and advocates women's incorporation into the institutional workings of society. Some of the transgressive women in the tales manage to access the privileges of inclusion by taking on masculine identities and behaviors. Zayas calls for the restoration of "proper" social order, suggests modifications to the existing system, and, in less conventional moments, explores fluid constructions of gender and desire. An examination of performativity can help us sort through the complex matrices of exclusion and inclusion, of appropriation and revisionism, of legitimization and devaluation present in the texts. Through these analyses of gender, transgression, and compliance, this chapter aims to contextualize and untangle the political and social implications of presenting gender–in any historical moment or context– as *the* operative category of difference.

I. MODELLING FEMININITY

Bound by social custom, laws, and church teachings, women's subordination to men was defined clearly and programmatically in early modern Spain. Many examples of sanctioned roles for women appear in Zayas's texts. We can use these markers of "proper" femininities to open up the question of gender representations in the novellas. First, it is important to note that the feminization of the collection occurs at the generic, stylistic, and structural levels. Through the choice of the framed novella–a genre that relies on orality and allows for the portrayal of women as agents in the telling

---

[3] One important aspect of this dynamic of identification and marginalization is the question of access. Who, indeed, can gain access to the center merely through compliance with prescriptive behavioral norms? As I discuss in the conclusion, the exclusionary matrix in Zayas's texts sets up a group of insiders (aristocrats) and outsiders (most others).

of stories—Zayas reproduces an accessible narrative structure that encourages gender inclusion both for delivery and reception.[4]

The framed novella provides a likely structure for Zayas's didactic purposes: like Zayas herself "speaking" through her texts to a reading public of men and women, the storytellers in the *Desengaños amorosos* speak to a mixed audience about problems with familial and love relations. As Boyer suggests in her introduction to *The Enchantments*,

> The stories have a dramatic, oral quality that almost demands that they be read aloud, acted out, that the songs be sung. Given the widespread illiteracy in that day and especially among women, this is undoubtedly how the book was read. (xxviii)

Commenting on Cervantes's mention in the *Novelas ejemplares* of private reading as a commonplace activity, Ife has suggested that in the Golden Age "listeners were gradually outnumbered by readers" (22). Even as literacy improved and *literatura de consumo* or popular literature became a mainstay of the growing book trade, many people continued to rely on oral reading for their contact with the written word.[5] Through her choice of genre, Zayas inscribes accessibility into the texts, validates the possibility for women's participation in the literary endeavor, and reproduces the reliance on orality that persisted well into the seventeenth century, when access to education remained limited.[6]

---

[4] Even the new generic denomination of *maravillas* and *desengaños* to denote the tales told, respectively, in the *Novelas amorosas* and the *Desengaños* authenticates and highlights feminine authority and authorship. With regard to orality and feminism, Spieker states that Zayas's feminist thesis influences her prose at every level (154). Donovan's study of the framed novella genre as having its own feminist tradition illuminates the various feminist strategies used by women before and after Zayas (esp. 966-69).

[5] The mark of private reading is evident in Zayas's texts to a certain extent. Brownlee has suggested, for example, that the taboo of homosexuality (especially as seen in the sexual encounter between men in "Mal presagio casar lejos") became a possible topic in the seventeenth century because of the shift to private reading: "Silent reading created an air of intimacy that shut out the outside world, permitting the reader to indulge in all types of fantasies" ("Elusive Subjectivity" 174).

[6] Describing the growing awareness that the masses could support a large book industry, Cruickshank analyzes the shift toward popular literature in "'Literature' and the Book Trade in Golden Age Spain." Nalle has found in Inquisition documents that many defendants testified that they did not own certain chivalric novels about which they were questioned, but did say, "No, but I have heard read aloud

That the collection presents a woman as its central frame tale protagonist underscores the importance of the feminine in Zayas's fictional world. With Lisis as the leader of the soiree and with storytellers taking turns in the narrators' seat, the frame tale mirrors the salons attended by aristocrats and intellectuals alike in the seventeenth century.[7] In turning to Lisis as an exemplary noblewoman, we see that her roles as courtly lady, generous hostess, accomplished poet/singer, and compliant daughter infuse the *Novelas amorosas* with a somewhat idealized portrait of women and femininity. Lisis is presented as a "proper" lady, in other words; but when she reacts angrily to Juan's rejection of her and eventually accepts another man as a suitor, we see that femininity is not circumscribed entirely by passivity in Zayas's textual economy. It is precisely because of Lisis's characterization as an exemplary woman that her defiant withdrawal to the convent in the *Desengaños* resonates as a prudent, albeit radical, course of action.

Offered up as a model of femininity, Lisis occupies the feminine center throughout the collection. The primary narrator and the frame characters recognize this exemplarity. In one scene that summarizes the view others have of her, Lisis is treated with reverence and described as articulate and divine (*Desengaños* 469). Through her we see that positive feminine traits predictably include beauty, virtue, prudence, and generosity. Somewhat less predictably, Lisis's intelligence, wit, independence, and fidelity in friendship and in love also form part of her positive characterization. Lisis's cohorts, the other *desengañadoras*, share her qualities, as do many of the female protagonists of the tales. In this sense, femininity seems limited in the frame tale to a small range of characteristics and abilities that, with the important exception that these are women who speak out, coincide with conventional representations of aristocratic women.

---

such and such a book" (89). See Whinnom's discussion of "The Problem of the 'Best-Seller' in Spanish Golden-Age Literature" for an analysis of fiction's role in the book market.

[7] The fact that women attended and sometimes participated in *academias* supports the appropriateness of the novella genre for Zayas's fiction. Zayas was one of the few women allowed to participate in an *academia*, which was no small achievement considering, as W. King indicates in *Prosa novelística y academias literarias en el siglo XVII*, that women's role in Spanish salons paled in comparison to the situation in France and Italy (59, n. 81). Also see Paun de García's "Zayas as Writer" for a suggestive, yet speculative, analysis of Zayas's attitudes toward *academias*.

Yet this legitimization of less conventional feminine traits in the frame tale directly challenges the dominant discourse of containment and control present in the novellas proper. The *Desengaños amorosos* makes this challenge explicit as the women narrate tales about men's destructive behavior. Throughout both volumes, the valorization of feminine speech and ideas undermines the cultural insistence on female servility and submission. For contrast, we need only consider Fray Luis's authoritative comments on proper femininity:

> es justo que se precien de callar todas, así aquellas a quien les conviene encubrir su poco saber, como aquellas que pueden sin vergüenza descubrir lo que saben, porque en todas es no sólo condición agradable, sino virtud debida, el silencio y el hablar poco. (175)

> [it is necessary that all women, from those who need to cover up their lack of knowledge to those who have no shame in telling all that they know, apply themselves to being quiet; because it is not only an agreeable condition but also an obligatory virtue for women to be silent and to speak little.]

Zayas's texts defy the dictum that women must be silent, and they break with the insistence on women's subordination. With typical complexity, however, Zayas embeds this defiance in seemingly conventional representations of women and gender. Lisis embodies such a contradiction: for all of her apparent compliance with conventional standards of graciousness and beauty, she encourages resistance, criticizes men, and opts for rebellion.

The potentially contradictory coexistence of defiance with compliance informs Zayas's constructions of femininity. By depicting women as witty and strong, the *Novelas amorosas* implicitly communicates the message that, in spite of women's lack of access to justice, arms, and education, they are capable of subverting and circumventing male power. Yet, as the violence against women in "La fuerza del amor" and "El juez de su causa" attests, even smart, steadfast women cannot always manage to escape victimization.

While the female frame tale protagonists share the narrative task with men and safely break with the dicta regarding feminine silence, women within the tales often are punished for speaking out.

The threat of women's speech is hinted at in the *Novelas amorosas*, in which several women provoke men's fear and anger. Jacinto kills a neighbor because he fears that she will tell others about his plan to have sex with Aminta, for example. The frustrated and humiliated Fadrique beats Violante in "El prevenido, engañado" because she takes another lover and because she ridicules his fear. When Laura in "La fuerza del amor" protests her husband's adultery, he beats her and then tries to kill her. Rape victim and angry avenger Hipólita is beaten by her lover when she confesses to murdering her rapist. In all of these cases, women's speech intensifies men's tendency to act violently. Threatened by women's voices–which are representative of the destabilizing female body–male characters respond with violence.

In a discussion of the cultural impetus toward containment, Christine Froula has analyzed the threat posed to men by women who speak out. For Froula, the "hysterical cultural script" is "the cultural text that dictates to males and females alike the necessity of silencing women's speech when it threatens the father's power" (623). The pattern hinted at in the *Novelas amorosas* and solidified in the *Desengaños* captures the stifling consequences of this script. However, as a counterpoint to women being punished for speaking out in the novellas proper, the women in the frame tale enjoy discursive freedom.

In terms of gender and decorum, the frame tale thus functions as a modelling device. Liberated from the cultural prohibition against women's speech, the women characters handily comply with the task of narration. Exploiting this newly granted freedom, the all-female cast of narrators in the *Desengaños amorosos* issues interrelated criticism of men's behavior, masculinist literature, and male-dominated society. While Isabel claims that her story serves as the best example of men's mistreatment of women, for example, Matilde assures us that men are inherently deceitful, and Lisis threatens that women will take up arms if men do not move hurriedly toward reform. Just as Lisis models femininity, the frame tale models a space in which women are encouraged to speak up and, in the *Desengaños*, to speak out.

Lisis uses her privileged position as leader of the soiree and hostess to the guests to summarize these feminist messages. At the end of the *Desengaños*, she inveighs against men for their treatment of women and for their degeneracy. In typical baroque fashion and in tune with early modern feminism, Lisis laments the passing of a time in which men "acted like men" and women did not live in fear. She says that men should be willing to protect women and "no digo yo a ir a la guerra, y a pelear, sino a la muerte, poniendo la garganta al cuchillo" (*Desengaños* 505) [I do not mean only to go to war and fight, but fight to the death, exposing your throat to the knife (400, mod.)]. Pointing to a crisis of the masculine subject, Lisis blames the decline of the Spanish state on men's mistreatment of women and on their effeminacy. Here, Lisis denigrates men's desire to merely show off the insignias that confirm their rank:

> Mas pienso que ya no las deseáis y pretendéis, sino por gala, como las medias de pelo y las guedejas. ¿De qué pensáis que procede el poco ánimo que hoy todos tenéis, que sufrís que estén los enemigos dentro de España, y nuestro Rey en campaña, y vosotros en el Prado y en el río [. . .]? De la poca estimación que hacéis de las mujeres [. . .]. (*Desengaños* 505)

> [But I think you seek and desire nobility only as adornment, like silk stockings and curly locks. Where do you think the lack of courage you all exhibit nowadays comes from; that lets you tolerate the enemy within Spanish borders, with our king doing battle, and you in the park and near the river [. . .]? It comes from your low regard for women. (400, mod.)]

This criticism of men's failed, effeminate masculinity suggests that the texts endorse the prevailing notion in early modern culture that "(the) stability of the social order rests on absolute distinctions between genders" (Howard 422). If things were in order, the texts imply, then men would act like men and women could act like women.[8] Yet, as the violence and victimization of the novellas attest, chaos reigns. And, even more radically, the systemic nature of violence in Zayas points to problems in a social order that sanctions men's control of women's bodies.

---

[8] In her analysis of crossdressing in the English theater, Howard suggests that the increased threat of social mobility in the period can be linked to the trope of crossdressing, as both phenomena directly relate to instability of the social order. Similarly, Garber discusses crossdressing as a "category crisis" that "permits border crossings from one (apparently distinct) category to another" (16). Maravall also mentions the anxiety about the effeminacy of men as a symptom of the larger crisis affecting the whole of society (*Culture of the Baroque* 37).

These critiques signal an important tactical move. Zayas's insistent criticism links the political crisis of the period with a crisis of masculinity. Lisis articulates this message clearly: if gender relations were dependable and, equally important, if they did not privilege men's humanity over women's, then there would be no need for threats (of women turning to violence) or for drastic action (of available women retreating to the convent). Moreover, Lisis's threat of violent action indicts men's misplaced anxieties and legitimizes women's self-protective violence in a topsy-turvy world (*Desengaños* 507).

The frame characters' comments and behavior thus define and specify the basic tenets of the gender schema and the feminist agenda. Lisis's concluding comments blame social and political problems on a crisis of masculinity. These statements, which constitute a response to all of the tales, justify her own entry into the convent. They also model a politicized reading of the gender politics of the novellas. Related to this inscribed feminist response to the texts, the modelling of gender in the frame tale departs from conventional representations of women in that it validates women's intellectual activity, independence, and control. In several fundamental ways, the frame tale functions as a corrective to the social problems brought to light in the novellas: unlike most of the novella protagonists, Lisis and her cohorts enjoy certain control over their lives and speak their minds without retribution. Cast in terms of obligation to self and state, these constructions of gender in the frame tale provide a framework for reading the appropriations of masculinity and femininity in the novellas.

II. PASSING: ACCESS THROUGH EMULATION

Zayas's feminist critiques have two basic facets: men's failure to treat women respectfully and women's lack of access to the body politic. These criticisms span the personal as well as the structural realities of women's dependence on men and their exclusion from the *polis*. This is communicated directly in statements such as, "... el que dijere mal de ellas [las mujeres] no cumple con su obligación" (*Desengaños* 507) [the man who speaks ill of women does not meet his obligations (401, mod.)], and in the characterization of legislators as men who "render women powerless" (*Novelas* 241). I reiterate these comments because they reveal Zayas's consciousness of the interconnectivity between the individual and society, a connection that legitimizes reaching out to individual men and women in her advocacy for cultural change.

In their reliance on the individual's ability to effect reform, Zayas's messages fall within the definition of baroque consciousness as summarized by Maravall in his landmark study, *Culture of the Baroque*. Maravall addresses the confluence of the optimism of humanist discourse with the anxiety over political crisis in the seventeenth century and concludes that, during the baroque period, the possibility for change was thought to lie in human hands (21-30).[9] The tension between the perceived power to control one's environment and the stark social realities plays out on Zayas's frustrated female subjects. Working against patriarchal structures that simply will not admit women as agents, Zayas's female characters fight for inclusion and survival.

Generally speaking, Zayas portrays women as marginal to the body social. In search of justice and refuge, female characters, particularly those of the *Desengaños*, find little relief from violence. Yet there are several tales in which characters challenge the social order by abandoning rigidly conceived gender codes. In these novellas, a fluid vision of gender and difference—familiar to aficionados of *comedia*—is made manifest through characters' disguises, crossdressing, and women's violent acts. These explorations of gender and sexuality locate in the body what Maravall identifies as one of the fundamental problems of the baroque period: the "living tension between authority and freedom" (*Culture* 172). As seen in the frame tale character Isabel's self-fashioning into the Moorish slave Zelima and back into the Christian Isabel, from free woman to slave

---

[9] Beverley echoes Maravall, noting that the paradox of the baroque era lies in the "principle of submission to authority" in conjunction with the "theoretical ideal of the self-willed, independent individual" (225). Cascardi argues that notions about "the accessibility of the good" and the nature of the will converged in the discourse of the period (121-22). With regard to who had access to the benefits of this changing society, Dewald suggests in *Aristocratic Experience and the Origins of Modern Culture* that the "preoccupation with ambition forced nobles to think about the problems of success and failure and to seek explanation of failure in the nature of the polity" (30). For more on literature and aristocratic ideologies, see Martínez Camino's "La novela corta del barroco español" and Otero-Torres, who claims that Zayas's narrative expresses the nobility's anxiety about social change (81).

to nun, the adoption and revelation of different identities question the success with which a culture can exert control over individuals. Dominant conceptualizations of gender topple or at least bend as characters seek to assert their individuality and act out their desire. More pointedly, these transformations and transgressions ask us to reconsider the supposedly fixed nature of categories of difference (gender, sexuality, ethnicity, class, religion, etc.).

A handful of tales in the collection specifically deal with transgressive gender behavior, and it is here that the connection between gender performance and gender politics becomes readily apparent. With plots revolving around female avengers, for example, "La burlada Aminta" and "Al fin se paga todo" show women appropriating and performing traditionally masculine, violent behavior in order to assert control over their (stained) honor. Estela in "El juez de su causa" adopts the identity of a male soldier after her abduction and near rape, and the Virgin Mary outfits Beatriz as a male healer in "La perseguida triunfante." The two tales involving male crossdressers, "La más infame venganza" and "Amar sólo por vencer," portray men who adopt female identities in order to rape and court women, respectively. These tales have been taken up individually by critics, but by reading them as a group of texts about gender performance, we can examine the collective constructions of gender put forth and often undone in Zayas's texts.[10]

Zayas's representations of transgressive women can be squarely located in the literature of the period. Everything from Byzantine novels to theater to *Don Quijote* depicts women crossing gender barriers in search of freedom of movement and behavior. Along with Carmen Bravo-Villasante's *La mujer vestida de hombre* (*The Crossdressed Woman*), McKendrick's study on *Woman and Society in the Spanish Drama of the Golden Age* continues to serve as a baseline for any consideration of the trope of the *mujer varonil* (the manly woman). McKendrick defines this character as "the woman

---

[10] Articles that deal with the avenger and crossdressing tales individually include: Boyer's "La visión artística," Senabre Sempere's "La fuente de una novela de Doña María de Zayas," Chevalier's "Un cuento, una comedia," and Charnon-Deutsch's "The Sexual Economy" (all on "El juez de su causa"); Williamsen's "Challenging the Code" (on "Al fin se paga todo"); Gorfkle's "Re-constituting the Feminine" and Mary Gossy's "Skirting the Question: Lesbians and María de Zayas" (on "Amar sólo por vencer"); and, on crossdressing in Zayas, Kahiluoto Rudat's "Ilusión y desengaño" and Felten's "La mujer disfrazada."

who departs in any significant way from the feminine norm of the sixteenth and seventeenth centuries" (ix) and rejects the notion that literary depictions of defiant women were based on historical changes (3-44). Shifting her analysis to dramatic traditions, McKendrick discusses Zayas's tales of women avengers within the literary context of the period and concludes:

> These writers [e.g., Lope, Mira de Amescua, Rojas Zorrilla, and Zayas] all used the traditional theme of the vengeful female to explore the idea of sexual equality within the terms of the reigning personal and social code of their day. A concern with the equality in honour of *all* human beings was, after all, a natural progression from that belief in the equality in honour of all men so strenuously upheld in the drama of the period. (275)

As Lisis's final exaltations of women's integrity and her exit to the safety of the convent confirm, the didactic framework of Zayas's novellas certainly endorses the notion of "equality in honour of all human beings" that McKendrick sees in drama. Zayas explores the shortcomings of her society, showing the harm that results from women's marginality.

Closely related to the trope of the female avenger is that of the crossdresser. The standard message expressed by the various discussions and depictions of female crossdressers throughout western Europe is that of a chaotic social order. In the English pamphlets *Haec Vir* and *Hic Mulier* as well as in European drama (including that of Lope, Calderón, Shakespeare, and Jonson), women's appropriation of male attire and behavior enacts the threat that, faced with men's incompetence, women might be forced to usurp male roles.[11] In *Cross Dressing, Sex and Gender*, Bullough and Bullough explain this threat:

> Wearing men's clothes not only symbolically lifted the restrictions put on them by the male-dominated society, but indicated that their husbands, fathers, or brothers were weak and effeminate. (79)[12]

---

[11] *Hic Mulier* and *Haec Vir*, published in 1620, both appear in abridged form in Henderson and McManus's *Half Humankind* (264-89).

[12] Bullough and Bullough historicize cross-dressing in the early modern period in "Playing with Gender" and "Crossdressing Men and Women" (chapters three and four of *Crossdressing, Sex, and Gender*), and Levine's *Men in Women's Clothing* deals extensively with fears of effeminization in English culture in the period.

On her way to exact revenge on the Comendador in *Fuenteovejuna*, Lope's Laurencia expresses her anger at the men's effeminacy, for example. The most obvious example of Zayas's direct attacks on masculinity is Lisis's previously mentioned vituperation on the weakness of the Spanish state, to which she adds an insult about Spanish men being "Frenchified": "Bien dice un héroe bien entendido que los franceses os han hurtado el valor, y vosotros a ellos, los trajes" (*Desengaños* 506, also 505) [Some clever writer has said that the French have stolen Spanish courage and you have stolen French fashion (401)].

Like the transgressive women in drama, the two women in Zayas's fiction who perform violent acts of vengeance are reintegrated into the patriarchal order through marriage.[13] Both Aminta and Hipólita marry, and both leave behind their active rebellion in the process. In this respect, these characters are not particularly innovative or unique. However, the avengers and crossdressers in Zayas's texts actually make visible the factors informing gender construction by appropriating and performing different gender roles. When considered as a group that challenges the boundaries of gender, Zayas's transgressors provide a rich source for the analysis of the interworkings of sexuality, gender, and violence that lie at the heart of the feminist explorations in the *Novelas amorosas* and the *Desengaños amorosos*.

The appropriation and repetition of gendered identities and behaviors–the characters' self-conscious performances of gender– open up moments of instability and indecision, moments in which gender and sexual identity are released from the strictures of cultural norms.[14] Based on tropes popular in early modern literature, Za-

---

[13] As McKendrick states in the conclusion to *Woman and Society*, the *mujer varonil* was "habitually compelled to conform to the social norm, however exciting her temporary departures from it had been" (334). It should be noted that other characters in Zayas might be considered avengers: Jacinta ("Aventurarse") ventures out in search of her lover; Zelima/Isabel ("La esclava") tries to force her rapist to marry her, only to be avenged by a suitor; and Florentina ("Estragos") tries to create a situation in which her lover must marry her. Even Lisis presents herself as an avenger in love to a certain extent. Since none of these characters performs a violent act herself, all are excluded from this analysis. In contrast to the violent avengers, all of these women enter the convent on a permanent basis.

[14] There are many ways to approach the questions of gender codes. Disposing of gender as a redundant category, Grosz argues, for example, that sexuality is "the label and terrain of the production and enactment of sexual difference" (*Space, Time, and Perversion* 213). I take up Butler's categorizations in *Bodies that Matter*

yas's tales of women's violence reinforce the political agenda of the texts. The tales also deconstruct gender by detailing the performances of female characters whose situations demand a circumnavigation of traditional feminine roles.

As Zayas's female characters seek to act or pass as men, they gain access to the freedoms—of movement, of speech, of action—denied them in society.[15] And, as seen in Juan's and Esteban's crossdressing in "La más infame venganza" and "Amar sólo por vencer," the appropriation of femininity allows male characters to penetrate the feminized domestic domain. Put succinctly, the women transgress to gain access to the body politic and the men crossdress to gain access to the female body. From the perspective of late twentieth-century feminism, these questions of access and emulation are linked inextricably. As Gatens summarizes in her consideration of the nation state,

> the modern body politic is based on an image of a *masculine* body which reflects fantasies about the value and capacities of that body. The effects of this image show its contemporary influence in our social and political behavior which continues to implicitly accord privilege to particular bodies and their concerns. . . . It refuses to admit anyone who is not capable of miming its reasons and its ethics, in its voice. (25)[16]

The issues on the table here—male political hegemony and its corporeal implications—play out through the process, as Gatens states, of miming.

Examples of this phenomenon with regard to various categories of difference abound in the Spanish context. The impulse toward

---

(of gender and sex) rather than Grosz's (of sex and sexuality) because Butler's assessment of gender as the performance of sex encompasses a wider range of possibilities of behavior and motivations than Grosz's inherently "sexualizing" collapse of the categories. That is, sex and sexuality do not seem to readily admit non-sexual impulses.

[15] A well-studied subject, literary crossdressing has held the attention of many scholars, particularly those of early modern Europe, who have mined this trope for its cultural and political implications. For general treatments of transvestism, see Bravo-Villasante's *La mujer vestida de hombre*; Bullough and Bullough's *Cross Dressing, Sex, and Gender*; Garber's *Vested Interests*; and Levine's *Men in Women's Clothing*.

[16] Gatens bases her arguments on Hobbes, Locke, and others. These thinkers postdate Zayas, but their observations, and the modern nation state, grew out of the model of the nation that arose in the early modern period.

unification and homogenization in the fifteenth and sixteenth centuries, and the concern with distinguishing between old and new Christians speak to the increasing pressure for religious and ethnic "others" either to mimic dominant identities or to face persecution. As we have seen, the discourses of religion, humanism, politics, and law went to great lengths to contain women. For women to gain even limited recognition and privilege, they had to comply with narrow definitions of femininity. Zayas's texts protest the injustice of the system and suggest that women cannot depend on mimicry to secure their safety.

Gatens's analysis of access to the body politic through imitation complements Butler's observations about the repetition of gender codes as a sign of identification with the cultural center. Gatens focuses on the *effects* of imitation (access to the political sphere) and Butler on the *process* of imitation (the reiteration of performative acts). Between the two we get a sense of the individual's (and the individual body's) relationship to the body politic. Zayas's tales involving women avengers and crossdressers instantiate the usurpation of masculinity–a performative imitation–as a means to gain access to male privilege. These processes of usurpation expose the constitutive elements of masculinity as well as the hegemony of the masculine subject.

A relatively contained, straightforward example of female crossdressing occurs in the ninth novella of the *Desengaños amorosos*. The Virgin Mary adorns Beatriz with all the accoutrements of a male healer so as to enable Beatriz to heal her evil brother-in-law's soul and to make amends with her husband. This tale does not mediate this act of crossdressing. Like the outfitting of Gracia ("El prevenido") with armor, Beatriz merely is dressed as a man. In the crucial moment of revelation, her queenly garb miraculously appears on her body. As with most female crossdressers in literature of the period, Beatriz's male identity allows her to travel into the public sphere. The twist to this conventional function of literary crossdressing arises in her actions as a doctor: the male garb legitimizes Beatriz's knowledge and, in a move reminiscent of male crossdressers' interest in gaining access to the opposite sex, permits her to have access to the male body.

The opening tale of the *Novelas amorosas*, "Aventurarse perdiendo," represents crossdressing as an automatic, obvious decision for a woman in danger in the public sphere. Motivated by the need to protect herself after being robbed by a male companion on the way to Barcelona, Jacinta secures her safety by selling a ring (a symbol of femininity and virtue) and using the money to buy men's clothes. Beyond this brief description of changing her outward appearance, the text does not allude to Jacinta's performance of masculinity. The superficiality of such an appropriation becomes apparent when Fabio finds her dressed as a shepherd in the hills, for he guesses her true identity almost at once. Showing little reluctance to forfeit her disguise, Jacinta welcomes his suggestion that she enter a convent, and agrees to obey Fabio's every command (*Novelas* 78).

In this tale, the privileges afforded by masculinity remain limited to safety in the public sphere. Endangered by the mere fact of her sex, Jacinta adopts a male identity only until a "real" man appears to take over the masculine role of protector. Her superficial appropriation of masculinity provides one model for performing gender: masculinity protects her from danger but, when given a chance, this female character returns to her true, "feminine" state. "Aventurarse perdiendo," like many early modern crossdressing texts, offers insight into male privilege and calls attention to social disorder through the temporary exchange of gender roles. In essence, this tale enacts the transvestism most familiar to us from its many examples on the stage, where women characters most commonly take on a male disguise as a means to gain mobility and guarantee their safety in public. Unlike the theatricality of such transformations seen on the stage or even in other prose fiction, here the implications of transvestism seem relatively narrow, particularly in that Jacinta limits the descriptions of her experience to the donning of clothes and the acceptance of a man's job.

A more profound exploration of gender performance occurs in the ninth tale of the *Novelas amorosas*. In "El juez de su causa," Estela transforms herself into a valiant soldier after venturing into the public sphere as a woman. The plot for this novella originates with a real-life female soldier, Catalina de Erauso, and the many fictionalized renderings of her life. The sandwiching of this novella between two fundamentally unbelievable stories suggests that, in terms of structure, the *Novelas amorosas* moves toward inverisimilitude. Indeed, the last three novellas–"El imposible vencido," "El juez de su causa," and "El jardín engañoso"–deal with unlikely scenarios involving kidnapping, war, devils, and resuscitation.

The novella that precedes "El juez de su causa" models a conventional vision of femininity through a virtuous female protagonist. In "El imposible vencido," Leonor faithfully waits for her lover to win his fortune and return to marry her. Anxious to marry Leonor off to a wealthier suitor, her parents convince her that her lover has died so that she will marry the man of their choice. This leads to Leonor's sudden death, from which her true love resuscitates her. They live, as we might expect from this fairy tale, happily ever after. In spite of its reliance on the trope of female weakness and male strength–the woman dies and the man restores life–this tale emphasizes loyalty in love. It also provides fodder for a message that arises sporadically in Zayas's texts: women should not be forced to marry against their will.[17]

In addition to their probable familiarity with the pre-texts relating to Catalina de Erauso's life, readers thus come to "El juez de su causa" prepared for conventional gender exemplarity and unlikely reunions like those found in Leonor and Rodrigo's saga of love lost and found. The positioning of "El juez de su causa" between farfetched tales about love ("El imposible vencido") and the devil ("El jardín engañoso") structurally highlights the fantastic nature of this, the ninth novella of the *Novelas amorosas*. Capitalizing on the remarkable example of an adventurous woman turned soldier, Zayas represents her protagonist's search for justice and love as a search for agency and power. Like Erauso in *Lieutenant Nun*, Estela also establishes a military identity for herself and relinquishes this male identity only when no other options remain. Like Erauso, Estela holds on to her male identity until forced by circumstance to relinquish it. Given the similar attention dedicated to Estela's experi-

---

[17] Although some critics have suggested that Zayas unambiguously endorses women's right to choose their husbands (e.g., Redondo Goicoechea, "Introducción" [36] and Montesa [116]), Yllera is correct in pointing out the textual ambivalence on this point (50-51). In support of the first opinion, we can look to several characters who, after marrying men whom they do not necessarily know or love, fall victim to their husbands' mistreatment or violence (e.g., in "El prevenido, engañado" and "Mal presagio casar lejos"). Others devise schemes to avoid unwanted marriage (e.g., in "El juez de su causa"). Yet the women in many other tales marry or agree to marry the men of their choice and also are abandoned or victimized (e.g., "La burlada Aminta," "La fuerza del amor," "La más infame venganza," "Estragos que causa el vicio," etc.). In fact, the latter pattern of women's willingness to marry and their subsequent victimization prevails in the collection as a whole, which suggests that Zayas does not sharply focus her didacticism on women's choice in marriage but, rather, on women's precarious position in male-female relationships.

ences as a woman and to her experiences as a "male" soldier, the tale erases the dichotomy between masculine and feminine characteristics. Finally, both the processes and results of gender imitation come to the surface in this story of kidnapping, violence, and eventual triumph.

Like other crossdressing stories, "El juez" highlights women's lack of access to individual and social power. Denied her choice of husband by parents who value social prestige over their daughter's happiness, Estela plots with her chosen suitor Carlos to steal away and marry secretly. The plan depends on his initiative, for he will have to make the arrangements for the journey. Restrictions on her movement in the public sphere are made explicit when the Moor Amete schemes to kidnap Estela by leading her to believe that Carlos will take her away and marry her. As the plot thickens, the reader's awareness of women's reliance on men heightens: like Estela, who waits for Carlos, another woman (Claudia) relies on Amete's plan, by which they will both pair up with the love objects of their choice. A noblewoman of "free customs" and ill-repute who is in love with Estela's lover, Claudia conspires with Amete to kidnap Estela. During a year of hardship for Estela, her family blames Carlos for her disappearance. Until this point, the tale parallels the trials of Leonor and Rodrigo in "El imposible vencido." Yet, with the introduction of violence, Estela's fate takes a turn that propels her into an extended, gender-bending adventure.

During the prolonged period spent with Amete and Claudia, Estela repeatedly laments her misfortune. In this way, the virtuous Estela–whose only act of rebellion was her intended defiance of her parents' wishes–continues to model femininity and grows weaker as the kidnapping ordeal continues. Assisted by Claudia, Amete arranges to rape Estela if she will not comply with his wishes to have sex with her. In spite of her debilitated state, Estela finds the strength to reject Amete's overtures, but he physically retaliates against her. According to the narrator, the beaten Estela relies on the last and most ordinary resort of women in danger: she screams (*Novelas* 386).

I have laid out the unfolding of the narrative and the characterization of Estela to this point precisely because I want to draw attention to their conventionality. Unable to plan an escape from her home but willing to trust Carlos's servant, Estela is complicit in her own kidnapping. Unable to defend herself with physical strength, she cries out for help. Even Claudia, who shows a certain resourcefulness when she crossdresses and becomes Carlos's servant, fails to exert influence over men. She, too, falls victim to Amete, who betrays her in spite of the assistance she gives him. Subordinated to a masculinist power structure and to individual men's power, women exert very little influence in the first half of this tale. Like many of Zayas's female characters, these women are not completely weak or guileless, yet they have little power in what is portrayed as a man's world.

Estela's inability to maneuver or to defend herself seems to relate to her female identity in the first section of the novella, but her rapid transformation into a "male" soldier urges the reader to reconsider this initial assumption. Estela's success as the soldier Fernando suggests that her previous lack of power related not to her own personal identity as a woman but, rather, to the circumstances in which she found herself because she was a woman. Her inability to choose her mate, venture into the public sphere, and avoid victimization underscores the problems resulting from the constraints placed on women.

Whereas Estela previously had no input into her parents' choice of spouse for her, no access to arms to defend herself, and no freedom of movement in the public sphere, she enjoys all of these privileges when dressed as a man. In that Estela enjoys her male role and easily makes the transition from woman to "man," this character's crossdressing highlights the material differences between men and women as the primary differences between the sexes. Most analyses of crossdressing focus on the freedom afforded women characters when they take on male disguise, as Yarbro-Bejarano suggests in a general discussion of the female crossdresser in literature: "Crossdressing frees her from the restrictions, enclosure, sexual vulnerability, and passivity that define the feminine position" (102). Indeed, once Estela adopts a male identity, she moves about successfully as an agent, free to pursue her desires and goals.

However, some gaps surround Estela's adoption of her masculine military identity. Estela's decision to change her appearance and behavior marks a point of ambiguity, for example. After the Prince of Fez sets her free and gives her Christian servants for protection, Estela hears that Charles V has begun fighting in North Africa. Without explanation, she dismisses two of her three companions, takes on a male disguise, and searches for the battlefields. Once again, the question of this character's motivations remains completely subordinated to her actions. But the silence surrounding Estela's possible motivations for this transformation suggests that this is an automatic decision, one that transparently presents her with an opportunity for action. Unlike Jacinta in "Aventurarse perdiendo," Estela does not adopt a male identity in order to secure safety in the public sphere. Given the first opportunity to make a decision for herself, she simply chooses access to the action and agency afforded men.

The actual process of imitation receives little attention here: Estela presents herself as Fernando and acts on this identity by showing military prowess and even saving the life of the Holy Roman Emperor. In addition to her military might, Estela also seeks power, accepting the king's rewards for her success on the battlefield and going so far as to request the position of viceroy of Valencia upon the death of the previous viceroy. Finally, Estela sits as the judge of her own case. Put in the powerful position of judging whether or not her lover should be held accountable for her disappearance, Estela performs authority with a certain zeal. Given that she takes so much time to decide in the case, she seems reluctant to surrender her male role. As Charnon-Deutsch has suggested about this protracted scene, "While *deciding* what for her and the reader is the unquestioned innocence of her former suitor, Estela is as dilatory as a reader's patience would probably allow" (124). She seems to enjoy her power, in other words, and does not immediately relinquish the male identity that allows for this power. Estela's imitation of masculinity consists primarily of action and of discursive power. Quickly mastering these behaviors, she easily passes as a man.

The rewards for successful usurpation of masculinity are tangible and plentiful. Even though Estela's lover reaps the benefits of her masculine performance in that he takes over her position and her titles, Estela does not forgo all of her rewards at the end. In fact, her success and power culminate in one final manipulation: Estela takes advantage of her parents' amazement at the revelation of her identity to secure their approval of her choice of husband. The gender dynamics of this story allow the reader to glimpse women's potential as leaders, warriors, and politicians. Estela's automatic decision to become a soldier, her success as a soldier, and her unapologetic hunger for power all point to the ease with which women might step into men's roles, the ease with which women might usurp masculinity, if given the chance.

The tale sets limits on this performative usurpation, however. Claudia, who attempts to steal Carlos away from Estela by crossdressing and becoming his servant, does not enjoy success as a "man." In fact, the condemnation of Claudia's actions by the male character Amete underscores the threat posed by women's performativity. Amete uses Claudia's performativity to his benefit, suggesting that her sins consist of trying to hurt the man she loves and of breaking with conventional femininity. These actions tell him that she has debased herself, becoming a woman "dispuesta a cualquier acción" (*Novelas* 378) [inclined to any sort of action (278, mod.)]. Similar to Manuel's dismissive treatment of Isabel in "La esclava de su amante," this comment hints at the dangerous enterprise of women's bodily transformation, the dangers of women daring to cross boundaries of behavior to achieve their desire.

These remarks, and the characterization of the ill-intentioned Claudia as a foil to Estela, bring questions of the body–the body politic and the individual body–to the fore. Crossdressing affords Estela freedom of choice and freedom of action, and this marks a fundamental difference between her life as a woman and her life as a man. This tale overtly decenters male privilege by demystifying masculinity: the process of gender imitation receives minimal attention (i.e., Estela suddenly *is* a male soldier), while the results of such imitation are potent. The threat of women usurping masculinity is tempered by Estela's unrealistic military ability and sudden rise to fame. The threat is contained in the final instant by Estela's revelation of her identity and the transfer of her titles to Carlos. So while Estela models masculinity for male characters and male readers, as Charnon-Deutsch has argued (125), the pleasure and success Estela achieves through her masculine identity suggest that masculinity is easily performable and fundamentally performative. Within the textual economy of Zayas's novellas, this capacity for successful performance is good news for the woman who seeks access to the *polis*, for the woman capable, to use Gatens's description of access to the modern body politic, of "miming its reasons and its ethics" (25).

The rewards of performance are circumscribed by certain factors, however. Claudia's inability to obtain her goal while dressed as a man relates to the dynamics of class and gender in Zayas's work. We should remember that, although noble, Claudia is portrayed as a woman who has failed to meet the expectations of her class and whose desire conflicts with that of the virtuous, aristocratic protagonist. In the end, Claudia remains unfulfilled in her quest for love and is executed for her complicity in Estela's kidnapping and near-rape. Like the cases of the intermediary who arranges for a prostitute to pose as Inés in "La inocencia castigada" and the black slave substituting for a white man's wife in "Tarde llega el desengaño," Claudia is punished. All three characters are condemned for their actions: the intermediary is whipped and exiled, and the slave and Claudia are killed. Contrasted with the successful ruses, disguises, and identity changes of the properly aristocratic protagonists (e.g., Aminta, Estela, Zelima/Isabel, Beatriz, etc.), the eventual failure of the minor characters suggests a larger dynamic that legitimates claims on performance only if the characters belong to and are accepted as legitimate members of the dominant class and ethnic group.

Sustained performances of masculinity help Zayas's crossdressing heroines achieve access to political power and physical freedom. The emulation of men leads to relief from the constraints placed on women just as it leads to other rights and privileges. Yet what of men who emulate women? A less frequently explored trope, male crossdressing nevertheless appears occasionally in the literature.[18] Zayas's examples of male crossdressing, which occur in the *Desengaños amorosos*, turn the question of access on its head: the male characters crossdress in order to gain access to the private sphere and, more precisely, to the female body. In "La más infame venganza," Juan fails in his courtship of the married woman Camila. Determined to have sex with Camila in order to take vengeance on her husband, he finally decides that the only way to gain an audience with her is by impersonating a woman:

> [don Juan] se vistió un vestido de los mejores que tenía su hermana, y tocándose y componiéndose de suerte que pudiese pare-

---

[18] Similar patterns of crossdressing arise in another woman-authored texts of the period. In Ángela de Azevedo's *El muerto disimulado* [*The Feigned Death*], a man and a woman crossdress for reasons similar to those in Zayas's texts: the female character, Lisarda, needs freedom of movement in the public sphere, while the male character, Clarindo, wants access to the private sphere. In her analysis of the play, Soufas contrasts the frivolity of Clarindo's crossdressed appearance with the gravity of Lisarda's own position: while Lisarda dresses as a man to avenge her family members' deaths, her brother Clarindo merely wants to test Jacinta's love for him (*Dramas* 129).

cer mujer, se entró, cubierto con su manto, en una silla, y se hizo
llevar a casa de Camila, llevando consigo dos amigos de su par-
cialidad, que le hiciesen resguardo. (*Desengaños* 192)

[don Juan donned one of his sister's best dresses, and, making
himself up so that he would seem to be a woman and covering
himself with a mantilla, he got into a hand-chair that took him to
Camila's house accompanied by two trusty friends to serve as
guards. (105, mod.)]

Juan's performance of femininity incorporates female clothes and
behavior. When he arrives at Camila's house, he presents himself as
a noblewoman in distress, covering his face as if out of humility
and letting Camila lead him by the hand into her private quarters.
With the door locked behind them, Juan abruptly sheds his costume and reasserts his masculinity by pressing a dagger against
Camila's breast and then raping her. The discrepancies between
the male and female protagonists in this novella dramatize the tensions between femininity and masculinity: Juan's passivity as a
woman and his actions as a man find their counterpoints in Camila's compassion for an unknown woman and Carlos's violent plan
for vengeance against his raped wife.

This short description of male crossdressing in "La más infame
venganza" introduces the connection between male transvestism
and deception that later is developed at length in "Amar sólo por
vencer." The plot of "Amar," like many of Zayas's novellas, contains
what seem to be two stories in one: first, Esteban dresses as a female servant in order to be closer to the fourteen year old he is pursuing; later, after confessing his identity and his love to Laurela, he
takes her away, only to have sex with and abandon her. The second
part of the tale deals with the mistreatment of Laurela by her father,
uncle, and aunt, who arrange to punish the young woman by top-
pling a wall onto her and her handmaid. The violence of the story
relates unequivocally to women's compromised position in the sexual
economy. Indeed, the dismissive and violent treatment of women
found here also appears in other novellas in the *Desengaños
amorosos*. The eroticism surrounding Esteban/Estefanía's presence
in the household creates a textual ambivalence that flies in the face
of the more rigidly cast dominant representations of masculinity
and desire found both in Zayas and in male-authored literature.

The success with which Esteban penetrates Laurela's space suggests that femininity, like masculinity, is reproducible and performable. While his transformation into a woman relies on a sartorial change, Esteban's sustained performance of femininity heavily depends on his ability to sew, write, and talk like a woman. He even sings at the behest of Laurela's father, Bernardo, who spends the next year trying to sleep with Esteban/Estefanía. Faithful to this character's change in appearance, the text refers to Esteban in the feminine throughout his crossdressing stint. The narrator calls attention to the entrenched sexual difference that remains despite his costume, indicating that Esteban/Estefanía complies with the request to sing because, "como no era mujer más que en el hábito, no la ocupó la vergüenza" (*Desengaños* 307) [(s)ince she was a woman in dress only, she didn't know the meaning of shame (215)]. Although layered in its repetition of feminine behaviors, Esteban's performance fails to convince the other female servants, who doubt Esteban/Estefanía's female identity. For the young Laurela–the object of this erotic attention–the question never arises.[19]

Esteban/Estefanía's repeated expressions of love for Laurela make the female servants wonder about this character's "true" sex and make what we now call sexual orientation the focal point for much of the first section of the story. Esteban/Estefanía's outspoken defense of homoeroticism complicates sexuality and gender for the other members of the household, who listen to numerous declarations of this presumed woman's love for Laurela. Esteban/Estefanía's defense of love–of what the others take to be love between women–brings us back to corporeality, for he casts love as a matter of the soul, not of the body. Like Zayas in "Al que leyere," Esteban/Estefanía insists on the soul's lack of sexual specificity. While Zayas means to legitimize her own intellectual production with the assertion of equality in the preface, Esteban/Estefanía seems to legitimize female homoeroticism:

---

[19] Zayas's use of pronouns that correspond to the character's appearance adds yet another dimension to the homoeroticism of this particular tale. Clearly, Laurela's sustained naivete vis-à-vis Esteban/Estefanía's disguise opens up a space for the exploration of female homoeroticism that is stifled by the "heterosexual order" (Gorfkle 84; Gossy 27). Gorfkle suggests that Laurela is positioned as her father's rival for Esteban/Estefanía, a fact that might contribute to the father's violence toward his daughter later in the story (82-84).

pues para amar, supuesto que el alma es toda una en varón y en la hembra, no se me da más ser hombre que mujer; que las almas no son hombres ni mujeres, y el verdadero amor en el alma está, que no en el cuerpo [. . .]. (*Desengaños* 317)

[with regard to love, since the soul is the same in male and female, it matters not whether I'm a man or a woman. Souls aren't male or female and true love dwells in the soul, not in the body. (224)]

This subordination of the physical to the metaphysical justifies erotic love between women, particularly since Esteban/Estefanía later condemns pure physical attraction ("apetito") as inferior to the love he purports to feel for Laurela. He even denounces men who love women briefly, men who wrongly proclaim their love when they seek only physical satisfaction.[20]

Now, the great irony (and some might say the great inconsistency) of this tale is that once Esteban reveals his true identity, he proves himself to be just like the men he previously condemned. He convinces Laurela to run off with him by claiming to be a devoted lover equal to her in lineage but not in wealth. Then, in spite of his elaborate scheme and his many proclamations of love, he abandons her after they have sex. In the end, Esteban reveals all of his lies: he is not a woman, not noble, not single, and not interested in risking his life for Laurela. In spite of his experiences as a woman, with women in women's space, Esteban proves himself unchanged.

Read in the context of the ideological framework of the *Desengaños amorosos*, Esteban's comportment comes as no surprise; like the male protagonists of this and other stories, he abuses women. But, when read against Zayas's crossdressed female characters, Esteban's performance of femininity highlights the processes by which femininity is enacted. In contrast to the women crossdressers, who free themselves from culturally imposed constraints by adopting mascu-

---

[20] This tale only endorses female homoeroticism, for it is important to note that this apparent endorsement directly contrasts with the vilification of male homosexuality in "Mal presagio casar lejos," in which two men are caught having sex and the wife then burns the bed. Historically, this differential treatment existed in legal codes and Church law, which condemned sodomy and usually dealt with "lesbian" sexuality when implements (dildos) were used to replicate the penis (cf. Brooten, Gossy, and Perry ["The 'Nefarious Sin'"]).

line postures, Juan and Esteban achieve their desire only when they reveal and reclaim their male identities. The women, on the other hand, act as agents of action when dressed as men, and then return their female identities only after meeting their goals.[21]

This gendered discrepancy in behavior focuses on the privilege of masculinity, on the action and agency made possible by the mere fact of male identity. It must be noted, however, that both the male and female crossdressers free themselves when they engage in these performative, transvestite acts. Freedom of movement is afforded the women–who move about in the public sphere when dressed as men–and the men–who move into intimate domestic space when dressed as women. Like the feminized frame tale, in which women's voices and concerns dominate, Juan's and Esteban's tales of crossdressing take readers into women's intimate spaces. In this sense, new worlds open up to both sexes when crossdressed. Through the processes of gender performance, the constitutive elements of masculinity and femininity are articulated. Such performances result in a layered, fluid conceptualization of gender that strengthens the critique of women's lack of access to the *polis*, validates women's capacity for intelligent action, and, in an intriguing moment of ambiguity, sanctions love between women.

III. Crossing Over: Women Who Kill

The self-conscious performance of gender on the part of the crossdressed characters discussed previously allows for the transcendence of otherwise rigidly defined gender categories. In their focus on men's domination of all facets of the public sphere, the female transvestite plots highlight the freedoms enjoyed by men. The two stories about violent women avengers make explicit similar issues of access: by combining elements of violence with those of gender restrictions, "La burlada Aminta" and "Al fin se paga todo" provide an apt starting point for a summative analysis of the complex relationships between gender, bodies, and culture in Zayas's fiction.

As slaves to the honor code, characters frequently seek vengeance in early modern Spanish literature. Most of the examples

---

[21] Charnon-Deutsch's observations on Estela apply to the other crossdressed women as well: "As a man, there is nothing she is incapable of doing" (124).

are of men seeking vengeance in order to cleanse their stained honor. As victims of men's deception and violence, Zayas's female avengers comply with this pattern to a certain extent. Like commoners and women who lay claim to honor in *comedia*, some of Zayas's women worry about their reputations so much that they kill their offenders rather than live with their dishonor.[22]

The violent acts committed by the female characters in "La burlada Aminta" and "Al fin se paga todo" present the reader, particularly the feminist reader, with the problem of interpreting women's violence. The onslaught of male violence in the *Desengaños amorosos* complicates this issue even further, for the context of increased violence casts the female avengers in a more favorable light, showing them as crusaders in what turns out to be a losing battle against men's aggression. In this sense, the homicides perpetrated by Aminta and Hipólita might be seen as merely reinforcing the patriarchal order, or, in Paul Julian Smith's view, as failing to transcend phallocentric logic (*The Body Hispanic* 31). Yet, as Williamsen has argued, the very act of inserting women into the honor code and giving them active roles speaks for female independence and initiative in a manner consistent with the portrayal of many female characters' autonomy in the *Novelas amorosas* ("Challenging" 140). In their usurpation of violence and assertion of agency, these avengers reinforce the claims on equality between men and women made throughout the collection.

These two tales stand out not only for their inversion of the patterns of violence–with women killing men–but also because they contain four of the eight murders in the *Novelas amorosas*. That women are depicted as capable of premeditated violent acts and, in several cases in "La burlada Aminta," of malevolence toward other women, gives testimony to Zayas's refusal to flatten her representations of gender relations.[23] Although the collection as a whole

---

[22] Among the many studies on honor and the Golden Age, I refer the reader to Castro's "Algunas observaciones acerca del concepto del honor"; Dutton's "The Semantics of Honor"; Honig's *Calderón and the Seizures of Honor*; Larson's *The Honor Plays of Lope de Vega*; Maravall's *Poder, honor y élites en el siglo XVII*; McKendrick's "Honour/Vengeance in the Spanish *Comedia*"; and Stroud's *Fatal Union*. There are many other studies, of course, but these provide a variety of perspectives on the topic.

[23] In *La vida española en el siglo de oro según los extranjeros*, Díez Borque quotes Madame Marie D'Aulnoy's *Relación del viaje de España*, in which she observes that Spanish women are willing to do "todo lo que sea necesario para ven-

moves toward an indictment of violence and injustice under patriarchy, the plot twists and characterizations demonstrate an inclination to account for the variability of human nature.

The representations of women avengers similarly support the feminist didacticism. First and foremost, the processes by which Aminta and Hipólita become violent differ significantly from male characters' violence in the collection. Zayas's examples of female avengers provide two of the few exceptions to violence that otherwise is enacted as an expression of misogyny and as an attempt to protect male interests. The depictions of women as murderers reiterate the patterns of retaliatory violence seen in other tales. The actions of these women avengers also expose the compulsion of men's violent impulses as they are portrayed in these and other novellas. Maintaining the *locus* of propriety in the female body, the tales of women avengers emphasize the need to protect women's integrity. As shown in the violent *Desengaños*, men seek to affirm the integrity of their own honor, which they locate in what is figured culturally as an unstable and unreliable female body. "La burlada Aminta" and "Al fin se paga todo," on the other hand, show that women turn to violence to repair an immediately tangible, provable, and invasive injustice–the violation of their own bodies.

Performing acts associated with masculinity and imposing their own violent solutions on dishonorable situations, the female avengers appropriate the justice that many other tales depict as unavailable to women in the culture. In doing so, these women model a feminized violence in which action is taken in response to concrete acts of physical violation. Both Aminta and Hipólita subvert the honor code by claiming honor for themselves in a system that views women as repositories, not holders, of honor. The feminization of violence occurs not in the mimicry of the violent act, however, but in the reconceptualization of the terms. Rather than jumping to conclusions, believing specious claims, or defending an abstract notion of honor, these women protect personal bodily integrity.

---

garse de sus amantes si las abandonan sin motivo; de suerte que los grandes amores acaban de ordinario con alguna funesta catástrofe" (qtd. in Díez Borque 123) [everything that might be necessary to take vengeance on lovers who abandon them without motive; so that many great loves end ordinarily with some horrific catastrophe]. While the *Relación* should not be taken as a reliable historical source, the comment does suggest that ideas about honor in the period might not have excluded the possibility of women's vengeance.

The narrator Matilde validates women's violence in her introduction to "La burlada Aminta." Speaking to the women listeners, she says that her tale will articulate women's obligation,

> que es a no dexarnos engañar de las invenciones de los hombres, o ya que como flacas mal entendidas caigamos en sus engaños, saber buscar la venganza, pues la mancha del honor, sólo con sangre del que le ofendió sale. (*Novelas* 81)
>
> [which is not to let ourselves be deceived by men's trickery. Foolishly and without thinking, we fall into their snares, when we should be learning how to avenge ourselves, since stained honor can be cleansed only with the blood of the offender. (45-46, mod.)]

In recapitulating the basic elements of the male-oriented honor code, this statement by Matilde claims violence as a woman's right. Keeping in mind that narrators and characters repeatedly lament the denial of women's access to arms, we can read Matilde's declaration of female agency as encouraging women to mimic men, to protect themselves by forging access to the male privileges of honor and violence. There is no paradigmatic change here; except for the fact that the honor code is made available to women, it remains intact. However, Matilde's comments do prepare us for a shift in the justification of violence that occurs with women avengers, whose motivations for revenge are based on concrete evidence of bodily violations.

Naive and young, the orphan Aminta allows herself to be led into a clandestine marriage with Francisco, a married man known under the alias of Jacinto. Francisco abandons Aminta and runs off with his lover. After she leaves her uncle's home, Aminta faces the consequences of her naivete: under suspicion of killing his niece, her uncle has been incarcerated, and Jacinto has escaped with a lover. Two women, the neighbor, Elena, and Jacinto's lover, Flora, take part in Aminta's deception. Both women meet their deaths, and they are condemned by the narrator as traitors to women's cause. The isolated Aminta makes a comment that applies to the honor code and, more generally, that demonstrates great insight into the devaluation of the feminine in her culture: she attempts to kill herself because "con la muerte de sola una mujer, se restauran las honras de tantos hombres" (*Novelas* 106) [With the death of one lone woman, the honor of many men will be restored (65, mod.)]. Prevented from carrying out this rash act by Martín, Aminta devises an elaborate scheme for avenging her honor.

When her new suitor, Martín, agrees to participate in the plan for vengeance, he agrees to play a feminine role. Committed to resolving her own problems, Aminta denies him access to violence, "porque supuesto que yo he sido la ofendida, y no vos, yo sola he de vengarme" (*Novelas* 108) [since I am the offended one, and not you, I alone must avenge my honor (66, mod.)]. Aminta decides to dress as a man for purposes of safety (*Novelas* 108) and to travel in search of Francisco and Flora. While Aminta works for Francisco as his servant, Martín grows jealous. Moreover, Martín reacts to the enclosure he must endure–an enclosure that clearly parallels that endured by women in other novellas. Martín complains "que no podía sufrir verse encerrado en casa, ni a ella en la de un hombre, que había sido su primer amor" (*Novelas* 116) [He could no longer stand staying shut indoors, nor could he bear the thought of her living in the house of the man who had been her first lover (72)]. Aminta's performance of masculinity effects an inversion of gender roles by limiting a man's actions and control. Like many of Zayas's female characters in similar situations, Martín reacts adversely to the constraints placed on him.

In contrast to Martín's dissatisfaction with the role reversal, Aminta enjoys tremendous gains in her crossdressed identity. Aminta acts out masculinity in her dress and her daily activity. She even takes on the name of Jacinto, the name by which she knew Francisco when they were a couple. But when Aminta speaks of love, she continues to speak in a feminine voice, singing a song that indicts an ingrate named Jacinto (i.e., Francisco himself) for his deception of a young woman:

> ¿para qué, Jacinto ingrato,
> causa de mi eterna pena,
> con falso y fingido amor
> engañaste mi inocencia?
>
> (*Novelas* 113)

[why, ungrateful Jacinto, cause of my eternal sorrow, with love false and feigned did you deceive my innocence? (70)]

Aminta looks like a man, yet adopts a female perspective in her song. She also impresses the others with her ability to sew; in addition to these 'feminine' skills, she demonstrates great dexterity with reading, writing, and counting (*Novelas* 112). Symbolic of Aminta's ability to perform masculinity, this convincing gender performance characterizes her masquerade to the very end. Aminta's violent acts are equally fraught with tension between her two identities. She stabs Francisco and, when his lover Flora awakens, she delivers Flora's death sentence: "Traidora, Aminta te castiga y venga su deshonra" (*Novelas* 117) [Traitor! Aminta punishes you and avenges her dishonor! (73)].[24] Delivered in the third person by a crossdressed woman, this statement is doubly ventriloquized.

Aminta's act of violence contrasts directly with Francisco's abuse of her and his murder of the servant Elena. Driven by desire, he first found pleasure in his deception of Aminta and later killed Elena so she would not turn him in. Aminta's autonomously achieved vengeance inserts her into the male-centered honor code. In that Aminta redresses the bodily harm done to her, her actions circumscribe vengeance in concrete, corporeal terms. This performance of masculinity relies on an overlay of gendered values, characteristics, and behaviors.

The other female protagonist who commits murder, Hipólita in "Al fin se paga todo," takes revenge on her rapist.[25] The frame narrator Miguel uses unproblematized language to capture the lesson of Hipólita's misadventures. Miguel declares that the tale proves that evil always is punished and goodness rewarded–a premise undermined by most of the other novellas:

---

[24] Flora's complicity in the deception of Aminta is clear from the beginning, but this does not minimize the implications of a woman murdering another woman. In the lack of resolution of this conflict, the text resists absolutism in the characterization of women. It also shows women as capable of violating the code of female solidarity. Women's solidarity in Zayas is the topic of Maroto Camino's "*Spindles for Swords*" and is discussed by Cruz in "Feminism" (43).

[25] As mentioned, there are two other female murderers in the collection. While courted by Fadrique, Beatriz kills a black man with her sexual appetite (*Novelas* 184) and another, unnamed, lover drowns her husband (*Novelas* 204). Since these women are secondary (and even tertiary) characters, I exclude the incidents from my analysis. See Brownlee's analysis of these women's actions ("Elusive" 166-69). Such definitional problems–of which characters to include in different analyses– also arise when discussing rape since characters such as Esteban in "Amar sólo por vencer" might be considered rapists (as he has sex with a woman intending only to abandon her later). However, for simplicity's sake, I have limited analyses to cases involving clearer definitions of violence among major characters.

> Que nadie haga tanto cuanto pague es cosa averiguada, porque el mal jamás dexa de tener castigo ni el bien premio, pues cuando el mundo no le dé, le da el cielo. Esto se verá más claro en mi maravilla [. . .]. (*Novelas* 292)
>
> [People get just what they deserve, that's common knowledge, because evil always has its punishment just as good has its reward, if not in this world, then certainly in the next. My *maravilla* shows this clearly [. . .]. (214, mod.)]

Such over-determined comments before this, the seventh novella, prepare the reader to accept Hipólita's violent actions as justified and to expect that all who commit wrongful acts–including Hipólita in her affair and her brother-in-law in his rape of her–will indeed be punished before the end of the tale.

Yet in "Al fin se paga todo," the question of "just desserts" does not obtain completely. What are we to make of the fact that the husband, unaware of his wife's attempted infidelities and his brother's violent behavior, dies a lonely death after the resolution of all other situations? In terms of the entire first volume, the problematic affirmation that "people get just what they deserve" is consonant with the relatively fair distribution of justice in the *Novelas amorosas*. Yet, when read in the context of the collection as a whole, this affirmation of justice presents no small measure of ambiguity. Like the lesson found in Tirso's tale of don Juan's insatiable desire and irrevocable condemnation, the reader here is advised that all evil eventually will be punished. Yet, the failure of the system to punish those who act with malice and violence, particularly in the *Desengaños*, makes this assertion of justice read as a highly ironic statement that criticizes the culture for not ensuring the protection of male and female citizens.

Since the entire story deals with sexuality, it is appropriate that "Al fin se paga todo" immediately centers our attention on the body. After the discovery of Hipólita's beaten body on the street, the rescuer García listens to her tale of rape, murder, and abuse. Hipólita exhibits sexual agency in startlingly open ways: she freely narrates her sexual adventures and the circumstances that led her to murder her brother-in-law, Luis. Hipólita reveals the autonomy with which she arranged assignations with a would-be lover. Later, she describes how she retaliated against Luis for raping her, showing once again her ability to assert her agency. These connections between sexuality and death, between desire and violence, give depth to the episodic structure of this novella.[26]

This tale hinges on the circulation of desire among several characters. The young wife Hipólita, happily married and worried only about her brother-in-law's constant proclamations of love, decides to give in to a suitor. With Hipólita arranging liaisons with the suitor, Gaspar, and the brother-in-law arranging to rape Hipólita, only the husband remains innocent. In spite of the humorous accounts of Gaspar's near-death experience in a clothes trunk and his escape from a tight squeeze in a window frame, the thrill of illicit sex is subordinated to what pans out to be the very real threat of violence connected with sexuality.[27] Gaspar and Hipólita are thwarted in their affair and never actually have sex. Foreshadowed by Gaspar's nearly fatal escapades, the dangers associated with sex culminate in rape and death. After the brother-in-law poses as Hipólita's husband in order to rape her, she retaliates by stabbing him to death and seeking refuge with Gaspar. Convinced that Hipólita has set him up repeatedly, Gaspar rejects her pleas for help, beating and robbing her before throwing her onto the street.

In that Hipólita and Gaspar are punished for their illicit meetings and Luis is killed for raping his sister-in-law, this is a moralistic tale that touts the virtues of marital fidelity. Yet the sympathetic characterization of Hipólita as a victim of male violence supersedes the culpability one might be inclined to ascribe to this woman who has tried several times to cheat on her husband. We must remember that Hipólita tells the story as she recovers from the beating her ex-lover gave her, a beating that followed her rape and, then, the murder of her rapist. This sequence of events depicts Hipólita as traumatized, as caught in the wheels of male violence. The narrative thus casts her as a victim, and the king's exoneration confirms this reading, for he sees "cuán justamente se había vengado doña

---

[26] Gartner's Girardian analysis of several of Zayas's novellas could easily be applied to the various functions of desire in "Al fin se paga todo."

[27] Although "Al fin se paga todo" takes a decisive turn toward violence, the catalog of mishaps suffered by Gaspar is similar to the list of sexual adventures in "El prevenido, engañado." For analyses of Zayas's comic tone and her use of irony, see Foa ("Humor and Suicide") and Williamsen ("Engendering Interpretation"), respectively.

Hipólita" (*Novelas* 326) [how rightly doña Hipólita had avenged herself (239)]. Ambivalence about sex and marriage permeates the resolution of the tale: declared innocent, Hipólita enters a convent and refuses to return to her husband. Then, in a twist that affirms female agency, Hipólita marries her rescuer García when her husband dies.

While many characters fall victim to each other's machinations in the tale, the reader is led to focus on Hipólita's victimization rather than on the husband's plight. The descriptions of the rape and of the ensuing murder dramatize the psychological and material effects of Luis's crime. Hipólita indicates that Luis snuck into her bed and "gozó cuanto deseaba, deshonrando a su hermano, agraviándome a mí y ofendiendo al cielo" (*Novelas* 320) [he proceeded to enjoy everything that he might ever have desired. He dishonored his brother, he injured me, he offended heaven (234, mod.)]. The next day, Luis smugly informed Hipólita that it was he, and not her husband, who had sex with her. In response, Hipólita went into his room at night and stabbed him in the heart. Unsatisfied, she gave herself over to more violence:

> le di otras cinco o seis puñaladas con tanta rabia y crueldad, como si con cada una le hubiera de quitar la infame vida. (*Novelas* 321)

> [I stabbed him five or six more times with such rage and violence, as if I were ending his vile life with each blow. (236, mod.)]

In relating these events to Gaspar, Hipólita takes full responsibility for her actions, saying she killed Luis with her own hands, "para lavar con su sangre la mancha de mi afrenta" (*Novelas* 323) [in order to cleanse the offense against my honor with his blood (237, mod.)].[28] These descriptions of rape and revenge make clear that Hipólita uses violence to redress material injury as well as offended honor.

---

[28] The description of the rapist brother-in-law Luis as a desperate lover ("amante desesperado") ties in with an ambiguous comment made about the rescuer García, who is said to love Hipólita "tanto que casi disculpaba a don Luis de su yerro" (*Novelas* 325) [so much that he almost excused don Luis's error (239, mod.)]. There is a possible slippage here between male desire and women's bodily integrity; the comment either sanctions rape or reveals the "stain" left by rape.

Hipólita's responses to Luis's trickery relate to her assertion of agency throughout the tale. She speaks of sexuality with candor, arranges several liaisons with her lover, and revels in the excitement of her adventures. Hipólita proves herself equally independent and industrious in the more serious matters of violence and retaliation. She does not hesitate to take revenge, for example, and she does not seek help from a man to do so. The above quotes are instructive because they point to Hipólita's claim on the emotions and actions that the honor code legitimizes for men, reminding readers that Hipólita unapologetically exacts vengeance in accordance with rules established to protect men.[29]

These tales of women avengers are distinct from the representations of male violence throughout the collection in significant ways. Most important, women set the terms of bodily integrity in "La burlada Aminta" and "Al fin se paga todo." Claiming the right to defend their bodies, the avengers enact the masculine behaviors of violence, anger, and redress as a means to restore order. Unlike Zayas's male characters–many of whom beat and kill women out of jealousy, fear, misogyny, and proprietariness–Aminta and Hipólita exact revenge based on direct evidence of their victimizers' guilt. In that women forge access to revenge based on evidence of personal injury, the resolutions to the tales sanction a more equitable configuration of the terms of violence and honor. These tales reward the women for the active role they play in putting a stop to male violence and in asserting control over their own bodies. Aminta escapes punishment from the authorities: even though she renounces her inheritance and never returns home, she takes on the name Victoria as an outward, and perhaps ironic, sign of her victory over Francisco.[30] Hipólita, on the other hand, receives a pardon from the king, enters a convent, inherits her husband's fortune, marries her rescuer, and has children.

---

[29] Notably, Hipólita expresses anger, an emotion often considered improper for women in the period. As Davis has shown in her analysis of pardon letters in early modern France, the expression of anger was common among men but not among women, who took great pains to justify their actions without expressing the rage common in the men's accounts (cf. *Fiction in the Archives*).

[30] Boyer suggests that Aminta is punished twice: first by having to renounce her fortune and her identity (when she crossdresses and when she becomes Victoria) and, later, by not having children ("La visión artística" 257-58). The text mentions children as the only thing lacking in Aminta's life at the end of the tale (*Novelas* 119).

While the tales of women avengers suggest that women should have the freedom to act on their own behalf, the notion of eye-for-an-eye justice is problematic regardless of the gender of the victims or the killers. I certainly do not want to argue that Zayas glorifies or endorses this type of violence. However, these tales of gender transgression help us glean a new perspective on Zayas's representations of gender and culture. Specifically, these stories of love, sex, and violence show women playing active roles and setting (or at least correcting) the terms of engagement between the sexes.

Read in association with each other, the female characters who transgress gender boundaries and successfully perform men's roles point to the possibility for women's active participation in the social order. At the very least, these feminine performances demystify and decenter masculinity. In doing the "manly things that men do," the female transgressors in these tales reiterate the constitutive elements of masculinity. With a similar dynamic of imitation at work in the stories about crossdressed men, Zayas's texts blur the boundaries between the sexes and emphasize that women and men have similar capabilities. These deliberate, successful emulations of masculinity and femininity reveal the arbitrary nature of gender construction and draw attention to the mechanisms by which women are excluded from full participation in the social order.

CONCLUSION

FEMINISM EMBODIED

> *No es trágico fin, sino el más felice que se pudo dar, pues codiciosa y deseada de muchos, [Lisis] no se sujetó a ninguno.*
> María de Zayas
>
> [*This end is not tragic but rather the happiest one you can imagine, for although courted and desired by many, Lisis did not subject herself to anyone.*]

LIKE many feminist discourses of our own time, the body-bound aesthetic of Zayas's novella collection privileges gender as the operative category of difference in interpersonal relations and, more broadly, in patriarchal culture. The description of Lisis's entry into the convent as the happiest possible ending to the soiree encapsulates Zayas's critique of women's subordinate status. This assertion of autonomy runs counter to the situations faced by many of the female characters in the *Desengaños*. The numerous depictions of victimization move Lisis to enter the convent, and they also indict the culture for leaving women at the mercy of men.

Potent for its shock value in a genre replete with marriage endings, Lisis's convent decision reiterates the feminist messages that permeate the entire collection. Beginning with the self-authorizing rhetoric of the preface and ending with Lisis's final speech, Zayas's fiction is both feminized and feminist. The texts leave little room for doubt that, at least in Zayas's fictionalized world, there are no guarantees for women's safety. Summing up this message, Lisis's last speech recounts the fate of the *Desengaños* heroines. She methodically lists the reasons for each female character's victimization and, in most cases, death. Isabel and Camila suffered for being raped; Ana, Beatriz, Mencía, and Magdalena suffered in their innocence;

and Elena "died a tortured death."[1] Lisis scolds women for believing themselves to be more fortunate than the victims of the tales:

> ¿Pensáis ser más dichosas que las referidas en estos desengaños? Ese es vuestro mayor engaño; porque cada día, como el mundo se va acercando al fin, va todo de mal en peor.... Y es la mayor desdicha que quizá las no culpadas mueren, y las culpadas viven; pues no he de ser yo así, que en mí no ha de faltar el conocimiento que en todas. (*Desengaños* 507)

> [Do you expect to be more fortunate than the women in these disenchantments we've been telling? This is your greatest deception, because every day the world draws to its end, things go from bad to worse.... The greatest misfortune is for the blameless women to die and the guilty to live. Well, that won't happen to me. I won't be lacking in judgment like other women. (402)]

Apocalyptic in its rhetoric, this statement about cultural decline and men's violence puts the burden for self-protection squarely on women's shoulders.

Using the compendium of female victims as justification for concern over her own personal safety, Lisis leaves the marriage market behind. We are meant to celebrate this decision because Lisis refuses, in the narrator's language, to "subject herself" to a man. From start to finish, Zayas's texts use the body–in all of its performative capacities–to encourage the reader to care about women. In Lisis, Zayas creates a character who elicits a sympathetic reading of this corporeal aesthetic. Through texts that explore the joys and perils of gender relations, Zayas encourages the reader to value women, to acknowledge the reliance of masculinity on violence, and to recognize the dangers of excluding women from the body politic.

Moreover, the similarities between Zayas's politics and current feminist concerns underscore the importance of these texts in the history of feminist thought. Gatens has summarized late twentieth-century Western liberal feminist beliefs, for example, and these match up in many ways with Zayas's own ideas about social justice:

---

[1] The long paragraph in which Lisis recalls the fates of the female protagonists functions as a springboard for her own choice to avoid marriage and enter the convent (*Desengaños* 507-08).

Equality, wealth, and opportunity are located in the public sphere. Hence the issue of providing women with access to power becomes an issue of providing them with equal access to the public sphere. (63)

With their emphasis on men's abuse of women–on their unchecked violence and uneven application of justice–Zayas's texts focus simultaneously on equality of access and on misconstrued conceptualizations of masculinity. These two aspects of her feminism merge in an aesthetic of violence that displays the consequences of individual and collective devaluations of the feminine. Aimed at critiquing the gender schema and its attendant unequal distribution of basic rights, Zayas's feminism demonstrates the dangers of reifying women's position as secondary citizens.

The innovation of Zayas's feminism lies in its deployment of gendered, politicized violence. Through an aesthetic of embodiment and violence, the texts guide readings of pervasive cultural injustice. Representations of systemic injustice and didactic responses to these social problems advocate a reconceptualization of women's place in the culture. Fundamentally, the *Novelas amorosas* and the *Desengaños amorosos* recast the terms by which the cultural center and margins should be defined. By showing women's lack of recourse to justice and self-protection, Zayas outlines the material disadvantages of a society in which women are subordinated to men.

To round out a discussion of Zayas's feminism, we need to consider the contradictory and sometimes exclusionary tactics at work. The issue of women's generalized exclusion raises the more particularized question: *Which* groups do the texts suggest should be integrated into political and social processes? Simply put, *which* bodies matter? Located in the novellas proper as well as in the comments and depictions of frame tale characters, the ideological framework of the collection accommodates a variety of political positions. By way of conclusion, I want to turn to the frame characters' attitudes about women's issues. This analysis of various feminist positions highlights the challenges and subtleties of Zayas's feminism, and it shows that, out of a multiplicity of female voices and images of women in the *Novelas amorosas* and the *Desengaños amorosos*, a coherent feminist vision emerges.

I. Framing Feminism

Just as Zayas manipulates images of violence to raise consciousness about the plight of women in society, her texts seek to correct the prevailing exclusion of women from cultural discourse in general. Lamented by eighteenth-century writer Josefa Amar y Borbón, the constraints placed on women merely reflect the practice of limiting women's worth to their domestic and/or religious roles:

> Saben ellas [las mujeres] que no pueden aspirar a ningún empleo, ni recompensa pública; que sus ideas no tienen más extensión que las paredes de una casa, o de un convento. Si esto no es bastante para sofocar el mayor talento del mundo, no sé qué otras trabas puedan buscarse. (147)[2]

> [Women know that they cannot aspire to any job or to any public compensation; that their ideas do not extend beyond the walls of a house or a convent. If this is not enough to suffocate the greatest talent of the world, I don't know what other difficulties can be found.]

From Amar's perspective, women's voices are only heard within the "walls of the home or the convent." Zayas's texts suggest that, even in the home, women are silenced by the same disadvantages pervasive in society at large.

One exception holds for the collection, however, as the safehouse atmosphere of the *Desengaños* soiree sanctions intimate, liberal expression on the part of the female frame characters.[3] In these characters' personalized comments, we find a plurality of feminist and anti-feminist positions. The diversity of stances expressed in the frame tale reconstructs the anxieties informing women's discursive production and, more generally, informing women's reluctance to challenge male hegemony. Perhaps the best example of women's

---

[2] Amar y Borbón's 1786 "Discurso en defensa del talento de las mugeres" was transcribed and reprinted by Tesser in *Dieciocho* 3.2 (1980), and I cite from that version but regularize the spelling.

[3] The decided feminization of the soiree in the *Desengaños* contrasts with the first volume in several respects. Most obviously, narration is shared by men and women in the *Novelas* and no rules govern content. The narrators' comments tend to be linked to their own gender as well. Three of the female narrators (Lisarda, Matilde, and Filis) introduce their tales by talking about women, while three of the male narrators talk about men (Álvaro, Alonso, and Lope).

inclination to remain silent can be found in the initial trepidation exhibited by several of the frame tale narrators.[4]

Lisarda and Filis demonstrate the greatest resistance to the mandate of speaking out against men in mixed company. Lisarda glances toward Juan as she prepares to tell her tale, and the principal narrator describes her body language as apologetic, as if it were saying: "Más por cumplir con la obligación que por ofenderte hago esto" (*Desengaños* 171) [I do this more out of duty than to offend you (85, mod.)]. Lisarda then verbalizes this trepidation and registers her discomfort with the narrative task. Declaring herself innocent of personal disenchantment in love, Lisarda tries to placate the male audience:

> Y para que ni ellos se quejen, y yo cumpla con lo que me es mandado, sucintamente referiré un caso . . . con lo que me parece que, sin agraviar, desengañaré a las que hubieren menester desengañarse. (*Desengaños* 171-72)
>
> [But, so that I may comply with your command without giving the men cause to complain, I shall briefly relate an account . . . that, without offending anyone, I hope will un-deceive anyone who has need of it. (85, mod.)]

With these remarks, this narrator posits a distance between herself and the narration, between herself and the women who need to hear the story.

In this individualist preface to her tale, Lisarda firmly states her resistance to the narrative act. Yet she relaxes into her role as narrator as she tells the story of Camila's rape and murder in "La más infame venganza." At certain points, Lisarda balances her criticism of men and women, berating women for their weak will and men for taking advantage of women. However, when Carlos tricks Octavia into entering a convent so that he can free himself of his obligation to her, Lisarda decisively connects his behavior to his gender: "¡Quién hiciera esta traición sino un hombre!" (*Desengaños* 187)

---

[4] Much of the resistance shown by the female frame narrators relates to the trope of humility and other conventions of women's writing. As Lerner indicates with regard to women writers' apologetic and seemingly uncertain attitudes, "Each thinking woman had to spend an inordinate amount of time and energy apologizing for the very fact of her thinking" (47). In her fascinating study on Santa Teresa, Weber has decoded these tropes, reading them in terms of a self-conscious "rhetoric of femininity."

[Who but a man could be so treacherous! (100, mod.)]. Finally, at the end of the tale, Lisarda concludes that misfortune, caused by men's trickery and women's own weakness, afflicts good and bad women everywhere (*Desengaños* 196).

The process of Lisarda's assumption of narrative and moral authority mirrors women's relationship to discursive power. She is wary of offending men, particularly her lover, who sits nearby. At first, she appears to comply only reluctantly with the act of narration. Yet, once she begins to speak, Lisarda becomes absorbed by the story; by the end of the tale, she has become invested in the plight of the heroine. Lisarda portrays the protagonist as a victim of her rapist and her husband, and the language used to describe the men decisively condemns their actions: Juan acts on his "infame deseo" [evil desire] when he rapes Camila; Camila dresses "honestamente" [chastely] when she leaves the convent; and Carlos allows the devil to "reign" in him when he kills his wife (*Desengaños* 194-96).

In spite of this harsh language, Lisarda immediately retreats into her original, reticent stance after telling the story. Hiding behind her own lack of bad experiences with men, she concludes by distancing herself from previous denunciations, reiterating her inability to advise others on matters of deception in love: "yo, como he dicho, si hasta ahora no conozco los engaños, mal podré avisar con los desengaños" (*Desengaños* 196) [I've never known any deception and so can scarcely give advice about disenchantment (109)]. The principal narrator connects Lisarda's embarrassment with her love for Juan, whom she does not wish to anger by blaming men for women's misfortune (*Desengaños* 196). Later in the soiree, this issue arises again when the narrator reminds us that Nise has never succumbed to love, "y por eso con menos embarazo que Lisarda había hablado" (*Desengaños* 222) [that's why she could speak with less restraint than Lisarda (135)].⁵ Without the distance provided by biography and without the freedom afforded unattached women, Lisarda leaves the task of deciphering the moral of the tale to her companions. In the end, Lisarda resorts to an individualistic stance in which she attends to her own relationship with men rather than to the larger project of educating women about men's abuses.

---

⁵ Yllera points out in her edition of the *Desengaños* that this emphasis on Nise's love-free life marks an inconsistency between the two volumes: at the outset of the *Novelas amorosas*, Nise and Alonso appear wearing each other's colors in testimony of their inclination toward each other (222-23 n. 6).

Filis's resistance follows a trajectory similar to Lisarda's. Filis believes that the soiree has not recognized women's own responsibility in their disenchantment, and so she disagrees with the basic proposition of trying to disabuse women of their naivete. She proposes that women bear more guilt than the tales have admitted, and men bear less (*Desengaños* 227). Yet her subsequent three-page diatribe advocating educational and social reform claims women's possible intellectual superiority and compares men's oppression of women to the Moors' castration of the Christians (*Desengaños* 228, 231).

After narrating "Tarde llega el desengaño," Filis offers some equally critical musings about men's attitudes toward women. She says that women are held in such low esteem that neither their innocence nor their suffering can change men's opinions. Indeed, Filis's language pinpoints an adversarial relationship between the sexes:

> Y es bien mirar, que en la era que corre, estamos en tan adversa opinión con los hombres, que ni con el sufrimiento los vencemos, ni con la inocencia los obligamos. (*Desengaños* 255)

> [We should also take into account the fact that, in these times, we women have such a bad name among men that we cannot overcome them with our suffering, nor change their minds with our innocence. (163, mod.)]

The rhetorical path taken by Lisarda and Filis leads them to the same political position. In spite of their initial discomfort with speaking out against men, these narrators' comments eventually line up with the feminist stances taken by other female characters in the frame tale.

The ten narrators of the *Desengaños* have different, individuated styles of presentation. Some of the women discuss their personal experiences in love while others merely comply with the task of narration. Despite such different characterizations, this group of women repeatedly indicts men for their abuses of women and power. The male characters in attendance at the soiree are said to cling to the women's words and, in several instances, to agree with the criticism. On the second night, the principal narrator indicates that Lisis would have spoken more, but that the men were already convinced by her,

> porque los nobles y cuerdos presto se sujetan a la razón, como se vio en esta ocasión, que estaban los caballeros tan colgados de

> sus palabras, que no hubo ahí tal que quisiese ni contradecirla ni estorbarla. (*Desengaños* 335)

> [because noble and intelligent men respond readily to reason as you could see on this occasion. All the gentlemen were absorbed in her words, and not one tried to argue with or contradict her. (240-41)]

If the men are absorbed in Lisis's speech, they also listen to the other narrators with intensity. After hearing the eighth tale, the men collectively admit that many innocent women have suffered because of male deception:

> Si bien los caballeros, o rendidos a la verdad, o agradecidos a la cortesía, dieron el voto por las damas, confesando haber habido y haber muchas mujeres buenas, y que han padecido y padecen inocentes en la crueldad de los engaños de los hombres. (*Desengaños* 399)

> [Now the gentlemen, either out of courtesy or convinced by the truth, voted in favor of the ladies. They confessed that there have been and are many good women who, being innocent, have suffered and continue to suffer from the cruelty of men's deceptions. (300)]

These reactions of the male characters model the destabilization of misogyny and the reeducation of men that are central to the didactic goals of the novellas.

Another indication of men's acceptance of criticism appears in the ever growing numbers of people in attendance at the soiree. By the last night, no room remains for more guests before the soiree officially begins. Such is the fame of the storytellers that people have come from far and wide to witness the final evening's events. The principal narrator indicates that the crowds have flocked to the soiree because the women's fame has spread. Specifically, the wise and levelheaded men have seen the error of their ways:

> a los cuerdos poco es menester para sacarlos de un error, que en esto más que en otra cosa se diferencian de los necios, viendo que las damas no los tachaban de otro vicio sino en que engañan a las mujeres y luego dicen mal de ellas, no sujetándose a

creer que hay mujeres buenas, honestas y virtuosas [. . .]. (*Desengaños* 403)

[It doesn't take much to disabuse the wise of error; this is precisely how they differ from the foolish. The gentlemen realized that the ladies were blaming them only for the vice of deceiving women and then speaking ill of them, and of refusing to acknowledge that there are good, chaste, and virtuous women. (305)]

If the men experience a conversion of sorts during the soirees, their realizations are limited in scope. After all, they do not admit to more than ruining women's reputations; and they make no admissions related to violent, abusive, or even manipulative behavior. While the novellas repeatedly point to systemic problems and misogyny, the men's acknowledgement of culpability minimizes the larger cultural implications of the critique. Nonetheless, the texts provide a starting point for change by inscribing a positive male response to problematic gender relations and by modelling a dialogue between men and women.

Through this dialectic between female narrators and male listeners, the frame tale sets a standard for the readers' response. Like the frame tale characters, readers should acknowledge that women have been mistreated. Like the wise and well-informed characters in the novellas, we should recognize that behavior and attitudes can and should be changed. This sets up the choice–which is really no choice at all–of either being wise and committing oneself to change, or of being stupid and refusing to see the error of one's ways. Like the rhetoric in "Al que leyere," these comments by the principal narrator leave little room for the resistant reader to maneuver. The frame tale thus reaches out to readers by portraying a seemingly comfortable space in which men and women can admit to the roles they play in the perpetuation of misogyny.

These points of contact between the many narrative styles and narrators' characterizations show that Zayas manipulates certain ideological positions, highlighting and legitimizing some, and rejecting others. Fundamentally, the strategies used to confine criticism soften the potentially alienating feminist element of the texts. This dynamic of ideological validation and disavowal depends on several key rallying points. First and foremost, of course, is the issue of class. Readers are addressed as members of the aristocratic elite, a group whose codes of behavior are represented everywhere from Zayas's initial chivalric plea for gentlemen to read these female-authored texts (i.e. "Al que leyere") to the severe criticisms of those male characters who fail to act as gentlemen. Descriptions of violence and violated bodies also play a crucial role in the validation of these feminist ideologies. The reader response mechanism in the frame tale and in the principal narrator's ideologically charged comments also underscore the means by which the collection validates certain beliefs. These aesthetic, thematic, and rhetorical manipulations of reader response constitute the dynamic by which Zayas presents and justifies her basic feminist ideas.

One remaining aspect of the politics of these texts has yet to be explained. If the novella collection is as pointedly feminist as these analyses have made it out to be, then why weren't Zayas's readers completely alienated? Entirely legitimate, although not wholly answerable, I think this question needs to be asked, for it points to a larger issue relevant not only to Zayas but to feminist analyses of all texts circulated, published, or performed during this period. A reading of Zayas's texts as cogently feminist is not incongruous with their popularity. In fact, we cannot preclude the possibility that they were read as adamantly pro-woman in their own period. However, Zayas's charged didacticism needs to be contextualized in terms of its coherence and limitations in order to decipher the possible impact of the feminist messages in the seventeenth century.

An explanation that accounts for contemporary readers' comprehension of the didacticism as well as the popularity of the texts can be found in one crucial means by which the texts guide reader response: the dispersion and channeling of social and cultural criticism. Clearly, men's abuses of women and the culture's exclusion of women receive the brunt of criticism in the novellas. Each tale's presentation of gender relations gone askew provides an occasion for readers to contemplate the implications of these problems. The *Desengaños amorosos* principally is concerned with giving women the space to reclaim their reputations and to air their complaints, for example. Claiming to speak out on women's behalf, the texts limit their advocacy primarily to aristocratic Christians. This seems logical enough, since Zayas addresses herself to an upper-class readership. In her appeal to this readership's sensibilities, other identities provide the most obvious lightening rods for the displacement of anger as the tales unfold. In fact, the frequent channeling of anger toward male victimizers is diffused through criticisms of specific minor characters, many of whom are of races, ethnicities, classes, and nationalities other than those of the frame tale and external *destinateurs*. While the texts elucidate the dangers of excluding women from the cultural center, they also displace much resentment onto a broadly configured Other, one that works in opposition to a gender-inclusive, aristocratic center.[6]

This is not to suggest that the repeated vilification of servants, slaves, female lovers, Moors, and others was included by Zayas as a self-conscious technique to divert some of the culpability for women's problems. The impact of these characterizations on the feminist agenda interests me far more than speculations about authorial intent. In terms of the function of this otherness, these characterizations afford frame characters and external readers an uncomplicated source for moral indignation. As scapegoats whom nobody defends, they are blamed (often unjustly) for their participation in violent acts which, nonetheless, usually are carried out by Christian male aristocrats.[7]

As Lisis's intention of "recovering women's good name" suggests, the masculinist dominant discourses of the period frequently denounced women. Zayas turns this tradition on its head, and indicts many men and a handful of women for their malicious treat-

---

[6] Zayas's representation of difference is extremely complex and merits an entire study unto itself. The xenophobia of "Mal presagio casar lejos" and the enigmatic depictions of slaves in several novellas (including "El prevenido, engañado," "Tarde llega el desengaño," and "Estragos que causa el vicio") are only a few examples of the presentation of difference throughout the texts. Boyer's "The Other Woman" addresses one facet of this problem by dealing with the female lover in Zayas and Cervantes. Fra-Molinero's *La imagen de los negros en el teatro del Siglo de Oro* and "La imagen de los negros en la literatura española de los siglos XVI y XVII" provide excellent starting points for further considerations of representations of difference in literature of the period.

[7] With the exception of servants, who are frequently blamed for betraying their masters in the tales, there are few non-Christian, nonaristocratic characters who actually engage in deception or in violence. The list of such characters and their actions includes the following episodes: Estela's Moorish kidnapper tries to rape her in "El juez de su causa"; the false accusations of adultery by Jaime's slave lead Jaime to enslave and abuse his own wife in "Tarde llega el desengaño"; and the foreign nationals kill their wives in "Mal presagio casar lejos." Although they do not commit violent acts per se, we also should consider the outsider status of those characters who cast spells on others (e.g., Lucrecia in "El desengaño amando" and the unnamed Moor in "La inocencia castigada").

ment of women. For the most part, Zayas's texts rebuke unvirtuous, undignified, and often lower-class or somehow othered women. The "evil" or "unvirtuous" women receive harsh criticism, condemned by the narrators as traitors to women's cause.

Like the large group of male characters who cause harm to wives, sisters, and lovers, the negatively portrayed female characters engage in a wide range of behaviors. This list of women includes: the lover in "La fuerza del amor," who refuses to give up her hold on Diego; Claudia in "El juez de su causa," who sets up Estela's kidnapping and (attempted) rape; the aunt in "Amar sólo por vencer," who assists the men with the murder of Laurela and her handmaid; the black slave in "Tarde llega el desengaño," who makes up a lie that is said to lead to her mistress' death; and a servant in "Estragos que causa el vicio," who is blamed for devising a plan that results in a slaughter. Some female characters' actions are portrayed as causing or enacting unwarranted violence against men as well (cf. "El prevenido, engañado" and "El jardín engañoso"). Many of the female characters whose actions lead to women's victimization are portrayed as breaking with female solidarity, as putting men's interests before women's.[8] Depicted as traitors to women's cause, these characters are easy targets for criticism because of their complicity in women's suffering.

Moreover, Lisis expresses the elitist tendencies present in the collection when she likens servants to animals that turn on their masters and kill them. In an extremely distasteful speech, Lisis warns readers about servants' lack of reliability:

> Porque los criados y criadas son animales caseros y enemigos no excusados, que los estamos regalando y gastando con ellos nuestra paciencia y hacienda, y al cabo, como el león, que harto el leonero de criarle y sustentarle, se vuelve contra él y le mata, así ellos, al cabo, matan a sus amos [. . .]. (*Desengaños* 508)

> [Servants are domestic animals and privileged enemies whom we spoil and on whom we spend our patience and our wealth. In the end, they're like the lion that turns against his keeper and kills him if he is negligent in feeding and pampering him; and so they, in the end, kill their masters [. . .]. (403, mod.)]

---

[8] Such betrayal of women's solidarity by disloyal women provides the focal point for Zayas's only known play, *La traición en la amistad*.

The frame characters' oversimplified readings of servants' and others' complicity in much of the injustice displace some blame onto groups (such as Moors, servants, and foreigners) often demonized in official state policies and literary discourse of the period.[9] These representations also sharpen the aristocratic agenda in that they define the specific category of person for whom the texts advocate change. This agenda has limited, yet clear, political ramifications: by investing in the safety of the aristocratic woman, the reader also invests in the health of the larger aristocratic body.[10]

While the foreign nationals of "Mal presagio" kill their Spanish wives, and the black slave in "Tarde llega el desengaño" betrays her mistress, many counterexamples to this pattern suggest that some slaves, servants, non-whites, and non-Spaniards share a commitment to protecting women. In some instances, these characters even sacrifice themselves and their own interests to the survival of the female protagonists. Many handmaids either are victims of the same violence to which their mistresses are subjected (e.g., "Amar sólo por vencer") or faithfully mourn their mistresses' fate (e.g., "Mal presagio casar lejos"). More dramatically, a slave in "Estragos que causa el vicio" sacrifices herself in order to save the adulterous Florentina from her brother-in-law's wrath. These layered characterizations confirm once again the complexity and ambiguity of Zayas's ideology and aesthetic.

---

[9] Yllera points out that such criticisms of servants were common in writings of the period (55 n. 148). Cushing analyzes the ways that Zayas's texts indict aristocratic men for not living up to their class privilege (4-41). The differentiation between aristocrats and others in Zayas's texts adds more support to Cushing's argument, for it shows yet one more strategy used by Zayas to encourage the upper classes to behave properly so as to avoid becoming like servants. For analyses of attitudes toward servants and the lower classes in Spain, see Maravall (*La literatura picaresca*, esp. 196-242). For other parts of Europe, see Burnett ("Masters and Servants in Moral and Religious Treatises, c. 1580-1642"), Fairchilds (*Domestic Enemies. Servants and their Masters in Old Regime France*), and Hill (*Servants: English Domestics in the Eighteenth Century*).

[10] I am suggesting that the homogenization effected by the focus on the aristocratic body can be read as a political tactic on many fronts. Three and a half centuries later and well into the third wave of contemporary feminism, Gatens suggested that feminists might also need to fight the implicit masculinity of the body politic with a "counterforce (that) will necessarily involve the assertion of a certain homogeneity in the specific situations of women" (56). While second- and third-wave feminism and postcolonial theory have exposed the dangers of such homogenization, it is interesting to note the similarity in tactics between Zayas and feminist philosophy.

Despite the forays into the purported malevolence of lower class, ethnic, religious, national, and racial others, the rift between men and women unquestionably draws the most fire in these texts. The emphasis on men's responsibility for women's mistreatment and for social change gains force in the collection. The *Desengaños* explicitly links men's obsession with the honor code to the dangers facing women. This charge appears, for example, in one of the most blatantly gendered discussions in the collection. After Nise's tale, "El verdugo de su esposa," the frame characters contemplate the implications of an innocent woman's murder by her husband. The men in the group defend the crime, saying that no proof of corruption is needed to kill a woman because "un marido no está obligado, si quiere ser honrado, a averiguar nada" (*Desengaños* 223) [a husband, if he wishes to protect his honor, has no obligation to prove anything (136)]. The women, on the other hand, condemn Pedro, "afirmando que no por la honra la había muerto, . . . sino que por quedar desembarazado para casarse con la culpada" (*Desengaños* 223) [asserting that don Pedro hadn't killed Roseleta for the sake of his honor . . . but rather to free himself to marry the guilty woman (137, mod.)]. The women see Pedro as a shameless adulterer and murderer, but the men fail to grasp the criticism of violence and injustice of the tale. This ignorance about women's plight suggests that men, even sympathetic gentlemen like those in attendance at the soiree, fail to perceive the insidious cultural problems exposed in the stories.

The increased number of guests who eagerly await women's tales of vindication on the third and final night of the soiree suggests that women have gained ground in the ideological battle throughout the course of the *Desengaños amorosos*.[11] In front of this huge audience, Lisis delivers a litany against men, calls for women to protect themselves, and refuses to marry Diego. Anticipated by Isabel's concluding song about the tragedy and cruelty of love, Lisis delivers a long speech in which she defends women and attacks men. With her final speech and bodily example, Lisis drives home most of the principal tenets of the corporeal, aristo-

---

[11] The large number of guests on the final night is also attributable to the many invitations extended by Diego, who expects people to bear witness to his marriage to Lisis. The introduction to this section emphasizes the fame of the women storytellers and the anticipation of their tales of vindication (*Desengaños* 404).

cratic feminism of the novellas. Conceding that many women are corrupt, she nonetheless points to men's prejudice toward women and to their predisposition to deceive women. As mentioned, she also attacks the lack of masculinity in Spain, suggesting that if men acted like men, if they would fight as in the days of old, proper order would be restored. Finally, she tells women to stop trusting men, who cannot be relied upon once their desire has been satiated.

Lisis's summary of the lessons learned in the texts privileges individual over structural change. Indeed, she does not mention the previously stated calls for educational reform and for access to arms. Arms and letters are linked, however, in a momentary conflation of Lisis's voice with the authorial voice. Here, as 'Lisis' claims that she has taken up the pen, she threatens to take up arms to defend women's good name:

> Y como he tomado la pluma, habiendo tantos años que la tenía arrimada, en su defensa, tomaré la espada para lo mismo, que los agravios sacan fuerzas donde no las hay [. . .]. (*Desengaños* 507)
>
> [I've taken up the pen, set aside for so many years, in their defense, and so shall I take up the sword for the same purpose, for affronts give strength to those who were weak before. (401, mod.)]

Connecting the power of the word with the power of the sword, the texts threaten men with women's capacity to fight both discursively and physically. Lisis reiterates this militaristic rhetoric at the end of her speech when, again in an authorial voice, she says to men: ". . . si mi defensa por escrito no basta, será fuerza que todas tomemos las armas para defendernos de sus malas intenciones" (*Desengaños* 509) [If my written defense doesn't suffice, then we'll all have to take up arms to defend ourselves against your evil intentions (404)]. The convergence of female authorship with military might encourages women to forge their own access to education, arms, and discursive freedom.

Finally, Lisis's choice to enter the convent at the end of the *Desengaños amorosos* asserts the rights over body and self that have been advocated throughout the collection. By making this choice, Lisis acknowledges that the controlled safehouse atmosphere of the soiree—one that allows women to speak freely to a captive male audience—cannot be sustained once the festivities come to an end. The impact of Lisis's announcement should not be underestimated. Before the decision is stated, the reader presumes that the end of the soiree will bring about the dissolution of female authority and the restoration of patriarchal order through marriage.

Instead, Lisis circumvents this restitution of order by declaring her allegiance to Isabel and to a feminine world that lies outside the soiree, outside the texts. Lisis's final example urgently communicates the need for women to find strategies that will guarantee their survival. While her actions underscore the imperative of protecting the individual, aristocratic, female body, they also convey a message for other women: the current cultural climate cannot protect women outside the convent. Lisis sees her choice as cowardly, as if she were a criminal taking refuge from the law. Yet she also has confidence in the decision, declaring that, from her safe vantage point, she will watch her sisters face off with men, whom she calls women's greatest enemy (*Desengaños* 509). Acting to protect herself, Lisis makes her personal decision political by urging other women to follow.

While this collection repeatedly calls for the expansion of women's limited social, legal, and educational rights, Lisis emphasizes and performs small scale change. While other early modern women, such as Moderata Fonte and Lucrezia Marinelli, envisioned entirely feminized societies, Zayas does not posit a permanent female utopia as a solution for the social crisis.[12] Instead, she suggests that women remove themselves to the convent until men change their ways, until society changes to accommodate women. Like the representations of violence against women in the novellas, the final scene uses the body to protest the dangers facing women in the sexual economy. This emphasis on corporeality humanizes women's plight, reminding us that issues surrounding the body are central to feminism.

---

[12] Jordan discusses Fonte's and Marinelli's utopian visions at some length (253-61).

II. FEMINISM EMBODIED

From beginning to end, Zayas's aesthetic binds bodies to politics. Her political agenda depends on an embodied aesthetic: the images of women's containment, of women's frustrated attempts to act on their desire, and of the violence done to their bodies all point to the need for reform. Zayas's representations of women's stifled existence raise the same issues articulated by Gatens in her consideration of a feminist philosophy of the body:

> If women are going to play an active part in contemporary politics it is important to begin the task of thinking through how one participates in a context where female embodiment is denied any autonomous political and ethical representation. (56)

Zayas seeks to legitimate women's participation in the public sphere. Her texts encourage a reconceptualization of contemporary sociopolitical and ideological frameworks by showing that codes of behavior and cultural practices work together to reinforce a perilous devaluation of women's bodies and minds.

In a multifaceted construction of feminist politics, the texts validate women as subjects and criticize male-centered culture. The possibilities for many female subjectivities are explored by assertive frame characters who secure agency through narration and extra-narrative commentary. Zayas's expansive criticism emerges in her representations of sexual double standards, wrongheaded compliance with the honor code, and women's lack of access to the body politic. Her body-bound aesthetic literalizes the impulses behind social control, inscribing the various effects of domination and exclusion onto the living text of the body.

On a more optimistic note, the collection offers a glimpse into what a reconceptualized, woman-friendly society might look like. In this world, women would be as safe and as educated as men, and they would have the same access to justice as men. Armed with education and weapons–the tools of self-defense–women would be able to protect and defend themselves both intellectually and physically. Women's minds *and* bodies would be valued.

Like other pre-Enlightenment feminists, Zayas's vision for change remains within the boundaries of patriarchy. While her texts do not call for a new social contract, they do call for serious, immediate reforms of detrimental codes of behavior and exclusionary practices. Narrative commentary and bold characterizations validate and defend women's potential to function successfully in the dominant order. Indeed, from drawing attention to her own role in the sphere of public discourse to depicting female characters who perform traditionally masculine roles, Zayas flouts women's intellectual, physical, and political capacities.

Combined with Lisis's prominent role, the emphasis on women's narrative adds a crucial dimension to the feminism of the texts. The frame tale characters are shown to be successful narrators and impressive thinkers, respected by the men around them. Lisis's own dissertations on the social crisis are well reasoned and well received. The collective enterprise of storytelling depends, to a large extent, on the interpretive powers of the women. The validation of the feminine in the tales is complemented by women's successful use of their discursive freedom in the frame tale.

Working within the confines of seventeenth-century patriarchy, María de Zayas finds the answer for women's survival in the feminine environment of the convent. Her texts recognize the unlikelihood that substantive social reform will take place. Proposing a temporary solution that will protect women and encourage cultural reform, Zayas endorses the convent as a place where women can protect themselves from violence.

Through a critique of women's devalued status, the *Novelas amorosas* and the *Desengaños amorosos* reclaim the female body as worthy of protection and respect. Through Lisis, Zayas returns to the body one last time and, in a decision that combines the female body with feminist protest, Lisis becomes a model of corporeal feminism. In the interest of self-preservation, she will not subject herself to any man. This, the narrator tells us, is the happiest ending possible.

* * *

Zayas's early modern thought forms part of a feminist history that has yet to be studied sufficiently. By making connections among feminists from different cultures and time periods, we can better understand the persistence of inequality in modern societies and glean strategies that we might adopt or avoid in future struggles.

Indeed, while Zayas's advocacy of social change and focus on corporeality continue to resonate with contemporary feminisms, other aspects of her texts strike modern readers as relatively narrow. Writing about the upper classes, Zayas emphasized the need to protect the aristocratic body and excluded large groups of people from any consideration of equality. In historical terms, these dynamics signal various ethnic, class, and political tensions of seventeenth-century Spanish society. In terms of feminist ideology, they serve as reminders of the changes that have occurred in liberal Western thought since this revolutionary writer first published her pro-woman texts.

To do justice to Zayas, we need to remember the expansiveness of her vision and the sophistication of her critique. In laying claim to the integrity of the female body, Zayas defied philosophical traditions and cultural practices that denied women intellectual and physical autonomy. Emphasizing access to the polity, equality under law, and control over one's body, she perceived questions of corporeality and justice as crucial to women's safety and survival. It is a sign of María de Zayas's lasting importance as a feminist writer that she focused on issues that remain central to discussions about women's rights all over the globe today.

WORKS CITED

Alberti, Leon Battista. *The Family in Renaissance Florence.* (*I Libri della famiglia*). 1441. Trans. Renée Neu. Columbia, SC: U of South Carolina P, 1969.

Alcalde, Pilar. "Estrategias temáticas y narrativas en María de Zayas: las prácticas de la femineidad." Diss. U of Southern California, 1998.

Álvarez-Amell, Diana. "El objeto del cuerpo femenino en el 'Quinto desengaño' de María de Zayas." *Actas: Irvine 1992. Asociación Internacional de Hispanistas. Vol. II: La mujer y su representación en las literaturas hispánicas.* Ed. Juan Villegas. Irvine: U of California, 1994. 25-33.

Amar y Borbón, Josefa. "Discurso en defensa del talento de las mugeres y de su aptitud para el gobierno y otros cargos en que se emplean los hombres." *Memorial Literario, Instructivo y Curioso de la Corte de Madrid* VIII.32 (agosto de 1786): 400-30. Rpt. and notes by Carmen Chaves Tesser. *Dieciocho* 3.2 (1980): 144-61.

Amezúa, Agustín G. de. "Prólogo." *Desengaños amorosos. Parte segunda del sarao y entretenimiento honesto.* María de Zayas y Sotomayor. Madrid: Real Academia Española, 1950. vii-xxiv.

———. "Prólogo." *Novelas amorosas y ejemplares.* María de Zayas y Sotomayor. Madrid: Real Academia Española, 1948. vii-l.

Amussen, Susan Dwyer. "'Being stirred to much unquietness': Violence and Domestic Violence in Early Modern England." *Journal of Women's History* 6.2 (1994): 70-89.

———. "Punishment, Discipline, and Power: The Social Meanings of Violence in Early Modern England." *Journal of British Studies* 34.1 (1995): 1-34.

Anderson, Bonnie S., and Judith P. Zinsser. *A History of Their Own: Women in Europe from Prehistory to the Present.* NY: Harper and Row, 1988.

Arenal, Electa, and Stacey Schlau. *Untold Sisters. Hispanic Nuns in Their Own Works.* Trans. Amanda Powell. Albuquerque: U of New Mexico P, 1989.

Atwood, Margaret. "The Female Body." *Michigan Quarterly Review* (Fall 1990): 490-93.

Aulnoy, Madame d' (Marie-Catherine). *Relation du Voyage d'Espagne.* 1691. Paris: C. Klincksieck, 1926.

Azevedo, Angela de. *El muerto disimulado.* Soufas, *Women's Acts* 91-132.

Azorín (José Martínez Ruiz). "Doña María de Zayas." *Los clásicos redivivos. Los clásicos futuros.* 3rd ed. Colección Austral. Madrid: Espasa-Calpe, 1958. 69-73.

Barbeito Carneiro, Isabel. "¿Por qué escribieron las mujeres en el Siglo de Oro?" *Cuadernos de Historia Moderna* 19 (1997): 183-93.

Barker, Francis. *The Culture of Violence: Essays on Tragedy and History.* Chicago: U of Chicago P, 1993.

Bassein, Beth Ann. *Women and Death: Linkages in Western Thought and Literature.* Westport, CT: Greenwood, 1984.
Benedict, Kitty, and Karen Covington, eds. *The Literary Crowd: Writers, Critics, Scholars, Wits.* Austin, TX: Raintree Steck-Vaughn, 2000.
Bennassar, Bartolomé. *Inquisición española: poder político y control social.* Barcelona: Editorial Crítica, 1981.
Bergmann, Emilie. "The Exclusion of the Feminine in the Cultural Discourse of the Golden Age: Juan Luis Vives and Fray Luis de León." Saint-Säens, *Religion, Body and Gender* 124-36.
Beverley, John J. "On the Concept of the Spanish Literary Baroque." Cruz and Perry 216-30.
Bilinkoff, Jodi. *The Avila of Saint Teresa: Religious Reform in a Sixteenth-Century City.* Ithaca: Cornell UP, 1989.
Blanqué, Andrea. "María de Zayas o la versión de 'las noveleras.'" *NRFH*, XXXIX.2 (1991): 921-50.
Bordo, Susan. *Unbearable Weight: Feminism, Western Culture, and the Body.* Berkeley: U of California P, 1993.
Bourland, Caroline. "Boccaccio and the *Decameron* in Castilian and Catalan Literature." *Revue Hispanique* XII (1905): 1-232.
Boyer, H. Patsy. "Introduction." *The Enchantments of Love: Amorous and Exemplary Novels.* María de Zayas y Sotomayor. Berkeley: U of California P, 1990. xi-xxxi.
———. "The Other Woman in Cervantes's *Persiles* and Zayas's Novelas." *Cervantes* 10 (1990): 59-68.
———. "'The Ravages of Vice' and the Vice of Telling Stories." *Voces a ti debidas. In Honor of Ruth El Saffar.* Ed. Marie Cort Daniels, Herving Madruga, and Susan Wilcox. Colorado Springs: Colorado College Studies No. 29, 1993. 29-34.
———. "Toward a Baroque Reading of 'El verdugo de su esposa.'" Williamsen and Whitenack 51-72.
———. "La visión artística de María de Zayas." *Estudios sobre el siglo de oro en homenaje a Raymond R. MacCurdy.* Ed. Ángel González et al. Madrid: Cátedra, 1983. 253-63.
———. "The War between the Sexes and the Ritualization of Violence in Zayas's *Disenchantments.*" Saint-Säens, *Sex and Love* 125-45.
Bravo-Villasante, Carmen. *La mujer vestida de hombre en el teatro español (Siglos XVI-XVII).* Madrid: Revista de Occidente, 1955.
Bray, Abigail, and Claire Colebrook. "The Haunted Flesh: Corporeal Feminism and the Politics of (Dis)Embodiment." *Signs* 24.1 (Autumn 1998): 35-68.
Breines, Wini, and Linda Gordon. "The New Scholarship on Family Violence." *Signs* 8.3 (1983): 490-531.
Bronfen, Elisabeth. *Over Her Dead Body: Death, Femininity, and the Aesthetic.* NY: Routledge, 1992.
Brooten, Bernadette. *Love between Women: Early Christian Responses to Female Homoeroticism.* Chicago: U of Chicago P, 1996.
Brown, Judith. *Immodest Acts: The Life of a Lesbian Nun in Renaissance Italy.* Oxford: Oxford UP, 1986.
Brownlee, Marina S. *The Cultural Labyrinth of María de Zayas.* Philadelphia: U of Pennsylvania P, 2000.
———. "Elusive Subjectivity in María de Zayas." *Journal of Interdisciplinary Literary Studies* 6.2 (1994): 163-83.
———. "Postmodernism and the Baroque in María de Zayas." *Cultural Authority in Golden Age Spain.* Ed. Marina S. Brownlee and Hans Ulrich Gumbrecht. Baltimore: Johns Hopkins UP, 1995. 107-30.

Bullough, Vern L., and Bonnie Bullough. *Cross Dressing, Sex, and Gender.* Philadelphia: U of Pennsylvania P, 1993.

Burnett, Mark Thornton. "Masters and Servants in Moral and Religious Treatises, c. 1580-1642." *The Arts, Literature, and Society.* Ed. Arthur Maverick. London: Routledge, 1990. 48-75.

Butler, Judith. *Bodies that Matter: On the Discursive Limits of "Sex."* NY: Routledge, 1993.

——. *Gender Trouble: Feminism and the Subversion of Identity.* NY: Routledge, 1990.

Bynum, Caroline Walker. *Fragmentation and Redemption: Essays on Gender and the Human Body in Medieval Religion.* NY: Zone, 1990.

——. *Holy Feast and Holy Fast: The Religious Significance of Food to Medieval Women.* Berkeley: U of California P, 1987.

Calderón de la Barca, Pedro. *La dama duende.* Ed. Antonio Rey Hazas and Florencio Sevilla Arroyo. Barcelona: Planeta, 1989.

——. *El médico de su honra.* Ed. D. W. Cruickshank. Madrid: Castalia, 1981.

——. *La vida es sueño.* Ed. J. M. Ruano de la Haza. Madrid: Castalia, 1994.

Camps, Victoria. *El siglo de las mujeres.* Madrid: Cátedra, 1998.

Caputi, Jane, and Diana Russell. "Femicide: Sexist Terrorism against Women." Radford and Russell 13-21.

Carvajal y Saavedra, Mariana de. *Navidades de Madrid y noches entretenidas, en ocho novelas.* Ed. Catherine Soriano. Madrid: Comunidad de Madrid, 1993.

Cascardi, Anthony J. *Ideologies of History in the Spanish Golden Age.* Penn State Studies in Romance Literatures. University Park, PA: Pennsylvania State UP, 1997.

Castro, Américo. "Algunas observaciones acerca del concepto del honor en los siglos XVI y XVII." *Revista de Filología Española* 3 (1916): 1-50.

Cavendish, Margaret (Duchess of Newcastle). *The Convent of Pleasure and Other Plays.* Ed. Anne Shaver. Baltimore: Johns Hopkins UP, 1999.

Cervantes, Miguel de. *Don Quijote de la Mancha.* 2 vols. Ed. John Jay Allen. Madrid: Cátedra, 1986.

——. *Novelas ejemplares.* 2 vols. Ed. Harry Sieber. Madrid: Cátedra, 1995.

Charnon-Deutsch, Lou. "The Sexual Economy in the Narrative of María de Zayas." Williamsen and Whitenack 117-32.

Chevalier, Maxime. "Un cuento, una comedia, cuatro novelas (Lope de Rueda, Juan Timoneda, Cristóbal de Tamariz, Lope de Vega, María de Zayas)." *Essays on Narrative Fiction in the Iberian Peninsula in Honour of Frank Pierce.* Ed. R. B. Tate. Oxford: Dolphin, 1982. 26-38.

Cixous, Hélène. "Laugh of the Medusa." *New French Feminisms.* Ed. Elaine Marks and Isabelle de Courtivron. Amherst: U of Massachusetts P, 1980. 245-64.

Clamurro, William H. "Ideological Contradiction and Imperial Decline: Towards a Reading of Zayas's *Desengaños amorosos.*" *South Central Review* 5.2 (1988): 43-50.

——. "Madness and Narrative Form in 'Estragos que causa el vicio.'" Williamsen and Whitenack 215-29.

Cobbe, Frances Power. "Wife Torture in England." *Contemporary Review* 32 (April 1878): 55-87.

Cocozzella, Peter. "María de Zayas y Sotomayor: Writer of the Baroque *Novela ejemplar.*" *Women Writers of the Seventeenth Century.* Ed. Katharina M. Wilson and Frank J. Warnke. Athens: U of Georgia P, 1989. 189-227.

Cohen, Sherrill. "Asylums for Women in Counter-Reformation Italy." Marshall 166-88.

Conboy, Katie, Nadia Medina, and Sarah Stanbury, eds. *Writing on the Body: Female Embodiment and Feminist Theory.* NY: Columbia, 1997.

Cornilliat, François. "Exemplarities: A Response to Timothy Hampton and Karlheinz Stierle." *Journal of the History of Ideas* 59.4 (Oct. 1998): 613-24.
Covarrubias, Sebastián de. *Tesoro de la lengua castellana o española*. Ed. Martín de Riquer. Barcelona: S. A. Horta, 1943.
Crenne, Hélisenne de. *The Torments of Love*. Ed. and intro. Lisa Neal. Trans. Lisa Neal and Steven Rendall. Minneapolis: U of Minnesota P, 1996.
Cruickshank, D. W. "'Literature' and the Book Trade in Golden Age Spain." *Modern Language Review* 73 (1978): 799-824.
Cruz, Anne. "Feminism, Psychoanalysis, and the Search for the M/Other in Early Modern Spain." *Indiana Journal of Hispanic Literature* 8 (Spring 1996): 31-54.
―――. "Studying Gender in the Spanish Golden Age." *Cultural and Historical Groundings for Spanish and Luso Brazilian Feminist Literary Criticism*. Ed. Hernán Vidal. Minneapolis: Institute for the Study of Ideologies and Literature, 1989. 193-222.
Cruz, Anne, and Mary Elizabeth Perry, eds. "Introduction." *Culture and Control in Counter Reformation Spain*. Minneapolis: U of Minnesota P, 1992. i-xxiii.
Cushing, Nancy K. "The Novellas of María de Zayas y Sotomayor: Preserving and Protecting the Feminine." Diss. U of California, Berkeley, 1996.
Davis, Natalie Z. *Fiction in the Archives: Pardon Tales in Sixteenth Century France*. Stanford: Stanford UP, 1987.
―――. *Society and Culture in Early Modern Europe*. Stanford: Stanford UP, 1975.
Deats, Sara Munson. "From Pedestal to Ditch: Violence against Women in Shakespeare's *Othello*." Deats and Lenker 79-93.
Deats, Sara Munson, and Lagretta Tallent Lenker, eds. *The Aching Hearth: Family Violence in Life and Literature*. NY: Plenum, 1990. 1-23.
Defourneaux, Marcelin. *Daily Life in Spain in the Golden Age*. Trans. Newton Branch. NY: Praeger, 1966.
de Lauretis, Teresa. *Technologies of Gender*. Bloomington: Indiana UP, 1987.
del Portal, María Martínez, ed. "Introducción." *Novelas completas*. María de Zayas y Sotomayor. Barcelona: Bruguera, 1973. 9-34.
Dewald, Jonathan. *Aristocratic Experience and the Origins of Modern Culture. France, 1570-1715*. Berkeley: U of California P, 1993.
Diccionario de literatura española. Vol. I. 2d ed. Madrid: Revista de Occidente, 1953.
Díez Borque, José María. "El feminismo de doña María de Zayas." *La mujer en el teatro y la novela del siglo* XVII. *Actas del II coloquio del Grupo de Estudios sobre Teatro Español*. Toulouse: Institut d'Etudes Hispaniques et Hispano-Américaines, Université de Toulouse Le Mirail, 1978. 63-83.
―――. *La vida española en el siglo de oro según los extranjeros*. Barcelona: Ediciones del Serbal, 1990.
Dobash, R. Emerson, and Russell Dobash. *Violence against Wives*. NY: Free Press, 1979.
Dolan, Frances E. *Dangerous Familiars. Representations of Domestic Crime in England, 1550-1700*. Ithaca: Cornell UP, 1994.
―――. "Household Chastisements: Gender, Authority, and 'Domestic Violence.'" *Renaissance Culture and the Everyday*. Ed. Patricia Fumerton and Simon Hunt. Philadelphia: U of Pennsylvania P, 1999. 204-25.
Donovan, Josephine. "Women and the Framed-Novelle: A Tradition of Their Own." *Signs* 22.4 (Summer 1997): 947-80.
Dutton, Brian. "The Semantics of Honor." *Revista Canadiense de Estudios Hispánicos* 4 (1979): 1-17.
Eire, Carlos M. N. *From Madrid to Purgatory: The Art and Craft of Dying in Sixteenth-Century Spain*. Cambridge: Cambridge UP, 1995.

Elliott, J. H. *Spain and Its World: 1500-1700*. New Haven: Yale UP, 1989.
El Saffar, Ruth. "Ana/Lysis and Zayas: Reflections on Courtship and Literary Women in the *Novelas amorosas y exemplares*." Williamsen and Whitenack 196-216.
Enríquez de Salamanca, Cristina. "Irony, Parody, and the Grotesque in a Baroque Novella: 'Tarde llega el desengaño.'" Williamsen and Whitenack 234-54.
Erauso, Catalina de. *Historia de la monja alférez (escrita por ella misma)*. Ed. Joaquín María de Ferrer. Paris: J. Didot, 1829.
———. *Lieutenant Nun: Memoir of a Basque Transvestite in the New World*. Trans. Michele Stepto and Gabriel Stepto. Foreword by Marjorie Garber. Boston: Beacon, 1996.
Fairchilds, Cissie. *Domestic Enemies. Servants and their Masters in Old Regime France*. Baltimore: Johns Hopkins UP, 1984.
Felten, Hans. "La mujer disfrazada: un tópico literario y su función." *Hacia Calderón. Octavo Coloquio Anglogermano (1987)*. Ed. Hans Flasche. Stuttgart: Franz Steiner, 1988. 77-82.
———. *María de Zayas y Sotomayor. zum Zusammenhang zwischen moralistischen Texten und Novellenliteratur*. Frankfurt: Vittorio Klostermann, 1978.
Fisher, Sheila, and Janet E. Halley, eds. "Introduction." *The Lady Vanishes. The Problem of Women's Absence in Late Medieval and Renaissance Texts*. Knoxville: U of Tennessee P, 1989. 1-17.
Flynn, Maureen. "Mimesis of the Last Judgment: The Spanish *auto de fe*." *Sixteenth Century Journal* 22.2 (1990): 281-97.
Foa, Sandra M. *Feminismo y forma narrativa*. Madrid: Albatros, 1979.
———. "Humor and Suicide in Zayas and Cervantes." *Anales Cervantinos* 16 (1977): 1-13.
Fonte, Moderata. *The Worth of Women*. Trans. Virginia Cox. Chicago: U of Chicago P, 1997.
Foucault, Michel. *Discipline and Punish*. Trans. Alan Sheridan. NY: Pantheon, 1977.
———. *The History of Sexuality*. Vol. I. Trans. Robert Hurley. NY: Random House, 1990.
Fra-Molinero, Baltasar. *La imagen de los negros en el teatro del Siglo de Oro*. Madrid: Siglo Veintiuno, 1995.
———. "La imagen de los negros en la literatura española de los siglos XVI y XVII." Diss. Indiana U, 1990.
Fraser, Nancy. *Justice Interruptus. Critical Reflections on the 'Postsocialist' Condition*. NY: Routledge, 1997.
Froula, Christine. "The Daughter's Seduction: Sexual Violence and Literary History." *Signs* 11.4 (1986): 621-44.
Fuss, Diana. *Essentially Speaking: Feminism, Nature, and Difference*. NY: Routledge, 1989.
Garber, Marjorie. *Vested Interests: Cross Dressing and Cultural Anxiety*. NY: HarperPerennial, 1993.
Gartner, Bruce. "María de Zayas y Sotomayor: The Poetics of Subversion." Diss. Emory U, 1989.
Gatens, Moira. *Imaginary Bodies: Ethics, Power, and Corporeality*. NY: Routledge, 1996.
Gilbert, Sandra, and Susan Gubar. *The Madwoman in the Attic*. New Haven: Yale UP, 1979.
Gilmore, Leigh. *Autobiographics: A Feminist Theory of Women's Self-Representation*. Ithaca: Cornell UP, 1994.
Girard, René. *Violence and the Sacred*. Trans. Patrick Gregory. Baltimore: Johns Hopkins UP, 1977.

Goldsmith, Elizabeth C., and Dena Goodman, eds. *Going Public: Women and Publishing in Early Modern France*. Ithaca: Cornell UP, 1995.
Gorfkle, Laura. "Re-constituting the Feminine in 'Amar sólo por vencer.'" Williamsen and Whitenack 75-89.
Gossy, Mary. "Skirting the Question: Lesbians and María de Zayas." *Hispanisms and Homosexualities*. Ed. Sylvia Molloy and Robert McKee Irwin. Durham: Duke UP, 1998. 19-28.
Gournay, Marie Jars de. *L'ombre: ouvre composé de méslanges*. Paris, 1626.
Goytisolo, Juan. "El mundo erótico de María de Zayas." *Disidencias*. Barcelona: Seix Barral, 1977. 63-115.
Greenberg, Mitchell. *Canonical States, Canonical Stages*. Minneapolis: U of Minnesota P, 1994.
Greenblatt, Stephen. *Shakespearean Negotiations: The Circulation of Social Energy in Renaissance England*. Berkeley: U of California P, 1988.
Greer, Margaret R. *María de Zayas Tells Baroque Tales of Love and the Cruelty of Men*. University Park, PA: Pennsylvania State UP, 2000.
———. "The (M)Other Plot: Psychoanalytic Theory and Narrative Structure in María de Zayas." Williamsen and Whitenack 88-114.
———. "Who's Telling this Story Anyhow? Framing Tales East and West: Panchatantra to Boccaccio to Zayas." *Laberinto* 1.1-2 (Autumn 1997): <http://www.utsa.edu/laberinto/fall 1997/greer1997.htm>.
Grieve, Patricia E. "Embroidering with Saintly Threads: María de Zayas Challenges Cervantes and the Church." *Renaissance Quarterly* 44.1 (Spring 1991): 86-106.
Griswold, Susan C. "Topoi and Rhetorical Distance: The 'Feminism' of María de Zayas." *Revista de Estudios Hispánicos* 14.2 (1980): 97-116.
Grosz, Elizabeth. *Space, Time, and Perversion*. NY: Routledge, 1995.
———. *Volatile Bodies: Toward a Corporeal Feminism*. Bloomington: Indiana UP, 1994.
Haliczer, Stephen. *Inquisition and Society in the Kingdom of Valencia, 1478-1834*. Berkeley: U of California P, 1990.
———. *Sexuality in the Confessional: A Sacrament Profaned*. NY: Oxford UP, 1996.
Hampton, Timothy. "Examples, Stories, and Subjects in *Don Quixote* and the *Heptameron*." *Journal of the History of Ideas* 59.4 (Oct. 1998): 597-612.
Harvey, Elizabeth. *Ventriloquized Voices: Feminist Theory and English Renaissance Texts*. NY: Routledge, 1992.
Heiple, Daniel. "Profeminist Reactions to Huarte's Misogyny in Lope de Vega's *La prueba de los ingenios* and María de Zayas's *Novelas amorosas y ejemplares*." *The Perception of Women in Spanish Theater of the Golden Age*. Ed. Anita Stoll and Dawn Smith. Lewisburg, PA: Bucknell UP, 1991. 121-34.
Henderson, Katherine Usher, and Barbara F. McManus, eds. *Half Humankind. Contexts and Texts of the Controversy about Women in England: 1540-1640*. Urbana: U of Illinois P, 1985.
Herrera Puga, Pedro. *Sociedad y delincuencia en el siglo de oro*. Madrid: Biblioteca de Autores Cristianos, 1974.
Hesse, José. "Introducción." *Las novelas de María de Zayas*. Madrid: Taurus, 1965. 7-31.
Hic Mulier and *Haec Vir*. Henderson and McManus 264-89.
Higgins, Lynn, and Brenda Silver, eds. *Rape and Representation*. NY: Columbia UP, 1991.
Hill, Bridget. *Servants: English Domestics in the Eighteenth Century*. NY: Oxford UP, 1996.

Hillman, David, and Carla Mazzio, eds. *The Body in Parts. Fantasies of Corporeality in Early Modern Europe*. NY: Routledge, 1997.
Honig, Edwin. *Calderón and the Seizures of Honor*. Cambridge, MA: Harvard UP, 1972.
Horsfall, Jan. *The Presence of the Past. Male Violence in the Family*. Sydney: Allen and Unwin, 1991.
Howard, Jean. "Crossdressing, the Theatre, and Gender Struggle in Early Modern England." *Shakespeare Quarterly* 39.4 (Winter 1988): 418-40.
Hunt, Lynn, ed. "Introduction: Obscenity and the Origins of Modernity, 1500-1800." *The Invention of Pornography: Obscenity and the Origins of Modernity, 1500-1800*. NY: Zone, 1993. 9-45.
Hunt, Margaret. "Wife Beating, Domesticity, and Women's Independence in Eighteenth-Century London." *Gender and History* 4.1 (1992): 10-33.
Ife, B. W. *Reading and Fiction in Golden Age Spain*. Cambridge: Cambridge UP, 1985.
Irigaray, Luce. *An Ethics of Sexual Difference*. Trans. Carolyn Burke and Gillian Gill. Ithaca: Cornell UP, 1993.
———. *This Sex which Is not One*. Trans. Catherine Porter. Ithaca: Cornell UP, 1985.
Jeannret, Michel. "The Vagaries of Exemplarity: Distortion or Dismissal." *Journal of the History of Ideas* 59.4 (Oct. 1998): 565-80.
Jehensen, Yvonne, and Marcia Welles. "María de Zayas's Wounded Women: A Semiotics of Violence." *Gender, Identity, and Representation in Spain's Golden Age*. Ed. Anita K. Stoll and Dawn L. Smith. Lewisburg, PA: Bucknell UP, 2000. 178-202.
Jerónima de la Ascensión, (Sor). *Exercicios espirituales*. Zaragoza: Miguel de Luna, 1661.
Jiménez, Lourdes Noemi. "La novela corta española en el siglo XVII: María de Zayas y Sotomayor y Mariana de Carvajal y Saavedra." Diss. U of Massachusetts, 1990.
Jordan, Constance. *Renaissance Feminism. Literary Texts and Political Models*. Ithaca: Cornell UP, 1990.
Juana Inés de la Cruz, (Sor). *La respuesta/The Answer*. Ed. Electa Arenal. Trans. Amanda Powell. NY: Feminist Press, 1994.
Kagan, Richard L. *Lawsuits and Litigants in Castile: 1500-1700*. Chapel Hill: U of North Carolina P, 1981.
———. *Lucrecia's Dreams. Politics and Prophecy in Sixteenth-Century Spain*. Berkeley: U of California P, 1990.
Kahiluoto Rudat, Eva M. "Ilusión y desengaño. El feminismo barroco de María de Zayas y Sotomayor." *Letras Femeninas* 1 (1975): 26-43.
Kamen, Henry. *European Society: 1500-1700*. London: Hutchinson, 1984.
———. *Inquisition and Society in Spain in the Sixteenth and Seventeenth Centuries*. Bloomington: Indiana UP, 1985.
———. *Spain in the Later Seventeenth Century, 1665-1700*. London: Longman, 1980.
Kaminsky, Amy Katz. "Dress and Redress: Clothing in the *Desengaños amorosos* of María de Zayas y Sotomayor." *Romanic Review* 79.2 (1988): 377-91.
Kelly, Joan. "Did Women Have a Renaissance?" *Women, History, and Theory: The Essays of Joan Kelly*. Chicago: U of Chicago P, 1984. 19-50.
Kelly, Liz, and Jill Radford. "The Problem of Men." *Law, Order, and the Authoritarian State: Readings in Critical Criminology*. Ed. Phil Scraton. Philadelphia: Open UP, 1987. 237-53.

Kerber, Linda K. "Separate Spheres, Female Worlds, Woman's Place: The Rhetoric of Women's History." *Journal of American History* 75.1 (June 1988): 9-39.
King, Margaret L. *Women of the Renaissance*. Chicago: U of Chicago P, 1991.
King, Willard F. *Prosa novelística y academias literarias en el siglo XVII*. Madrid: Anejos del Boletín de la Real Academia Española X, 1963.
Kohn, Mary Ellen. "Violence against Women in the Novels of María de Zayas y Sotomayor." Diss. U of Illinois, Urbana-Champaign, 1994.
Kothe, Anamaria H. "Displaying the Muse: Print, Prologue, Poetics, and Early Modern Women Writers Published in England and Spain." Diss. U of Maryland, College Park, 1996.
La Fayette, Madame de (Marie-Madeleine Pioche de la Vergne). *La Princesse de Clèves*. Ed. Jean Mesnard. Paris: Impr. Nationale, 1980.
Lakoff, George, and Mark Johnson. *Philosophy in the Flesh*. NY: Basic, 1999.
Langle de Paz, Teresa. "Las voces del cuerpo. El arte narrativo de María de Zayas." Diss. Brown U, 1997.
Lanser, Susan Sniader. *Fictions of Authority: Women Writers and Narrative Voice*. Ithaca: Cornell UP, 1992.
Laqueur, Thomas. *Making Sex: Body and Gender from the Greeks to Freud*. Cambridge, MA: Harvard UP, 1990.
Larson, Donald. *The Honor Plays of Lope de Vega*. Cambridge, MA: Harvard UP, 1977.
Lemoine-Luccioni, Eugénie. *Partages de femmes*. Paris: Seuil, 1976.
Lerner, Gerda. *The Creation of Feminist Consciousness: From the Middle Ages to 1870*. Oxford: Oxford UP, 1993.
Levine, Laura. *Men in Women's Clothing. Anti-Theatricality and Effeminization, 1579-1642*. Cambridge: Cambridge UP, 1994.
———. "Rape, Repetition, and the Politics of Closure in *A Midsummer Night's Dream*." Traub, Kaplan, and Callaghan. 210-28.
Levisi, Margarita. "La crueldad en los *Desengaños amorosos* de María de Zayas." *Estudios literarios de hispanistas norteamericanos dedicados a Helmut Hatzfeld con motivo de su 80 aniversario*. Ed. Josep Sola-Solé et al. Barcelona: Hispamérica 1974. 447-56.
Littlejohn, Gary, et al., eds. *Power and the State*. London: Croom Helm, 1978.
Lockert, Lucía Fox. "María de Zayas." *Women Novelists in Spain and Spanish America*. Metuchen, NJ: Scarecrow, 1979. 25-35.
Luis de León, (Fray). *La perfecta casada*. Ed. Javier San José Lera. Madrid: Espasa-Calpe, 1992.
Maclean, Ian. "Constance Jordan. *Renaissance Feminism*." Rev. of *Renaissance Feminism*. *Renaissance Quarterly* 47.1 (Spring 1994): 214-16.
Mancuso, Emilia. *Donna María de Zayas y Sotomayor: una donna in difesa delle donne nella Spagna del Seicento*. Roma: Il Ventaglio, 1980.
Maravall, José Antonio. *Culture of the Baroque*. Trans. Terry Cochran. Minneapolis: U of Minnesota P, 1986.
———. "From the Renaissance to the Baroque: The Diphasic Schema of a Social Crisis." Trans. Terry Cochran. *Literature Among Discourses. The Spanish Golden Age*. Ed. Wlad Godzich and Nicholas Spadaccini. Minneapolis: U of Minnesota P, 1986. 3-40.
———. *La literatura picaresca desde la historia social*. Madrid: Taurus, 1986.
———. *Poder, honor y élites en el siglo XVII*. Madrid: Siglo Veintiuno, 1979.
Marinelli, Lucrezia. *La nobilità et l'eccellenza delle donne co'diffetti et mancamenti de gli huomini*. Venice: n.p., 1601.
Maroto Camino, Mercedes. "*Spindles for Swords*: The Re/Dis-Covery of María de Zayas's Presence." *Hispanic Review* 62.4 (Autumn 94): 519-36.

Marshall, Sherrin, ed. *Women in Reformation and Counter-Reformation Europe*. Bloomington: Indiana UP, 1989.
Martínez Camino, Gonzalo. "La novela corta del barroco español y la formación de una subjetividad señorial." *BHS* LXXIII.1 (1996): 33-47.
McKendrick, Melveena. "Honour/Vengeance in the Spanish *Comedia*: A Case of Mimetic Transference?" *Modern Language Review* 79 (1984): 313-35.
———. *Woman and Society in the Spanish Drama of the Golden Age: A Study of the Mujer Varonil*. Cambridge: Cambridge UP, 1974.
Mexía, Fray Vicente. *Saludable instrucción del estado de matrimonio*. Córdoba: Juan Baptista Escudero, 1566.
Monter, William. *Frontiers of Heresy. The Spanish Inquisition from the Basque Lands to Sicily*. Cambridge: Cambridge UP, 1990.
Montesa Peydro, Salvador. *Texto y contexto en la narrativa de María de Zayas*. Madrid: Dirección General de la Juventud y Promoción Sociocultural, 1981.
Nadelhaft, Ruth. "Domestic Violence in Literature: A Preliminary Study." *Mosaic* 17.2 (Spring 1984): 242-59.
Nalle, Sara. "Literacy and Culture in Early Modern Castile." *Past and Present* 125 (November 1989): 65-96.
Nash, Mary. "Two Decades of Women's History in Spain: A Reappraisal." *Writing Women's History. International Perspectives*. Ed. Karen Offen, Ruth Roach Pierson, and Jane Rendall. Bloomington: Indiana UP, 1991. 381-415.
Nussbaum, Martha. *Sex and Social Justice*. Oxford: Oxford UP, 1999.
Oltra, José Miguel. "Zelima o el arte narrativo de María de Zayas." *Formas breves del relato*. Ed. Yves-René Fonquerne. Zaragoza: Casa de Velázquez, 1986. 177-90.
Ordóñez, Elizabeth J. "Woman and Her Text in the Works of María de Zayas and Ana Caro." *Revista de Estudios Hispánicos* 19.1 (1985): 3-15.
Orso, Steven N. *Art and Death at the Spanish Habsburg Court. The Royal Exequies for Philip IV*. Columbia, MO: U of Missouri P, 1989.
Ortega Costa, Milagros. "Spanish Women in the Reformation." Marshall 89-119.
Osuna, Francisco de. *Norte de los estados en que se da regla de vivir a los mancebos . . . enseñando que tal ha de ser la vida del cristiano casado*. Sevilla: Impreso por Bartolomé Pérez, n.d.
Otero-Torres, Dámaris Milagros. "The Construction of the Female Subject in the Spanish Golden Age." Diss. U of California, San Diego, 1993.
Pardo Bazán, Emilia. "Breve noticia sobre doña María de Zayas y Sotomayor." *Novelas de Doña María de Zayas*. Biblioteca de la mujer (3). Madrid: Agustín Avrial, 1892. 5-16.
Park, Katharine. "The Rediscovery of the Clitoris. French Medicine and the Tribade, 1570-1620." Hillman and Mazzio 171-93.
Pauley, Caren Altchek. "Social Realism in the Short Novels of Salas Barbadillo, Céspedes, and Zayas." Diss. City U of New York, 1979.
Paun de García, Susan. "Magia y poder en María de Zayas." *Cuadernos de ALDEUU* 9.1 (abril 1992): 43-54.
———. "Zayas as Writer: Hell Hath No Fury." Williamsen and Whitenack 40-50.
Penyak, Lee M. "Safe Harbors and Compulsory Custody: *Casas de Depósito* in Mexico, 1750-1865." *Hispanic American Historical Review* 79.1 (February 1999): 83-100.
Pérez, Janet. *Feminist Encyclopedia of Iberian Literature*. Westport, CT: Greenwood, forthcoming.
Pérez Baltasar, María Dolores. *Mujeres marginadas: Las casas de recogidas en Madrid*. Madrid: Gráficas Lormo, 1984.
Pérez-Erdelyi, Mireya. *La pícara y la dama. La imagen de las mujeres en las novelas picaresco-cortesanas de María de Zayas y Sotomayor y Alonso de Castillo Solórzano*. Miami: Ediciones Universal, 1979.

Perona, Ángeles J., and Ramón del Castillo Santos. "Pensamiento español y representaciones de género." *Sociología de las mujeres españolas.* Coor. María Antonia García de León, María García de Cortázar, and Félix Ortega. Madrid: Editorial Complutense, 1996. 325-49.
Perry, Mary Elizabeth. *Crime and Society in Early Modern Seville.* Hanover, NH: UP of New England, 1980.
———. "Crisis and Disorder in the World of María de Zayas." Williamsen and Whitenack 23-39.
———. *Gender and Disorder in Early Modern Seville.* Princeton: Princeton UP, 1990.
———. "Magdalens and Jezebels in Counter Reformation Spain." Cruz and Perry 124-44.
———. "The 'Nefarious Sin' in Early Modern Seville." *Journal of Homosexuality* 16.1-2 (1988): 67-90.
Pfandl, Ludwig. *Historia de la literatura nacional española en el Siglo de Oro.* Trans. Jorge Rubió Balaguer. Barcelona: Sucesores de J. Gili, 1933.
Pizan, Christine de. *The Book of the City of Ladies.* Trans. Earl Jeffrey Richards. NY: Persea, 1982.
Place, Edwin B. "María de Zayas: An Outstanding Woman Short-Story Writer of Seventeenth-Century Spain." *The University of Colorado Studies* 13 (1923): 1-57.
Pleck, Elizabeth. *Domestic Tyranny: The Making of Social Policy against Family Violence from Colonial Times to the Present.* Oxford: Oxford UP, 1987.
Radford, Jill, and Diana Russell, eds. *Femicide: The Politics of Woman Killing.* NY: Twayne, 1992.
Redondo Goicoechea, Alicia, ed. "Introducción." *Tres novelas amorosas y ejemplares y tres desengaños amorosos.* María de Zayas y Sotomayor. Madrid: Castalia, 1989. 7-44.
———. "La retórica del yo-mujer en tres escritoras españolas: Teresa de Cartagena, Teresa de Jesús y María de Zayas." *Compás de Letras* 1 (dic. 1992): 49-63.
Reverby, Susan M., and Dorothy O. Helly, eds. "Introduction." *Gendered Domains. Rethinking Public and Private in Women's History.* Ithaca: Cornell UP, 1992. 1-26.
Rhodes, Elizabeth. "Skirting the Man: Gender Roles in Sixteenth-Century Pastoral Books." *Journal of Hispanic Philology* 11 (Winter 1987): 131-49.
Rigolot, François. "The Renaissance Crisis of Exemplarity." *Journal of the History of Ideas* 59.4 (Oct. 1998): 557-64.
Rincón, Eduardo, ed. "Prólogo." *María de Zayas y Sotomayor: Novelas ejemplares y amorosas o Decamerón español.* Madrid: Alianza, 1968. 7-21.
Rivers, Elias L., ed. *Renaissance and Baroque Poetry of Spain.* Prospect Heights, IL: Waveland, 1988.
Rosaldo, Michelle, and Louise Lamphere, eds. *Women, Culture, and Society.* Stanford: Stanford UP, 1974.
Rose, Gillian. *Feminism and Geography. The Limits of Geographical Knowledge.* Minneapolis: U of Minnesota P, 1993.
Routt, Kristin. "El cuerpo femenino y la creación literaria en 'La inocencia castigada' de María de Zayas." *RLA* VII (1995): 616-20.
Rupp, Leila J., and Verta Taylor. "Forging Feminist Identity in an International Movement: A Collective Identity Approach to Twentieth-Century Feminism." *Signs* 24.2 (Winter 1999): 363-86.
Saint-Saëns, Alain, ed. *La historia silenciada de la mujer.* Madrid: Editorial Complutense, 1996.

Saint-Saëns, Alain, ed. *Religion, Body, and Gender in Early Modern Spain.* San Francisco: Mellen Research UP, 1991.
———, ed. *Sex and Love in Golden Age Spain.* New Orleans: UP of the South, 1996.
Salstad, M. Louise. "The Influence of Sacred Oratory on María de Zayas: A Case in Point, 'La fuerza del amor.'" *MLN* 113.2 (March 1998): 426-32.
Sánchez Lora, José Luis. *Mujeres, conventos y formas de la religiosidad barroca.* Madrid: Fundación Universitaria, 1988.
Sánchez Ortega, María Helena. *La mujer y la sexualidad en el antiguo régimen: la perspectiva inquisitorial.* Madrid: Ediciones Akal, 1992.
———. "Woman as Source of Evil in Counter-Reformation Spain." Cruz and Perry 196-215.
Sawday, Jonathan. *The Body Emblazoned: Dissection and the Human Body in Renaissance Culture.* London: Routledge, 1995.
Scarry, Elaine. *The Body in Pain.* Oxford: Oxford UP, 1985.
Sedgwick, Eve Kosofsky. *Between Men: English Literature and Male Homosocial Desire.* NY: Columbia UP, 1985.
Senabre Sempere, Ricardo. "La fuente de una novela de Doña María de Zayas." *Revista de Filología Española* 46 (1963): 163-72.
Serrano Poncela, Segundo. "Casamientos engañosos. Doña María de Zayas, Scarron, y un proceso de creación literaria." *Bulletin Hispanique* 64 (1962): 248-59.
Sharp, John McCarty. "Costumbrismo in the *Novelas exemplares* of Doña María de Zayas y Sotomayor." Diss. U of Chicago, 1942.
Sharpe, J. A. "Domestic Homicide in Early Modern England." *The Historical Journal* 24.1 (1981): 29-48.
Smith, Paul Julian. *The Body Hispanic: Gender and Sexuality in Spanish and Spanish-American Literature.* Oxford: Oxford UP, 1989.
Smith, Sidonie. "Identity's Body." *Autobiography and Postmodernism.* Ed. Kathleen Ashley et al. Amherst: U of Massachusetts P, 1994. 266-92.
———. *A Poetics of Women's Autobiography.* Bloomington: Indiana UP, 1987.
Soufas, Teresa. *Dramas of Distinction.* Lexington: U of Kentucky P, 1997.
———, ed. *Women's Acts.* Lexington: U of Kentucky P, 1997.
Spain, Daphne. *Gendered Spaces.* Chapel Hill: U of North Carolina P, 1992.
Spieker, Joseph B. "El feminismo como clave estructural en las novelas de doña María de Zayas y Sotomayor." *Explicación de Textos Literarios* 6.2 (1978): 153-60.
Spivak, Gayatri. "Love Me, Love my Ombre, Elle." *Diacritics* 14 (Winter 1984): 19-36.
Stackhouse, Kenneth. "Narrative Roles and Style in the 'Novelas' of María de Zayas y Sotomayor." Diss. U of Florida, 1972.
———. "Verisimilitude, Magic, and the Supernatural in the *Novelas* of María de Zayas y Sotomayor." *Hispanófila* 62 (1978): 65-76.
Stallybrass, Peter. "Patriarchal Territories: The Body Enclosed." *Rewriting the Renaissance.* Ed. Margaret Ferguson et al. Chicago: U of Chicago P, 1986. 123-42.
Stallybrass, Peter, and Allon White. *The Politics and Poetics of Transgression.* Ithaca: Cornell UP, 1986.
Stierle, Karlheinz. "Three Moments in the Crisis of Exemplarity: Boccaccio, Petrarch, Montaigne, and Cervantes." *Journal of the History of Ideas* 59.4 (Oct. 1998): 581-95.
Stone, Marilyn. *Marriage and Friendship in Medieval Spain.* NY: Peter Lang, 1990.
Stroud, Matthew. *Fatal Union: A Pluralistic Approach to the Wife-Murder Comedias.* Lewisburg, PA: Bucknell UP, 1990.
Stuurman, Siep. "Literary Feminism in Seventeenth-Century Southern France: The

Case of Antoinette de Salvan de Saliez." *Journal of Modern History* 71 (March 1999): 1-27.
Suelzer, Amy Carol. "The Representation of the Noble Subject in María de Zayas's *Novelas amorosas y ejemplares* and *Desengaños amorosos*." Diss. Washington U, 1997.
Sylvania, Lena. *Doña María de Zayas y Sotomayor: A Contribution to the Study of her Works*. NY: Columbia UP, 1922. [Rpt. by AMA Press in 1966.]
Thurston, Herbert. *The Physical Phenomena of Mysticism*. London: Burns and Oates, 1952.
Ticknor, George. *History of Spanish Literature*. Vol. III. 3rd ed. Boston: Ticknor and Fields, 1866.
Tirso de Molina (Fray Gabriel Téllez). *El burlador de Sevilla*. Ed. Alfredo Rodríguez López-Vázquez. Madrid: Cátedra, 1989.
Traub, Valerie. *Desire and Anxiety: Circulations of Sexuality in Shakespearean Drama*. NY: Routledge, 1992.
——, M. Lindsay Kaplan, and Dympna Callaghan, eds. *Feminist Readings of Early Modern Culture: Emerging Subjects*. Cambridge: Cambridge UP, 1996. 1-15.
Valbuena, Olga Lucía. "Sorceresses, Love Magic, and the Inquisition of Linguistic Sorcery in *Celestina*." *PMLA* 109.2 (March 1994): 207-24.
Vasileski, Irma. *María de Zayas y Sotomayor: Su época y su obra*. NY and Madrid: Plaza Mayor, 1972.
Vega Carpio, Lope de. *El castigo sin venganza*. Ed. Antonio Carreño. Madrid: Cátedra, 1990.
Velasco, Sherry. *Demons, Nausea, and Resistance in the Autobiography of Isabel de Jesús (1611-1682)*. Albuquerque: U of New Mexico P, 1996.
Vigil, Mariló. *La vida de las mujeres en los siglos XVI y XVII*. Madrid: Siglo Veintiuno, 1986.
Vollendorf, Lisa, ed. *Recovering Spain's Feminist Tradition*. NY: MLA Publications, 2001.
Walker, Gillian. *Family Violence and the Women's Movement*. Toronto: U of Toronto P, 1990.
Walker, Lenore. *The Battered Woman*. NY: Harper & Row, 1980.
Wall, Wendy. *The Imprint of Gender. Authorship and Publication in the English Renaissance*. Ithaca: Cornell UP, 1993.
Walliser, Marta. "Recuperación panorámica de la literatura laica femenina en lengua castellana (hasta el siglo XVII)." Diss. Boston College, 1996.
Warner, Marina. *Alone of All Her Sex*. NY: Random House, 1976.
Weber, Alison. *Teresa of Avila and the Rhetoric of Femininity*. Princeton: Princeton UP, 1990.
Welles, Marcia L. "María de Zayas y Sotomayor and her novela cortesana: A Reevaluation." *Bulletin of Hispanic Studies* 55 (1978): 301-10.
——. *Persephone's Girdle. Narratives of Rape in Seventeenth-Century Spanish Literature*. Nashville: Vanderbilt UP, 2000.
——. "Violence Disguised: Representation of Rape in Cervantes's 'La fuerza de la sangre.'" *Journal of Hispanic Philology* XII.3 (Spring 1989): 240-52.
Whateley, William. *A Bride Bush or A Direction for Married Persons*. London: n.p., 1623.
Whinnom, Keith. "The Problem of the 'Best-Seller' in Spanish Golden-Age Literature." *BHS* LVII (1980): 189-98.
Whitenack, Judith A. "Introduction." Williamsen and Whitenack 1-10.
——. "'Lo que ha menester': Erotic Enchantment in 'La inocencia castigada.'" Williamsen and Whitenack 170-91.

Williamsen, Amy R. "Challenging the Code: Honor in María de Zayas." Williamsen and Whitenack 131-49.

———. "'Death Becomes Her': Fatal Beauty in María de Zayas's 'Mal presagio casar lejos.'" *RLA* VI (1994): 619-23.

———. "Engendering Interpretation: Irony as Comic Challenge in María de Zayas." *RLA* III (1991): 642-48.

———. "Questions of Entitlement: Imposed Titles and Interpretation in Sor Juana and María de Zayas." *Revista de Estudios Hispánicos* 31.1 (enero 1997): 103-12.

Williamsen, Amy R., and Judith A. Whitenack, eds. *María de Zayas: The Dynamics of Discourse*. Madison: Fairleigh Dickinson UP, 1995; London: Associated University Presses, 1995.

Wilson, Margo, and Martin Daly. "Till Death Do Us Part." Radford and Russell 83-98.

Wittig, Monique. "One Is not Born Woman." *Feminist Issues* (Fall 1981): 47-54.

———. "The Straight Mind." *Feminist Issues* (Summer 1980): 103-11.

Wofford, Susanne L. "The Social Aesthetics of Rape: Closural Violence in Boccaccio and Botticelli." *Creative Imitation. New Essays on Renaissance Literature in Honor of Thomas M. Greene*. Ed. David Quint et al. Binghamton: Medieval and Renaissance Texts and Studies, 1991. 189-238.

Yarbro-Bejarano, Yvonne. *Feminism and the Honor Plays of Lope de Vega*. Purdue Series in Romance Literatures. West Lafayette, IN: Purdue UP, 1994.

Yegidis, Bonnie. "Speaking the Unspeakable: Family Violence in America in the 1990s." Deats and Lenker 23-32.

Yllera, Alicia, ed. "Introducción." *Desengaños amorosos*. María de Zayas y Sotomayor. 2d ed. Madrid: Cátedra, 1993. 11-110.

Zavala, Iris. *Breve historia feminista de la literatura española*. Vols. I-VI. Ed. Iris Zavala. Vol. I edited with Myriam Díaz-Diocaretz. Barcelona: Anthropos, 1993-98. (Ongoing series.)

Zayas y Sotomayor, María de. *Desengaños amorosos*. 2d ed. Ed. Alicia Yllera. Madrid: Cátedra, 1993.

———. *The Disenchantments of Love*. Trans. H. Patsy Boyer. Binghamton, NY: SUNY, 1997.

———. *The Enchantments of Love*. Trans. H. Patsy Boyer. Berkeley: U of California P, 1990.

———. *Novelas amorosas y ejemplares*. Ed. Agustín G. de Amezúa. Madrid: Real Academia Española, 1948.

———. *Novelas amorosas y ejemplares*. Ed. Julián Olivares. Madrid: Cátedra, 2000.

———. *Primera y segunda parte de las novelas amorosas y exemplares*. Madrid: Melchor Sánchez, 1659.

———. *Traición en la amistad*. Ed. and notes Valerie Hegstrom. *Friendship Betrayed*. Trans. Catherine Larson. Lewisburg, PA: Bucknell UP, 1999.

———. *Traición en la amistad*. Soufas, *Women's Acts* 277-308.

———. *Tres novelas amorosas y ejemplares y tres desengaños amorosos*. Ed. Alicia Redondo Goicoechea. Madrid: Castalia, 1989.

INDEX

Al fin se paga todo, 35-36, 97-99, 135, 139, 186-96
Al que leyere, 63-69, 206
Alberti, Giannozzo, 158-60
Alcalde, Pilar, 24
Amar sólo por vencer, 109, 111, 183-86
Amar y Borbón, Josefa, 201
Amezúa, Agustín G. de, 16, 20, 43, 98
Amussen, Susan Dwyer, 52
Anderson, Bonnie, 22
Arenal, Electa, 55, 79, 137
Astell, Mary, 23
Atwood, Margaret, 125
Aventurarse perdiendo, 88-90, 95-97, 139, 175-76
Azevedo, Ángela de, 182
Azorín (José Martínez Ruiz), 20, 62

Barbeito Carneiro, Isabel, 17
Barker, Francis, 52
Bassein, Beth Ann, 88
Behn, Aphra, 23
Benedict, Kitty, 22
Bergmann, Emilie, 149
Beverley, John, 68, 170
Bilinkoff, Jodi, 50
Blanqué, Andrea, 43
Bordo, Susan, 61
Bourland, Caroline, 40
Boyer, H. Patsy, 16-17, 24, 31, 41, 156, 164, 171, 195
Bravo-Villasante, Carmen, 171, 174
Bray, Abigail, 61
Breines, Wini, 113
Bronfen, Elisabeth, 83, 87-88, 117-22

Brooten, Bernadette, 185
Brown, Judith, 79, 137
Brownlee, Marina S., 21, 24-25, 31, 40, 73, 104, 164, 191
Bullough, Bonnie, 27, 172, 174
Bullough, Vern, 27, 172, 174
La burlada Aminta y venganza del honor 45, 96-99, 186-96
El burlador de Sevilla, 84
Burnett, Mark Thornton, 209
Butler, Judith, 30, 61, 73, 161-63, 173-74
Bynum, Caroline Walker, 55-56

Calderón de la Barca, Pedro, 38, 53-54, 94, 133
Callaghan, Dympna, 26-27, 42, 125-26
Camps, Victoria, 18
Caputi, Jane, 113
Cascardi, Anthony, 126, 170
El castigo de la miseria, 97-102, 134-35
Castro, Américo, 187
Cavendish, Margaret, 23
Cervantes Saavedra, Miguel de, 23, 25, 38, 40, 47, 89-90, 100-01, 164
Charnon-Deutsch, Lou, 77, 79, 171, 180, 186
Chevalier, Maxime, 40, 171
Cixous, Hélène, 61, 69
Clamurro, William, 41, 44, 93, 127
Cobbe, Frances Power, 93
Cocozzella, Peter, 17, 24
Cohen, Sherrill, 136
Colebrook, Claire, 61
Conboy, Katie, 61

Cornilliat, François, 19, 107
Covarrubias, Sebastián de, 46-47
Covington, Karen, 22
Crenne, Hélisenne de, 23, 93
Cruickshank, D. W., 68, 164
Cruz, Anne J., 41-42, 50-51, 132, 154-55, 191
Cushing, Nancy, 40, 135, 209

Daly, Martin, 112-13
Davis, Natalie Zemon, 126, 195
Deats, Sara Munson, 94
Defourneaux, Marcelin, 50
de Lauretis, Teresa, 30, 87
El desengaño amando, 97, 137-39
Dewald, Jonathan, 170
Díez Borque, José María, 24, 187-88
Dobash, R. Emerson, 113
Dobash, Russell, 113
Dolan, Frances, 46, 52-53, 142
Donovan, Josephine, 40, 164
Dutton, Brian, 187

Eire, Carlos, 140
Elliott, J. H., 126-27
El Saffar, Ruth, 67
Erauso, Catalina de, 38
La esclava de su amante, 43, 69-81, 99, 108, 144-46
Estragos que causa el vicio, 42-46, 90-95, 99, 110-12, 117-18, 141-42

Fairchilds, Cissie, 209
Felten, Hans, 40
Fisher, Sheila, 38, 42
Flynn, Maureen, 52
Foa, Sandra, 17-18, 21, 24, 41, 90-91, 193
Fonte, Moderata, 156, 212
Foucault, Michel, 61-62
Fra-Molinero, Baltasar, 207
Fraser, Nancy, 18, 30
Froula, Christine, 167
La fuerza del amor, 47-49, 59, 97, 99, 135-39
Fuss, Diana, 61

Garber, Marjorie, 168, 174
Gartner, Bruce, 44, 193
Gatens, Moira, 30, 61, 83, 125-26, 130, 174-75, 209, 213
Gilbert, Sandra, 141, 145
Gilmore, Leigh, 73

Goldsmith, Elizabeth, 128
Goodman, Dena, 128
Gordon, Linda, 113
Gorfkle, Laura, 171
Gossy, Mary, 171, 185
Gournay, Marie de, 66
Goytisolo, Juan, 43-44
Greenberg, Mitchell, 38
Greer, Margaret, 21, 24, 31, 96-97
Grieve, Patricia, 40, 43, 55
Griswold, Susan, 24-25
Grosz, Elizabeth, 25-26, 28, 30, 35, 39, 60-61, 86, 173-74
Gubar, Susan, 141, 145

Haec vir, 172
Haliczer, Stephen, 50, 114
Halley, Janet, 38, 42
Hampton, Timothy, 107
Harvey, Elizabeth, 38
Heiple, Daniel, 17, 24
Helly, Dorothy, 131-32
Herrera Puga, Pedro, 57, 114
Hesse, José, 20
Hic mulier, 172
Higgins, Lynn, 76
Hill, Bridget, 209
Hillman, David, 58
Honig, Edwin, 187
Horsfall, Jan, 93
Howard, Jean, 168
Hunt, Lynn, 94
Hunt, Margaret, 46

Ife, B. W., 68, 106, 164
El imposible vencido, 97-98
La inocencia castigada, 42, 99, 109-11, 151-57
Irigaray, Luce, 30, 61, 65, 78

El jardín engañoso, 97-98, 105
Jeannert, Michel, 107
Jerónima de la Ascensión, (Sor), 55-56
Jiménez, Lourdes Noemi, 40
Johnson, Mark, 61
Jordan, Constance, 18, 22, 51, 64, 110-11, 156, 212
Juana Inés de la Cruz, (Sor), 45
El juez de su causa, 97-100, 176-82

Kagan, Richard, 50-51, 57
Kahiluoto Rudat, Eva M., 171
Kamen, Henry, 52, 57

Kaminsky, Amy Katz, 43-44, 71, 74
Kaplan, Lindsay, 26-27, 42, 125-26
Kelly, Joan, 126
Kelly, Liz, 108
Kerber, Linda, 131-32
King, Margaret, 22, 115
King, Willard, 165
Kohn, Mary Ellen, 40
Kothe, Ana, 40

La Fayette, Madame de, 23
Lakoff, George, 61
Langle de Paz, Teresa, 40
Lanser, Susan, 71
Larson, Donald, 187
Lenker, Lagretta Tallent, 94
Lerner, Gerda, 18, 22, 201
Levine, Laura, 117, 172, 174
Levisi, Margarita, 44, 55
Lockert, Lucía Fox, 17
Luis de León, (Fray), 64, 128, 132, 139-40, 166

Maclean, Ian, 22
Mal presagio casar lejos, 36-37, 99, 109, 113-15, 118-22
Mancuso, Emilia, 17
Maravall, José Antonio, 41, 52, 57-58, 168, 170, 187, 209
Marinelli, Lucrezia, 212
Maroto Camino, Mercedes, 24, 191
Martínez Camino, Gonzalo, 170
Martínez del Portal, María, 98
La más infame venganza, 42, 108, 146-48, 159-61, 182-83, 201-02
Mazzio, Carla, 58
McKendrick, Melveena, 18, 38, 50, 171-73, 187
Medina, Nadia, 61
Mexía, Vicente, 49
Monter, William, 57
Montesa Peydro, Salvador, 20, 40-41, 177

Nadelhaft, Ruth, 94
Nalle, Sara, 68, 164-65
Nash, Mary, 50
Navarre, Marguerite de, 40
Nussbaum, Martha, 30

Olivares, Julián, 98
Oltra, José Miguel, 143
Ordóñez, Elizabeth, 40, 92, 106, 143

Orso, Steven, 140
Osuna, Francisco de, 46-48
Otero-Torres, Dámaris Milagros, 25, 40, 73, 170

Pardo Bazán, Emilia, 62-63
Park, Katharine, 27
Pauley, Caren Altchek, 43
Paun de García, Susan, 165
Penyak, Lee, 136
Pérez Baltasar, María Dolores, 136
Pérez-Erdelyi, Mireya, 40, 72
Perona, Ángeles, 18
Perry, Mary Elizabeth, 24-25, 39, 50-51, 114, 126, 129, 132, 136, 154, 185
La perseguida triunfante, 110, 121, 144-46
Pfandl, Ludwig, 43
Pizan, Christine de, 23, 85
Place, Edwin, 40, 43
Pleck, Elizabeth, 46
El prevenido, engañado, 97-98, 102-05, 139
Prólogo de un desapasionado, 44, 68

Radford, Jill, 108, 117, 142-43
Redondo Goicoechea, Alicia, 24, 72, 98, 177
Reverby, Susan, 131-32
Rhodes, Elizabeth, 149
Rigolot, François, 107
Rincón, Eduardo, 20
Rivers, Elias, 54
Rosaldo, Michelle, 131-32
Rose, Gillian, 132
Routt, Kristin, 87
Rupp, Leila, 30, 225
Russell, Diana, 113, 117, 142-43

Saint-Saëns, Alain, 50
Salstad, Louise, 24, 40
Sánchez Lora, José Luis, 51
Sánchez Ortega, María Helena, 50, 126
Sawday, Jonathan, 58
Schlau, Stacey, 55, 79, 137
Sedgwick, Eve Kosofsky, 78
Senabre Sempere, Ricardo, 40, 171
Sharp, John McCarty, 43
Sharpe, J. A., 46
Siete Partidas, 49-50, 129-30
Silver, Brenda, 76
Smith, Paul Julian, 187
Smith, Sidonie, 70, 73, 75

Soufas, Teresa, 161, 182
Spain, Daphne, 132
Spieker, Joseph, 24, 164
Stallybrass, Peter, 78, 127-30, 140-41
Stanburg, Sarah, 61
Stierle, Karlheinz, 107
Stroud, Matthew, 37
Stuurman, Siep, 156
Suelzer, Amy Carol, 73

Tarde llega el desengaño, 42, 109, 111, 150-51, 203
Taylor, Verta, 30, 225
Thurston, Herbert, 56
Ticknor, George, 43
Traición en la amistad, 21, 208
El traidor contra su sangre, 99, 110, 115-17, 120-22
Traub, Valerie, 26-27, 42, 125-26

Vasileski, Irma, 22, 43
Vega Carpio, Lope de, 20, 23, 38, 40, 54, 172-73
Velasco, Sherry, 55
Verdella, Aurelia, 156
El verdugo de su esposa, 42, 45, 59-60, 99, 109, 148-50, 159-61

Vigil, Mariló, 46, 49-50, 126, 130
Vives, Juan Luis, 149
Vollendorf, Lisa, 18

Walker, Gillian, 93
Walker, Lenore, 112-17
Wall, Wendy, 128
Walliser, Marta, 40
Warner, Marina, 55
Weber, Alison, 201
Welles, Marcia, 47
Whateley, William, 51
Whinnom, Keith, 165
White, Allon, 78
Whitenack, Judith, 21-22
Williamsen, Amy, 17, 21, 35, 43, 154, 171, 193
Wilson, Margo, 112-13
Wittig, Monique, 61
Wofford, Susanne, 47

Yarbro-Bejarano, Yvonne, 38
Yllera, Alicia, 15, 17, 20, 24, 35, 41, 43, 62, 177, 202, 209

Zavala, Iris, 18
Zinsser, Judith, 22

NORTH CAROLINA STUDIES IN THE ROMANCE LANGUAGES AND LITERATURES

I.S.B.N. Prefix 0-8078-

Recent Titles

THE ALLEGORICAL IMPULSE IN THE WORKS OF JULIEN GRACQ: HISTORY AS RHETORICAL ENACTMENT IN *LE RIVAGE DES SYRTES* AND *UN BALCON EN FORÊT*, by Carol J. Murphy. 1995. (No. 250). *-9254-8.*

VOID AND VOICE: QUESTIONING NARRATIVE CONVENTIONS IN ANDRÉ GIDE'S MAJOR FIRST-PERSON NARRATIVES, by Charles O'Keefe. 1996. (No. 251). *-9255-6.*

EL CÍRCULO Y LA FLECHA: PRINCIPIO Y FIN, TRIUNFO Y FRACASO DEL *PERSILES*, por Julio Baena. 1996. (No. 252). *-9256-4.*

EL TIEMPO Y LOS MÁRGENES. EUROPA COMO UTOPÍA Y COMO AMENAZA EN LA LITERATURA ESPAÑOLA, por Jesús Torrecilla. 1996. (No. 253). *-9257-2.*

THE AESTHETICS OF ARTIFICE: VILLIERS'S *L'EVE FUTURE*, by Marie Lathers. 1996. (No. 254). *-9254-8.*

DISLOCATIONS OF DESIRE: GENDER, IDENTITY, AND STRATEGY IN *LA REGENTA*, by Alison Sinclair. 1998. (No. 255). *-9259-9.*

THE POETICS OF INCONSTANCY, ETIENNE DURAND AND THE END OF RENAISSANCE VERSE, by Hoyt Rogers. 1998. (No. 256). *-9260-2.*

RONSARD'S CONTENTIOUS SISTERS: THE PARAGONE BETWEEN POETRY AND PAINTING IN THE WORKS OF PIERRE DE RONSARD, by Roberto E. Campo. 1998. (No. 257). *-9261-0.*

THE RAVISHMENT OF PERSEPHONE: EPISTOLARY LYRIC IN THE *SIÈCLE DES LUMIÈRES*, by Julia K. De Pree. 1998. (No. 258). *-9262-9.*

CONVERTING FICTION: COUNTER REFORMATIONAL CLOSURE IN THE SECULAR LITERATURE OF GOLDEN AGE SPAIN, by David H. Darst. 1998. (No. 259). *-9263-7.*

GALDÓS'S *SEGUNDA MANERA*: RHETORICAL STRATEGIES AND AFFECTIVE RESPONSE, by Linda M. Willem. 1998. (No. 260). *-9264-5.*

A MEDIEVAL PILGRIM'S COMPANION. REASSESSING *EL LIBRO DE LOS HUÉSPEDES* (ESCORIAL MS. h.I.13), by Thomas D. Spaccarelli. 1998. (No. 261). *-9265-3.*

'PUEBLOS ENFERMOS': THE DISCOURSE OF ILLNESS IN THE TURN-OF-THE-CENTURY SPANISH AND LATIN AMERICAN ESSAY, by Michael Aronna. 1999. (No. 262). *-9266-1.*

RESONANT THEMES. LITERATURE, HISTORY, AND THE ARTS IN NINETEENTH- AND TWENTIETH-CENTURY EUROPE. ESSAYS IN HONOR OF VICTOR BROMBERT, by Stirling Haig. 1999. (No. 263). *-9267-X.*

RAZA, GÉNERO E HIBRIDEZ EN *EL LAZARILLO DE CIEGOS CAMINANTES*, por Mariselle Meléndez. 1999. (No. 264). *-9268-8.*

DEL ESCENARIO A LA PANTALLA: LA ADAPTACIÓN CINEMATOGRÁFICA DEL TEATRO ESPAÑOL, por María Asunción Gómez. 2000. (No. 265). *9269-6.*

THE LEPER IN BLUE: COERCIVE PERFORMANCE AND THE CONTEMPORARY LATIN AMERICAN THEATER, by Amalia Gladhart. 2000. (No. 266). *9270-X.*

THE CHARM OF CATASTROPHE: A STUDY OF RABELAIS'S *QUART LIVRE*, by Alice Fiola Berry. 2000. (No. 267). *-9271-8.*

PUERTO RICAN CULTURAL IDENTITY AND THE WORK OF LUIS RAFAEL SÁNCHEZ, by John Dimitri Perivolaris. 2000. (No. 268). *-9272-6.*

MANNERISM AND BAROQUE IN SEVENTEENTH-CENTURY FRENCH POETRY: THE EXAMPLE OF TRISTAN L'HERMITE, by James Crenshaw Shepard. 2001. (No. 269). *-9273-4.*

RECLAIMING THE BODY: MARÍA DE ZAYAS'S EARLY MODERN FEMINISM, by Lisa Vollendorf. 2001. (No. 270). *-9274-2.*

When ordering please cite the *ISBN Prefix* plus the last four digits for each title.

Send orders to: University of North Carolina Press
P.O. Box 2288
CB# 6215
Chapel Hill, NC 27515-2288
U.S.A.

www.ingramcontent.com/pod-product-compliance
Lightning Source LLC
Chambersburg PA
CBHW020651230426
43665CB00008B/396